How to Deal with
Anxiety

Dr Lee Kannis-Dymand &
Dr Janet D Carter

Contents

Acknowledgements

Lee

My deepest gratitude to my wife Rachael and my children, for their support while I worked on this book and their tolerance of my lengthy working hours and crankiness. Thanks to my Mum and Liz Bennetts, who are endless sources of support. I am grateful to the training programmes in clinical psychology at the University of Canterbury, New Zealand, and in cognitive behaviour therapy at the University of Oxford, both of these programmes and their lecturers and supervisors shaped my clinical knowledge and skills. I am particularly thankful for my experience working at the Anxiety Disorders Service in Christchurch, New Zealand, the Centre for Anxiety Disorders and Trauma at the Maudsley Hospital in London, and the Priory Hospital in Bristol. Thanks to the many multidisciplinary colleagues I have worked with and learned so much from over the past years. I owe considerable thanks to the clinical supervisors I have received supervision from; more than anything they have enabled me to bring CBT to life in my practice. Thank you to the University of the Sunshine Coast, Australia, for its support of me while writing this book.

Janet

A heartfelt thank you to Bill for your never-ending support, constructive feedback and proofreading during the writing of this book. To all the clinicians who have contributed to my ongoing training and clinical expertise in cognitive behavioural therapy over many years, thank you. This book represents a culmination of all of your input. Thank you to the University of Canterbury for enabling me to continue to work clinically, teach, research and write this book on a topic so important to me.

We would both like to thank those who reviewed early drafts of this book and provided valuable feedback – thanks to Bill Bryce, Rachael Kannis, Kim Bennetts Shields, Gina Dymand, Dr Helen Colhoun, Dr Dixie Statham, Colette Woolcock and Benjamin Lane.

Lastly, we would like to gratefully acknowledge the clients who have shared their life experiences and stories with us and, importantly, who have collaborated with us to work on their anxiety and to increase their wellbeing. Kia kaha.

Authors' note

The case studies in this book are an amalgamation of many real-life examples and do not depict any specific individuals. Any resemblance to an individual person is purely coincidental.

Introduction

'Worrying is like a rocking chair: it gives you something to do but never gets you anywhere.' Erma Bombeck (1927–96)

How often have you heard the saying 'Don't worry, be happy'? While the person saying it means well, they may not realize how challenging coping with worry and anxiety can be for someone.

The good news is that you can learn ways to deal with worry so that it does not rule your life and cause you anxiety and distress. Through reading this book you can develop your ability to manage worry and anxiety in different ways, which means they have less impact on you.

We have worked as clinical psychologists for a number of years and one of the most common problems that people have sought our help for has been worrying too much and anxiety. Using evidenced-based practices we have seen our clients move from being overwhelmed by anxiety to being able to lead lives that are not controlled by worry and anxious feelings, as well as experiencing improved wellbeing.

This book is based on evidenced-based traditional and contemporary cognitive behavioural approaches that have been shown to be very effective for the treatment of anxiety and worry difficulties. These interventions work with the way we think, feel and behave to diminish worry and anxiety in our lives. Self-help therapy, such as using this book, has some advantages over face-to-face treatment with a mental health professional. It is convenient, inexpensive and you can work through at a pace that suits you.

Is this book for you?

If you find that worrying is like a habit that you can't seem to let go of, or that anxiety is a presence in your life more often than not, then this book can offer guidance and coaching in tackling and reducing your anxiety. If you are reading these words, then it is likely that you, or someone you care about, is affected by anxiety. Whether it is this book or another form of support and help that you choose, the important point is that there are proven approaches to reduce worry and anxiety that you can learn to use in your life.

If you are still unsure if this book is for you, consider the following:

- Do you often find yourself worrying throughout the day or week?
- Are you often thinking about the worst that could happen to you or to those you care about?
- Do you often feel nervous or anxious?
- Does anxiety interfere with your ability to socialize, work, study or be a parent or partner?
- Does anxiety or worry make you focus on negative things and make you feel less confident in yourself or doubt your decisions?
- At times, does worry and anxiety overwhelm you or does it feel out of control?

If you answered 'yes' to a number of these questions, then it is likely that worry and anxiety is causing you problems and distress. The evidence-based approach of this book aims to increase your ability to deal with worry and anxiety leading to more enjoyment of life.

How to use this book

How to Deal with Anxiety features the **STEP P**ast method for overcoming anxiety and worry. **STEP P**ast is a five-step approach, drawing on cognitive behavioural therapy techniques, to give practical and emotional support to anyone affected by anxiety and worry.

S – Support helps you come to terms with the problem, and maps out the road to recovery. This part focuses on understanding worry and anxiety, including the different ways we experience anxiety. It gives an overview of the cognitive behavioural approach to dealing with anxiety, and you develop goals for change so you can progress towards where you want to be.

T – **Tackle** the negative thoughts and behaviour patterns that hold you back. This step introduces you to developing your own model of worry and anxiety so that each of the steps you need to take to tackle your worry and anxiety becomes clearer. You will start to learn ways to make changes and deal with anxiety using evidence-based strategies.

E – **Escape** the behaviours and situations that make your life a struggle. This part shows you how to put strategies in place to weaken the grip that anxiety and worry has on you. You learn how to think differently in order to deal with the unhelpful thinking that triggers your anxiety, and ways to use your attention differently, making it more flexible, so you don't get caught in worry.

P – **Practice** involves using your strategies on a daily basis so that they become a new way of responding to unhelpful thinking, worry and anxiety. It also shows you ways to build your resilience to stress and life's difficulties.

P – **Progress** to healthier emotional wellbeing and a happier life – with tools to manage setbacks and relapse. This part helps you to maintain your progress and also provides useful information for those supporting you.

Most chapters contain worksheets, which are designed to help you practise using the techniques you are being shown. These worksheets are also available free online at www.teachyourself.com/howtodealwith when you purchase this book. In addition, the website provides free access to online audio recordings of many of other strategies and exercises in the book.

Two people, Sarah and Luke, who have struggled with worry and anxiety, are described throughout the book to show how anxiety can affect people. They also illustrate how the strategies in this book can be used. These case studies are not real people but are an integration of the experiences of many actual examples of people with worry and anxiety. These case studies are a helpful and realistic way to demonstrate the cognitive behavioural approach to dealing with anxiety and worry.

Take your time reading this book. While you might be keen to read through it quickly, the book takes a *skills-based* approach, each chapter building your skills step by step, similar to how you would work with a cognitive behavioural therapist. From the middle chapters onwards, the practice you do in between chapters is the key to making progress and achieving change. So although you can read through the first few chapters quite quickly, it is important from Chapter 5 onwards to give yourself time between each chapter to put into practice the strategies that have been presented. Pace yourself to allow time to apply the strategies in this book and to develop the skills you will use to change your worry and anxiety.

Importantly, if at any time you believe that your anxiety is becoming too difficult to manage by yourself, then contact your general practitioner or an accredited therapist (see Chapter 15 for contact details). It is always okay to ask for help and support; anxiety can be just as disabling as any other illness.

PART 1

Support

Understand where you are now and where you want to be

CHAPTER 1

What is anxiety?

Overview

While people experience anxiety in individual ways, there are common features of anxiety. In this chapter we will:

- consider what anxiety is
- look at the way anxiety is typically experienced
- work out what specifically causes you to feel anxiety; once you understand this, you can target the anxiety effectively.

There are two worksheets in this chapter: one to help you to identify how anxiety affects you personally and where your anxiety problems may have come from; and one to help you consider the benefits of tackling your anxiety.

What is anxiety?

Anxiety may mean different things to different people in terms of how they feel it, show it and manage it. Anxiety can be distressing and disabling. Before tackling your anxiety, we need to help you to understand it as much as possible. This helps you to know what to do with your anxiety so you experience it less often. We would like to empower you to feel less threatened by your anxiety too.

As you read through this book and put into practice the strategies to reduce your anxiety, it is important to bear in mind that anxiety is experienced by all of us to some degree. Many people, at some point in their life, may battle overwhelming anxiety or even develop an anxiety disorder (see also Chapter 2). Briefly, an anxiety disorder occurs when anxiety becomes overpowering, persistent, causes the person ongoing distress and starts to affect their day-to-day life. There are various anxiety disorders and they are varied in their nature, but they have some common features and symptoms, such as:

- beliefs that something bad will happen in the future or in certain situations
- constant worrying or anxious thoughts that can be hard to control
- physical feelings of anxiety, like an increased heart rate, feeling shaky, feeling panicky, feeling hot, getting a churning stomach, or muscle tension
- feeling fearful, nervous, and anxious
- avoiding any things or situations that are believed to trigger anxiety or make it worse.

Anxiety problems and disorders are common. The current worldwide occurrence for anxiety disorders is 7.3 per cent of people, suggesting that one person in every 14 around the globe has an anxiety disorder at any one point in time. It is estimated that 11–22 per cent of the world's population will suffer with an anxiety disorder in any one-year period (Bromet et al., 2011; Baxter et al., 2013); that's up to *1 in 5* people. Given the high rates of anxiety experienced worldwide, it is not surprising that you or people you know are struggling with anxiety problems.

Having anxiety problems does not mean you are abnormal or weak, especially given how common anxiety is. Many people, including some well-known individuals, have suffered with problematic anxiety; examples include the singers Adele, Robbie Williams and Justin Timberlake, the actors Jennifer Lawrence, Johnny Depp and Scarlett Johansson, and sports people such as the footballer David Beckham, NFL player Ricky Williams, former Irish rugby player Alan Quinlan and former All Blacks player John Kirwan.

So having excessive anxiety does not mean you are abnormal or a failure; it just means that for you a number of factors in life have contributed to anxiety developing into a problem. It is the excessive anxiety that is the problem, *not you*!

Strange though it may seem, anxiety can be useful at times. To understand this we have to go back to the earliest periods in the history of the human species. When we were often exposed and vulnerable in the wild outdoors, a key to survival and protecting ourselves from harm was being able to respond quickly to threat. This is where anxiety comes in; basically, anxiety gets us moving quickly, fleeing from whatever is threatening us, or it prepares us to fight the threat. Sometimes, anxiety may lead to people feeling so overwhelmed that they freeze, much like a deer that has been stalked by a tiger will freeze to remain undetected. This is often referred to as the **flight, fight or freeze response**. It is unlikely that humans would have survived the dangers of the wild if we had not had this response. Remaining relaxed and not responding in ways that saved ourselves would have led to our species being wiped out.

Despite the millenia since, our bodies are still wired to react to threat. We still have the flight, fight or freeze response that goes hand in hand with anxiety. This can be valuable now too, for example if you are driving and another car pulls out in front of you, or if you have a child who is pulling something off a high shelf that may fall on top of them. In these situations, we react quickly because of the flight, fight or freeze response and because of anxiety. In these types of situations our anxiety is adaptive and protective. However, sometimes our anxiety occurs at other times and is out of context or it appears 'out of the blue' which is unhelpful and makes us feel distressed or apprehensive.

How is anxiety different from fear?

Often the words 'fear' and 'anxiety' are used interchangeably and this can create confusion. Researchers of emotions have reported that anxiety and fear are different but overlapping states (Sylvers et al., 2011). Two well-known researchers in the field of anxiety and the treatment of anxiety disorders, David A. Clark and Aaron Beck (2011), noted that fear is a basic and automatic judgment of threat or danger and is the central part of anxiety disorders. In contrast, they noted that anxiety is a more lasting condition of threat or apprehension that involves fear but also beliefs about things or events being uncontrollable or uncertain. They added that the person with anxiety believes they are vulnerable or helpless. Therefore, fear is the main emotion we feel but anxiety is the continuous state of being in 'threat mode' and can involve emotions such as fear but also physical reactions, like an increased heart rate, and responses or behaviours aimed at protecting ourselves or avoiding the thing we think is dangerous.

How do we experience anxiety?

Anxiety can be experienced in many ways. There are four components of anxiety reactions: our thinking, our emotions, our physical responses and our behaviour.

Our thinking

Our thoughts or thinking, often referred to in psychology as **cognitive processes**, are a key part of our anxiety response. Thoughts or beliefs related to feeling threatened in some way are the core feature in anxiety. Often if we have experienced anxiety a few times we may start to believe we are more vulnerable to harm. These beliefs about threat, and possibly our inability to manage anxiety, means that our thinking can become biased so that we might read danger into situations that may not be dangerous. Some examples of anxious thinking are: 'I won't cope'; 'Something bad is going to happen to me'; or 'No one will help me'. Also, our thinking can occur in the form of **worry** about danger or harm. Worry is a seemingly endless chain of ongoing and repetitive anxious thoughts that something awful or serious may happen. Worry is often experienced as 'What if …?' thoughts, such as 'What if I can't cope?', 'What if I fail?', or 'What if my child gets abducted?'. We might also experience our thoughts in the form of distressing pictures or images in our mind, as if an film projector in our head is showing our worst fears on the screen.

Our emotions

Anxiety itself can be an emotion. However, when we are anxious, we may feel other emotions or feelings too, such as fear, nervousness or apprehension. We may feel embarrassed about getting anxious. We can also feel frustrated, for example if we are fed up with feeling anxious or if our anxiety is preventing us from doing things or going places. Sometimes we may feel angry at ourselves for getting anxious, or angry with others because we think they are putting us in situations that make us anxious and they do not understand how difficult it is to manage anxiety and worry. Sometimes, if the anxiety has been around for a long time, we may start to feel sad, low or depressed because of the impact the anxiety is having on us and on our ability to enjoy life.

Our physical response

As mentioned above, when we are anxious we can experience the flight, fight or freeze response. This response can be helpful if we are under threat, for example if someone is trying to hurt us, or an animal is chasing us. However, worry and anxiety may often occur when there is no clear or present danger. The brain will trigger the flight, fight or freeze response when a visible and immediate danger is not in front of us if we *believe* there is a threat of some sort. The thought of danger itself can set-off the physical anxiety reaction in our body! Some of the physical sensations we might experience include:

- the heart beating faster – this sends more blood to the muscles so that we are more able to fight or run away
- a tight chest and quicker, shallower breathing - this enables us to take in more oxygen and readies the body to fight or run away
- tension in the muscles – this is the body readying itself to fight or run away, and can cause tembling
- feeling dizzy or light-headed – this is a result of the quicker, shallower breathing
- feeling hot – this is because the body sweats to keep cool, which makes it more efficient

- feeling a bit detached from what's going on around you – our thoughts race to evaluate and respond quickly to a threat, which can make it difficult to concentrate on anything else.

Other common physical anxiety responses can include headaches, an upset stomach, feeling restless, sweating, and being tired.

Perhaps this may help you to see that these physical sensations are normal reactions to threat and are not dangerous. That is, our body is reacting normally and just as it should to a perceived danger. Our body is trying to protect us by getting us ready to fight or flee. It is our **anxious thinking** triggering this response too frequently that is the problem, not the sensations themselves. While these physical sensations may feel very uncomfortable, they are not dangerous; they are just sensations.

Our behaviour

There are certain things we may do or not do when we are anxious. When we have anxious thoughts, feel nervous and experience some of the physical sensations noted above, we may behave in certain ways to try to avoid the anxiety occurring or to escape it. Common behaviours include:

- avoiding situations that might trigger the anxiety, e.g. someone who worries about getting cancer may avoid watching television programmes set in hospitals or reading the newspaper in case cancer is mentioned
- leaving situations to escape anxiety, e.g. leaving a shopping mall or a social event because they experience anxiety being around other people
- trying to avoid uncertainty, e.g. they may avoid things that don't have a clear outcome or set plan, or that seem beyond their control
- trying to do everything perfectly so that no mistakes will occur or nothing will go wrong

● being overly controlling of themselves and those around them to ensure the worst does not happen.

There are many other behavioural reactions related to anxiety. These behaviours may appear to be good ways to reduce anxiety but, for reasons discussed in later chapters, these behaviours tend to feed anxiety in the long term. An important focus of this book is to help you to work out which behaviours may be keeping your anxiety going and what behaviours may be more helpful to you in overcoming your anxiety.

Self-assessment ✓

Write down below how your anxiety shows itself. It might be helpful to think of a recent time when you experienced anxiety.

Worksheet 1A: My anxiety

How does your body feel when you are anxious? (e.g. *tense, heart races*)

_____

_____

_____

_____

_____

What emotions do you experience? (e.g. *scared, fearful*)

_____

_____

_____

_____

_____

_____

What do you think when you are anxious? (e.g. *I can't do it,
I will get it wrong*)

_____

_____

_____

_____

_____

_____

What do you do when you are anxious? (e.g. *leave the situation, don't go*)

_____

_____

_____

_____

_____

_____

Is anxiety bad?

Earlier we said that anxiety can be protective when there is a clear
threat. A small amount of anxiety can help us to stay alert and even to
perform better than if we were relaxed. Think about driving a car or

riding a cycle on a busy road and you will see how some anxiety could help us to be watchful and alert for anything that may collide with us. Also, if you have ever sat an exam or played a sport, you might have noticed that some anxiety helps us be sharper in our thinking and performance. If a rugby or netball player goes to the field or court to play a game, they will play better if they are a little anxious or 'hyped up' than if they were too relaxed. However, too much anxiety can make it hard to focus or perform to the best of our abilities.

So it's important to remember anxiety itself is not necessarily bad; it has a function. Worrying about getting anxious and wanting to get rid of anxiety will contribute to it reoccurring because it is not possible to be completely without some anxiety in your life. If you have too much anxiety or if anxiety is occurring without good reason or unexpectedly, then we can 'turn the anxiety down' by viewing anxiety differently and engaging in less worry. This may seem like an impossible task but the cognitive behavioural techniques in this book have been shown to be effective in helping people reduce all the different aspects (thoughts, emotions, physical reactions and behaviours) of anxiety.

How does anxiety affect our lives?

Sometimes people with excessive worrying and anxiety experience less enjoyment or a poorer quality of life. Anxiety can impact on our friendships and our family and romantic relationships. Worrying and the related anxiety can lead to emotional distress, interfering with peoples' ability to carry out daily activities at home, at work or in their studies. We may worry so much or be so anxious that it interferes with our concentration or ability to remember things. Also, if you worry about not being able to manage something at work or in other areas of your life, you may avoid taking on new tasks or new responsibilities because of beliefs that it will all go wrong.

Often when we are anxious we may turn to a loved one or a friend for support or to feel safe. While this is helpful and healthy at times, when worry or anxiety is the driving force behind seeking support, continual reassurance-seeking may tire out our loved ones and put stress on our relationships with them. For example, a worried person may frequently ask their partner if everything will be all right, or will continually check up on them to ensure they are safe. Don't be hard on yourself if this is the case for you. It's understandable when you feel distressed that you want to do whatever you can to reduce it. Sometimes, though, the people around you may not know what to say or how to support you when you are anxious; Chapter 14 explains how partners, family and friends can support you in ways that help to reduce your worry and anxiety over the long term rather than contributing to keeping it going.

If you have children, you may be wondering if your worrying and anxiety is affecting them. First, it is important to recognize that many factors in our children's lives shape how they develop, think and behave. It would be unhelpful to think that your worrying and anxiety is the main factor in their wellbeing. However, for some children, a parent worrying excessively or being overly anxious may mean the child learns or adopts these ways of responding to stress also. Fortunately, there are steps you can take to overcome this, such as identifying some of the worry behaviours you might be using and then decreasing them. The good news is that these worry behaviours will be worked on as you progress through this book.

One of the benefits of change and of working on your anxiety is that its negative impact on your home and work life, your social life and your relationships with others can be lessened. This means you can improve your wellbeing and your enjoyment of life! Use this thought to fuel the effort needed for tackling your anxiety.

What causes excessive anxiety or anxiety disorder?

Generally, anxiety problems do not have a single cause but are arise from a combination of factors. Some of us may be born with a genetic or biological predisposition or increased likelihood of developing anxiety difficulties. As with other physical conditions, like asthma or diabetes, if there is a family history of anxiety we may be more likely to develop it. This genetic disposition or vulnerability does not guarantee we will get anxiety; it just means we may be more susceptible to it in certain circumstances, like a tendency to asthma being triggered by living in an area with poor air quality.

There usually need to be factors other than genetics involved in the development of an anxiety problem, such as experiences we had when we were young or perhaps an event that triggered it, like a car accident or a health scare. It may be also that we have learned to cope with life's challenges and difficulties by using worry or by trying to avoid anything that may not go the way we want or that involves some uncertainty. Therefore, we may not have fully developed the skills to manage anxiety or stress in a way that prevents it from continuing or getting worse.

Early experiences that can contribute to developing worry or anxiety problems later in life include whether or not people in your family worry. If we see a family member frequently using worrying as a way of managing stress or if they believe that worrying will prevent the worst from happening, we as children may learn that worrying is a way to cope with life's stresses or a way to stop bad things from happening. If our caregivers were often anxious, we may have developed the belief that we need to be on the lookout for harm or to be anxious about life. Other experiences in life that can contribute to the growth of worry as a problem include having had experiences as children or young people that felt or may have been out of our control, such as:

- parents separating, or a family member getting sick or dying
- one of our parents leaving us

- being involved in an accident, like a car accident
- experiencing some type of disaster
- being bullied or teased badly
- being repeatedly hurt or harmed by people in our lives
- not doing as well as we would like at school or at other activities
- being very ill
- family, teachers or others telling us or leading us to believe that we can't cope with things or that we make bad decisions
- growing up with uncertainty, such as a chaotic household or our parents struggling with employment, finances or managing their own emotions.

In Chapter 4, we will consider how our biological make-up and early experiences shape our beliefs, thinking and self-talk, and how these in turn can generate worry and anxiety.

What if I can't find causes for my worry?

We understand that you may want a straight answer about where your anxiety came from, but if you have been unable to identify possible causes, don't spend too much time going over this in your mind; repeatedly searching for an answer can become unhelpful in itself as the process can cause anxiety and needless worry! Even if you learned the cause it may not stop the anxiety and worry from happening now. Think about someone who suffers with asthma; focusing on what caused their asthma originally rather than what's affecting it now is unlikely to help them. For example, if they did not exercise and lived in an area that had bad air quality or they smoked cigarettes, these factors, regardless of how the asthma started, would worsen their asthma and keep their breathing problems going. However, if they started to exercise, quit smoking and worked or lived somewhere with better air quality, their asthma would probably improve greatly. It's much the same with anxiety problems and worrying, i.e. identifying and addressing the factors that maintain your worry and anxiety will help you to reduce it. Throughout this book we help you to identify the maintaining factors of your worrying and anxiety, as well as explaining ways to fade out, diminish or let go of them.

The benefits of tackling your anxiety

If you are reading this book, you are already considering trying to deal with your anxiety and worry, or you may be feeling stuck and not sure what to do. Learning new ways to address anxiety and putting these strategies in place can be challenging and take time. This might seem like a barrier and put off some people, but remember that while it may be tough at times to tackle your anxiety, the benefits of reducing the hold that worry and anxiety have on you will be extremely valuable.

It is important to look at the advantages of changing and tackling your worry and anxiety. In Worksheet 1B you will have the opportunity to think about what some of the benefits will be. We encourage you to complete this exercise even if you already feel strongly about working on your anxiety, because if things get tough you will be able to look back at these benefits, which will help motivate you and give you the strength to keep going.

Reviewing behaviour

Write down the benefits of having less worry and anxiety in your life. It can help to think about what benefits there may be in the next few weeks, as well as in the longer term.

The following questions and the examples shown below may help you to identify benefits.

- What is your motivation for change – why do you want to change?
- How will you feel with less anxiety?
- What will you be able to do more of without worry and anxiety?
- How will your social, work or family life be different?

Worksheet 1B: The benefits of tackling my worry and anxiety

Feel less distress
Be able to focus on the present moment more and not get caught up in worry
Feel more relaxed and able to enjoy activities more because I'm not so stressed and anxious
Get to sleep better
More energy for myself and others

_____

_____

_____

_____

_____

_____

_____

_____

_____

_____

_____

Now that you have completed your benefits worksheet, where does that leave you? It's likely that there are many benefits that will make the effort to change worthwhile. Given that you have now identified the positives to tackling your anxiety, how will you remember them? When we are worrying or anxious it is hard to remember helpful thoughts. So we need to stamp those benefits and reasons for change into your mind to make them so well-known to you that they cannot be blotted out by worry and anxiety. Below are some ideas about how you could do this. The key is to make sure you are reminded about the benefits of change in your day-to-day life and that these benefits are on hand when the road to tackling your anxiety gets challenging.

- Put a copy of your completed Worksheet 1B somewhere you will see it often at home, such as on your fridge, your bedroom wall or in your home office.
- Tell a loved one or a support person what your benefits to change are so they can remind you of these regularly or when the going gets tough.
- Write out the benefits on a small card and put it in your wallet or purse so you see it often.
- Put the benefits on your phone, maybe as a photo of the worksheet, or keyed as a memo or as a voice recording.
- Visualize in your mind how things will be when you have reduced the anxiety. What would your benefits look like in a picture or image? Come up with an image in your mind of you relaxing or enjoying time with friends or family that symbolizes your benefits for change.

Two people's stories of worry and anxiety

Here is some background about our two case studies, Luke and Sarah, and their experiences with worry and anxiety. As we go through the book we will talk more about their worry and how they use some of the techniques for tackling worry and anxiety covered in this book.

Case study: Luke, aged 24

Luke has battled with worry since he was a teenager, when he used to worry about how he was doing at school, with his friends and at sport. He was a bit anxious when he started school and didn't like to be away from his parents much.

He is now working for a computer graphics company and is also completing a part-time degree in design and marketing. He has been with his girlfriend, Amanda, for about a year and she often spends time with him at his flat, which he rents with his friend Mike.

Luke's worry and anxiety have been particularly persistent over the past few years owing to the pressure of his job and taking on more study. He also broke up with his previous girlfriend about two years ago after a four-year relationship, and this really affected him badly. He has a good relationship with his parents, who separated when he was eight years old. While he loves them both, he found that his mother had high expectations of him as he grew up, while his father has always been a bit of a 'worrier' and Luke doesn't want to end up like that.

Luke notices his worry is worse in the mornings and on Sunday nights before work. He feels quite anxious in the mornings and has trouble eating because his stomach is upset and he just doesn't feel hungry. Sometimes at work or when a university assignment is due he gets worked up with worry, experiencing muscle tension and headaches, and feeling very overwhelmed and irritable. He often worries he will get things wrong, won't get his work tasks or assignments done, and that Amanda will leave him. Luke hasn't really spoken much about his worry and anxiety to anyone because he is embarrassed about it.

Case study: Sarah, aged 38

Sarah's anxiety and worry really became noticeable to her when her grandmother had cancer when Sarah was 12 years old. Sarah was close to her grandmother and was upset by her being ill. Her grandmother survived her cancer but Sarah started to worry lot about dying or getting seriously ill herself. Her mother also told her that when Sarah was a young girl she used to worry about something happening to her or her parents, would often have bad dreams and end up sleeping in her parents' bed, and was afraid of something bad happening to her or her family.

Nowadays, Sarah believes that she worries daily about anything and everything. She particularly worries about something happening to her children, Jacob (10 years old) and Ella (13 years old). She is worried that they'll be abducted or physically harmed in some way by someone, or that they'll be in an accident. She constantly thinks about how they are doing at school and whether they are liked and have friends. She worries a lot about her husband, Steve, a sales rep whose job involves a lot of driving; she is concerned he might crash. She also worries about the stability of his work and their finances. Steve is often short with her and says there is nothing to worry about, especially as Sarah does some part-time hairstyling work. Sarah also worries greatly about getting cancer or some other serious illness that will mean she won't be around for her kids.

Sarah's worries lead to anxiety and nervousness every day and difficulties getting to sleep at night as she thinks about all the things that could go wrong. Her worry and anxiety feels relentless and often leaves her with a sense of dread. At times she feels down because of the energy that the worry drains from her. Her doctor told her she has generalized anxiety disorder and some occasional low mood, and that exercising and relaxation might help.

Chapter summary

In this chapter you have learned:

- what anxiety is and that it is a common problem for many; you're not alone!
- how anxiety can be experienced in our thinking, our emotions and our physical responses, and how it may affect our behaviour
- that at times we need some anxiety and it can be beneficial in the right setting or context
- where your anxiety may have come from
- the benefits of tackling your anxiety
- about Luke and Sarah, who also struggle with worry and anxiety.

You have also completed worksheets on your experience of anxiety (Worksheet 1A) and the benefits of tackling anxiety (Worksheet 1B). Keep Worksheet 1B handy to remind yourself of what you will gain from reducing the role of anxiety in your life. For ongoing motivation and self-support it is good to refer to this worksheet from time to time as you work through this book.

In Chapter 2 we will look at what worry is, and generalized anxiety disorder and the other types of anxiety disorders and related conditions that people may experience.

What is worry and generalized anxiety disorder?

Overview

Winston Churchill once reflected, 'When I look back on all these worries, I remember the story of the old man who said on his deathbed that he had had a lot of trouble in his life, most of which had never happened'. Indeed, many of us worry about things that may never happen.

In this chapter we will learn about:

- what worry is
- how worry is related to generalized anxiety disorder, or GAD
- some conditions that may occur with GAD or worry, such as low mood and depression
- other types of anxiety-related disorders, such as panic disorder and social anxiety disorder.

It's important to keep in mind that mental health problems are not uncommon; about 1 in 5 people may be currently experiencing a mental illness.

What is worry?

Worry is a core feature of anxiety. Worry is basically when people frequently think a thought or related thoughts over and over again without finding an answer or some way forward. Worry is like a chain of thoughts that seem unstoppable and cause us to feel anxious. Such thoughts tend to be negative, or may be upsetting mental images. People may keep going over and over these thoughts or images because they believe that worrying will help them find an answer to a problem, or that worrying about something bad taking place will actually stop it from happening. However, worries and the beliefs that we may have about worrying, such as it being helpful or harmful, are often unfounded.

Worrying about events that we may have no control over does nothing to change the likelihood of such an event taking place. If you placed a bet on a horse in the Grand National, Kentucky Derby or Melbourne Cup and then stood in front of the television thinking over and over again 'My horse is going to win', this repetitive thinking would not influence or change the outcome of the race or the likelihood of your horse winning. The same is true of repeatedly thinking or worrying that something bad will happen; these thoughts and worries are just thoughts and will not change the likelihood of something happening or not happening.

People worry about many different things, but over the years researchers and therapists have found some common issues that people tend to worry about. These include:

- their own safety or the safety of those they love
- their own health or the health of others
- issues in their relationships
- issues at work
- their future
- broader world events, such as natural disasters, terrorism or environmental issues.

For many people, worry may come and go and not be problematic. However, for some people the worry may continue for extended periods of time or start to cause them distress. The worry is often accompanied by some of the physical symptoms of anxiety, such as feeling restless, an increased heartbeat, butterflies in the stomach or other sensations described in Chapter 1. When worry starts to cause recurrent distress, it may be developing into generalized anxiety disorder.

What is generalized anxiety disorder?

Anxiety or worrying is called generalized anxiety disorder (GAD) when the worry is:

- repetitive
- occurs most days
- is about a variety of things
- is difficult to control
- has been happening for at least six months.

GAD is basically a condition of chronic worry. The worry is associated with a variety of emotional and physical anxiety symptoms, which, together with the worry, cause distress, affect a person's ability to function on a daily basis and get things done, or reduces a person's ability to enjoy their life. The symptoms can include feeling restless, tired and lacking in energy, and experiencing muscle tension, concentration problems, sleep problems and increased irritability. Sometimes people with GAD experience panic attacks, which are a rush of anxiety symptoms or flight, fight, freeze sensations that often seem to occur unexpectedly; more information about panic attacks is given later in this chapter.

The things that people worry about are varied, may change over time and can include health, family, work, relationships, and social and financial worries. Often people experience these worries as relentless 'What if …?' questions in their mind. GAD is one of the more commonly experienced psychological problems. The average age at which people develop GAD is around 30 years, but most people with GAD report that they have experienced nervousness, anxiety and worry for most of their lives. The severity and frequency of the worry and anxiety for people with GAD tends to fluctuate throughout their lives, sometimes being continual and persistent and at other times less intense. It has been estimated that up to 9 per cent of people may experience GAD at some point during their lifetime (American Psychiatric Association, 2013).

Problems often associated with GAD

Rumination

Rumination is a similar process to worry because, like worry, it is a form of repetitive negative thinking. The difference between rumination and worry is that worry mainly focuses on things in the present or future going wrong or turning out badly, or apprehension about harm occurring. Worry mainly leads to anxiety. Ruminative thinking tends to dwell on past problems and negative past experiences. These past experiences can be related to what a person believes are their shortfalls or failures, or people may ruminate about losses or problems of some sort. Rumination typically leads to feelings of sadness, shame, worthlessness and depression; sometimes ruminating on past unpleasant experiences may lead to feelings of anger, hurt, resentment and anxiety too. At times people may just brood over why they feel so unhappy or ruminate about how bad or depressed they feel, which in turn worsens their mood.

While rumination and worry differ in the content of the thoughts that are running through a person's mind, both are persistent and repetitive forms of unhelpful thinking, and they often occur together for some people.

Depression

It is common for people who have anxiety problems like GAD to sometimes experience depression. All of us may feel low from time to time, but depression occurs when this low mood is ongoing. One of the core features of depression is experiencing negative and critical thoughts such as 'I am useless' or 'I am unlovable'. People suffering with a depressive illness often experience the belief that the future is hopeless or bleak. Depression causes people to see day-to-day life through a dark lens, perceiving life as pointless and without any pleasure, and they may believe that others do not care about or need them. Often these negative thoughts become the subject of rumination.

Major depressive disorder is what most people mean when they talk about depression. There are a variety of debilitating symptoms that characterize a major depressive episode. People often feel sad or numb and lose pleasure in many, if not all activities, including socializing and time with family, as well as experiencing a reduced sex drive. They can suffer weight changes, sleeping problems, difficulty with concentration and problems with memory and decision making. Also common are feelings of worthlessness, guilt, anxiety, hopelessness and helplessness, loss of energy, fatigue, feeling slowed up or wound up, and thoughts of death or suicide. Depression may be experienced by up to 7 per cent of people each year and by 9–18 per cent of people in their lifetime.

Depression can lead to anxiety and vice versa. Living with anxiety for a long time can be very disheartening, leading to feelings of hopelessness and periods of low mood. Anxiety compromises a person's ability to concentrate and impairs their attention and their ability to enjoy life, all of which can contribute to depression. Depression can also lead to anxiety. When depressed, people feel sad much of the time, their pleasure in simple things is noticeably reduced and they often struggle to keep up with their normal activities. People can become very worried and anxious about their ability to keep on top of things and cope when they are depressed. Also, they may feel anxious about the pressure they are experiencing from others to be their 'old self', and about letting others or themselves down. In addition to anxiety leading to depression or depression leading to anxiety, people can experience both anxiety and depression concurrently.

Anger

Anger is a normal emotion that we all experience. For some, anger becomes a problem when they start to experience it too much or express it in ways that are harmful to themselves or others. People battling with persistent worry and anxiety may find that they get angry with themselves or frustrated by feeling overwhelmed most of the time. Also, worry and anxiety can wear people down, leading to irritability towards others. If you are experiencing increased levels of anger or anger difficulties that are related to your worry, then it's likely that the strategies in this book will reduce your anger problems as your worry and anxiety lessens. However, if you are having anger problems or are expressing your anger in ways that are distressing to others, we would encourage you to talk to your doctor about this or seek help from a registered therapist (see Chapter 15).

Alcohol and drugs

Some people turn to alcohol and drugs to deal with worry and anxiety or to help them relax. This may seem like a helpful way to reduce anxiety or worry at first, but alcohol and drugs can make anxiety worse. Once the initial effects of alcohol or drugs wear off (the relaxed feeling or the 'high'), the substances are processed by your body and can cause sleep problems during the night and can also cause anxiety and mood problems in the following days; even small amounts of alcohol can disrupt your sleep that night. There are long-term effects too, including keeping your anxiety going, and other mental and physical health problems, such as feeling low and placing a strain on your liver and kidneys. Alcohol and drugs can also interfere with prescribed medication, making them less effective or causing unfavourable reactions.

Other anxiety and related disorders

People with GAD can also experience other types of anxiety conditions. All of these conditions have two things in common: they are associated with a great deal of distress for the person concerned, and they make it difficult for the person to lead or enjoy a normal life.

Panic attacks

Panic attacks are an extreme anxiety experience. They are very frightening for those experiencing them, sometimes occuring out of the blue or sometimes being triggered by a stressful event. When people have a panic attack, they experience a sudden rush of fear or intense distress accompanied by a number of the following:

- increased heart rate or palpitations
- chest pain or ache
- sweating, trembling or shaking
- chills or hot flushes
- feeling short of breath or breathing fast
- tightness in the throat or feelings of choking
- feeling sick
- dizziness, light-headedness or feeling faint
- numbness or tingling in the skin, especially in fingers, toes or lips
- feelings of unreality or being detached – feeling 'spaced out' or as if the world you're in is not real
- thinking you're going to faint or collapse, suffocate, have a heart attack or stroke, lose control of your bladder or bowels, or lose control of yourself and 'go crazy'.

Attacks typically last for five to 20 minutes.

Panic attacks can occur with different types of anxiety disorders. For example, if someone has GAD and their worry is becoming overwhelming, they may experience a panic attack. For someone with social anxiety, a panic attack might occur in a social situation that they are fearful of. Someone with a phobia (intense fear) of heights may have a panic attack if they are on the top floor of a building.

It is important to note that we all might feel panicky or stressed from time to time when we are in a nerve-racking situation, such as an interview for a job or going on a thrill ride, or if something startles us or gives us a fright. This is not the same as having a full-scale panic attack. Also, many people may experience a panic attack at some point in their life without developing an ongoing or reoccurring difficulty or a disorder.

Panic disorder

Unlike panic attacks related to general worries, social situations or a phobia, panic disorder occurs when a person believes their panic attacks or panic sensations will lead to losing control in some way or to physical or mental harm (such as having a heart attack or a stroke, or 'going crazy') or to death. To be classified as panic disorder, the panic attacks need to be recurrent for at least a month with a person fearing them happening again or trying to avoid triggering an attack. The reoccurring panic attacks often seem unexpected and can occur while people are sleeping, so that they wake feeling distressed. Up to 7 per cent of people may develop panic disorder during their life.

Some people with panic disorder also experience **agoraphobia**, which causes them to avoid places that they believe will trigger a panic attack. People with agoraphobia only feel safe when they are in certain environments or 'safe places' like their home. The thought of going out, being in a cinema, shopping mall or crowded area, on public transport, or standing in a queue, for example, is very distressing and is avoided at all costs. If agoraphobia is untreated, the number of places in which a person feels safe shrinks, sometimes to the point that the person becomes a prisoner in their own home.

Social anxiety disorder

Although it's normal to experience nervousness in social situations at times, some people can experience severe anxiety when around others. Social anxiety disorder occurs when the anxiety a person experiences is focused on social situations or doing things in front of others. The person worries about being scrutinized or judged by others or worries that they will embarrass themselves, often to the point that they will avoid social gatherings. Such anxiety is more extreme than the shyness some people experience. Those with social anxiety disorder become very anxious or may experience panic attack symptoms in social situations. They are often very apprehensive prior to social situations, particularly if they might have to meet or interact with unfamiliar people. Each year 8 per cent of people may experience social anxiety disorder and 13 per cent of people will have it at some point during their life.

Specific phobia

Specific phobia occurs when a person is extremely fearful of certain situations or objects, to the extent that the fear interferes with their life. When they are confronted by these situations or objects they become extremely anxious and may have a panic attack. They will do all they can to avoid the feared object or situation. Common phobias include an extreme fear of heights, enclosed spaces, flying, needles, vomiting and animals such as spiders, snakes or dogs. It is estimated that 9 per cent of people may experience a specific phobia each year, with up to 18 per cent of people experiencing a specific phobia during their life.

Post-traumatic stress disorder

At some point in our life, we might experience or witness a traumatic experience, such as a natural disaster, an accident, war or being assaulted or abused by others. At the time such an experience occurs, it is expected and understandable that people feel overwhelmed and distressed. For many, this distress passes in the days or weeks following the event. However, some people develop post-traumatic stress disorder

(PTSD). This occurs when they continue to suffer with distress and anxiety related to the traumatic event for months or years after the event, such as experiencing unwanted thoughts, images or memories of the event when awake and dreams or nightmares about it when asleep. They may also experience emotional and physical reactions to any reminders of the traumatic event, including feeling anxious or fearful or experiencing a racing heart or panic attacks. They might have sleep problems, difficulties with anger, feel overly alert and are easily startled. Understandably, the person may also try to avoid anything that is associated with or that reminds them of the event. It is estimated that around 10 per cent of people will experience PTSD in their lifetime.

Obsessive compulsive disorder

Obsessive compulsive disorder (OCD) is a complex and disabling condition that is characterized by someone experiencing recurrent unwanted and negative thoughts, images or urges (obsessions). These thoughts or obsessions can be quite illogical and distressing, and are about activities that are highly unlikely to occur, e.g. thoughts about keeping something very clean to avoid catching germs or thoughts that the house might burn down if certain rituals about turning off the heating are not followed. Sometimes the intrusive thoughts are about doing harm to others, such as their children, or engaging in sexual activities that are objectionable to themselves, even though these are things they would never want to do or act on.

Compulsions are the behaviours or actions, sometimes called rituals, that people do in response to their obsessions. These rituals are done to prevent the feared 'worst' event occurring and to reduce the person's anxiety related to the obsessional thoughts, e.g. spending many hours cleaning to prevent getting sick or repeatedly checking that the heater is turned off to stop a fire starting. Sometimes the compulsion includes trying to push the obsessional thoughts or images away because they are so upsetting or saying a prayer to counteract the obsessional thought. OCD is experienced by 2 per cent of people every year.

Body dysmorphic disorder

For many of us there is something about our body or the way we look that we are not particularly happy about, but people with body dysmorphic disorder (BDD) spend much of their time preoccupied with the flaws they perceive in their looks. They might be worried about a single feature of their body or several parts. Their preoccupation with their believed or slight imperfections leads to endless worry and anxiety about their appearance. This is associated with a number of behaviours, such as looking in the mirror excessively, spending hours grooming, frequently comparing themselves to others, picking their skin to make it free of imperfections, continually asking others for reassurance about how they look, doing too much exercise or weight lifting to change their body, or trying to cover up the part of their body they don't like. In some cases people with BDD have cosmetic surgery but usually this does not take away their concerns or anxiety. About 2.5 per cent of people may have BDD at any time.

Health anxiety

Health anxiety (also called hypochondriasis, or illness anxiety disorder) is a preoccupation with or strong fear about having or getting a serious illness. This means the person experiences substantial worry and anxiety about getting a severe health condition such as cancer or something else that will make them terminally ill. This often leads to the person believing that normal bodily sensations or physical occurrences such as headaches or minor pains are signs of a life-threatening serious illness. The person may repeatedly check their body for any indication of disease or illness or may repeatedly see their doctor or go on the internet to seek reassurance. Despite reassurances that they are okay, the person continues to be plagued with anxiety and worry about becoming unwell. The rates of health anxiety are estimated to be 3–10 per cent of people in a one-year period.

There are many similarities between health anxiety and GAD. The core feature of both is worry. In GAD it's usually worry about a number of things, which can include health worries, while in health anxiety the main content of the worry is getting a serious illness. If health worries are your main concern, you can benefit from the approach used in this book. However, if your health anxiety persists or does not improve, please seek guidance from your doctor or an accredited therapist.

Luke

After reading about worry Luke realized that worry was a problem for him. He also began to understand that he did feel anger at times when he was worrying a lot or if he had been ruminating or dwelling on his last relationship. He didn't believe he had depression, but recognized that his mood dipped a bit when he felt he had 'messed' something up at work or in his studies. It made sense to him that he felt anxious and irritable because of all the worry that was going round and round in his mind. Luke became more aware that he was sometimes drinking beer during the week to help get rid of his worry.

Sarah

Sarah found some of the points in this chapter upsetting because they really mirrored her experiences with worry. She now understood more that she was actually suffering with an illness, generalized anxiety disorder, which helped her to make sense of why she felt so overwhelmed. She recognized that she did feel so plagued with worry at times that she got panicky. When she read the information about health anxiety, it seemed to fit with some of the worries she had too.

Chapter summary

In this chapter you have learned about:

- worry and generalized anxiety disorder (GAD)
- some of the common difficulties that people with worry or GAD may experience, such as depression, anger or over-use of alcohol
- other anxiety and related disorders, which may or may not apply to you, such as panic disorder, social anxiety disorder and health anxiety.

Before moving on, use your Worksheet 1B to remind yourself of the benefits of tackling anxiety.

In Chapter 3, the cognitive behavioural approach to managing anxiety will be explained, including the relationship between our thoughts, emotional feelings, physical sensations and behaviours. It also covers the key factors that will help you to use this approach effectively in your day-to-day life, and helps you to create goals for tackling your anxiety.

Ways to help you change and reduce anxiety

Overview

In this chapter you will learn about:

- the cognitive behavioural approach to managing anxiety
- key factors that will help you to use this approach successfully in your everyday life
- developing specific goals, and planning how you will achieve them.

The worksheets will also help you to identify the people who can support you as you work through this book and assist you in monitoring your progress.

The cognitive behavioural approach to anxiety

The term 'cognitive behavioural' describes a broad framework or approach, which underpins a short-term talking therapy called cognitive behavioural therapy, often referred to as CBT. CBT is an effective therapy for treating many mental health problems and is particularly useful for treating and managing anxiety. Although CBT is the recommended treatment for anxiety, it is not always available through the health system or affordable for individuals. Research (Pittaway et al., 2008) indicates that self-help CBT (e.g. via books, online) can be used successfully and is recommended, among other things, for people who are experiencing mild to moderate anxiety problems.

At the heart of all CBT is the assumption that a person's anxiety levels are directly related to his or her patterns of thinking (cognitive) and the strategies or actions (behaviour) a person uses to try to cope with or reduce the anxiety they are experiencing.

A key message in the cognitive behavioural approach is that the way we think directly impacts on how we feel emotionally and physically, which in turn influences our actions. Figure 3.1 shows this link.

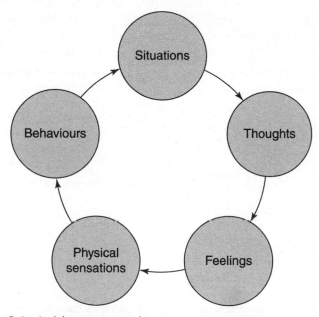

Figure 3.1: A vicious worry cycle

The table below shows what we mean by thoughts, feelings, physical sensations and behaviours.

Thoughts	Your mental chatter, thinking, beliefs, self-talk, words, images, mind pictures or videos.
Feelings	All of your emotions, such as feeling nervous, sad, fearful, frustrated, happy, contented.
Physical sensations	What we experience in our body, e.g. butterflies in the stomach, heart racing faster, headaches, shortness of breath.
Behaviours	Your actions, the things you do or don't do, e.g. crying, yelling, not speaking, repeatedly checking things, avoiding what you believe will trigger your anxiety.

When people are anxious their whole self is anxious, that is, their attitudes, emotions, physical state and their behaviour. Excessive dwelling on the 'What if' thoughts and thinking that things will go wrong might lead to a person feeling anxious and fearful, having stomach upsets and sleep disturbance, and avoiding anxiety-provoking situations. Look at the example below of someone going to an appointment and how the worry 'What ifs' can impact on a person. Notice the links between the thoughts, feelings, physical sensations and behaviours.

Situation	Leaving later than planned for an important meeting
Thoughts	What if I am late? What if my boss gets angry ... That would be terrible!
Feelings	Apprehension Fear
Physical sensations	Stomach upset Sweaty
Behaviours	Drive faster in the car Fidgety Text while driving

A vicious cycle can result, so that the person feels there is no way to stop the anxiety and worry, which in turn can affect their sense of self-worth and they may become depressed about life and the state of anxiety they find themselves in. Their ability to live a full and happy life is reduced. Figure 3.1 shows an example of a vicious worry cycle.

The goal of the cognitive behavioural approach is to teach you how to weaken the links in these anxiety and worry cycles. This approach shows you how to alleviate your anxiety by gradually learning to recognize unhelpful and unrealistic thoughts and worry patterns. You then learn to respond differently to those thoughts and to develop more helpful ways to manage. A cognitive behavioural approach for worry and GAD can produce sustained improvements for people and involves relatively simple, systematic steps to follow. The skills that you develop to manage anxiety can be used for the rest of your life to help you deal with problems in the future and as a way of improving your wellbeing.

The principles of cognitive behavioural anxiety management are:

- helping you to help yourself
- focusing on your 'here and now' problems and difficulties
- taking a structured and practical approach to anxiety reduction
- providing specific manageable techniques to learn and apply one step at a time
- systematically developing and increasing skills so that managing worry and anxiety gradually gets easier
- working at your own pace
- directly targeting the thoughts and behaviours that create and maintain your anxiety
- providing beneficial activities you can do each day.

The cognitive behavioural approach is not about:

- being more positive
- suppressing worrying
- avoiding worry
- telling yourself everything will be alright or fine
- 'just' getting over it
- 'just' believing in yourself
- 'just' telling yourself you can do it
- getting busy or distracted to avoid your anxiety.

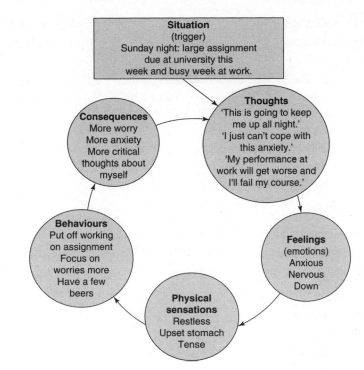

Figure 3.2: Luke's vicious worry cycle about his university work

The cognitive behavioural approach will help you to develop helpful and balanced thinking and be realistic in your day-to-day thoughts and fair in the thoughts you have about yourself. It's about letting go of unhelpful behaviours and learning and strengthening adaptive, healthy ones. It's about looking after yourself.

How to make progress

In the rest of the book you will learn about specific cognitive and behavioural strategies for dealing with anxiety and how to apply these strategies in everyday life to manage your anxiety. But first you need to consider the following points and plan how to make progress so that you increase the likelihood of being successful when you apply the strategies.

Set realistic goals

Think about the **goals** you would like to achieve.

1. Think about the 'big picture' – how would you like things to be in a few months or a year?
2. Break down the 'big picture' into small specific goals.
3. Put the specific goals in order according to how much anxiety they provoke or how difficult they are right now. Use a scale from 0–10, where 0 = no anxiety or no difficulty and 10 = extreme anxiety or difficulty. Consider working towards smaller, less difficult or the least anxiety-provoking goals first.

Then use the SMART method to create goals you can attain. 'SMART' is a mnemonic (memory aid) that stands for **S**pecific, **M**easureable, **A**chievable, **R**elevant and **T**ime-related.

- **S**pecific – goals should be very specific and concrete. When thinking about your goals, think about what you want to be different, where you want it to be different (home, work, relationships, etc.), and how you want it to be different.
- **M**easurable – goals need to be quantifiable so that you can measure your progress. How will you know when you have reached your goal?
- **A**chievable – goals need to be realistic so that they are achievable and attainable. Having lots of small specific goals that build upon one another, even if very slowly, is more realistic and achievable than having large goals which require big leaps.
- **R**elevant – goals need to be relevant to you and your life. Ask yourself if your goals make sense. Will your goals help you overcome your anxiety?
- **T**ime-related – setting a date for achieving your goals can help you stay on track and focused. Make sure the dates you set to reach your goals are not so far away that they seem irrelevant, but not too soon either as you don't want to overload yourself or rush yourself. Think about what is happening in your life at present, and what your responsibilities are to family, work etc. How do your goals fit with these in terms of the time needed to reach them?

Goals record

Develop your own specific goals using the SMART method – Specific, Measureable, Achievable, Relevant, Time-related – and record them below.

Worksheet 3A: My SMART goals

What is your SMART goal?	How will you measure progress?	Timeframe	Progress

Luke and Sarah both used the SMART worksheet to work out their goals. They listed them in order of difficulty, with what they viewed as the least difficult first.

Luke's SMART goals

What is your SMART goal?	How will you measure progress?	Timeframe	Progress
Get to sleep more easily at night.	Not take up to two hours to get to sleep at night and have at least 5 nights a week when I can get to sleep easily.	4–6 months	
Be less irritable with Amanda.	Be more patient and less cranky with her. Amanda will tell me if I'm doing okay with this.	2 months	
Be more confident in myself.	Not get caught in critical thoughts about myself and do things without worrying too much that I'll muck it up.	2 months	
Feel less controlled by worry.	When problems come up, not spend hours worrying. Be able to step away from worry when it starts.	4–6 months	

Sarah's SMART goals

What is your SMART goal?	How will you measure progress?	Timeframe	Progress
Have more energy and not be so tired.	My energy levels at the moment are about 2/10, so would like them to be 7–8/10 most days.	3 months	
Feel less anxious and panicky, have less worry.	Spend less than 10% of my day worrying. Don't feel panicky sensations in my body so much. Maybe only every now and then, rather than 2–3 times a week.	4 months	
Not be so worried about getting a serious illness.	Not spend every day worrying about dying or getting sick. If I have a cancer worry, to be able to let it go rather than it spiralling out of control.	Not sure, this seems really hard but maybe in 5 months' time.	

Be able to relax and not be beside myself with worry when the kids aren't home.	When the kids are out, not be pacing and restless and feeling anxious. Not have to ring or text Ella so much to see if she is okay.	4 months	

Progress

Make sure you update your progress on your goals worksheet each week so you can keep track of progress towards your goals, what you have been doing and how you are going. Keep track of all the small steps you take. Small steps and small gains or changes are very important; they are, after all, what larger changes are made up of.

Get support

It is easier to manage anxiety and apply the cognitive behaviour strategies if you have good support in place. Good support is having one or two key people who understand the approach you are taking to manage your anxiety; people who you trust and can count on to support you. Make sure your support people know your plan. Ask your support people to read this book, or you could go over each chapter and discuss each exercise as you go through the book. Talk to your support people regularly about the things you have learned and are working on as you progress through the chapters and learn new strategies for tackling your worry and anxiety. Talk with them when you are stuck but also make sure you tell them about your progress. Perhaps talk with your GP about your plans for change. The more people who know about your plans for change, the more likely it is that they will be able to help you.

Who could your support people be?

_____

_____

_____

_____

_____

Chapter 14 is intended for your support person(s) to read. It provides useful information and ideas to help your support person to help you manage your worry better. You don't have to wait until you get to Chapter 14 to ask them to read it; it might be helpful to ask to your support person to read it now if they are willing to.

Sometimes when people feel overwhelmed by worry, anxiety or depression they may start to feel hopeless and find it difficult to see a future. They may also be very hard on themselves and believe they are worthless or just want a way out and consider harming themselves. If you ever feel this way, contact your doctor immediately or talk to someone close to you. Chapter 15 lists some services you will also find helpful. If you think it would be helpful, write down the 24 hours contact details of your local mental health emergency service here:

_____

_____

_____

_____

Regular practice

The key to making progress with tackling your worry and anxiety is regular repetition and practice. Cognitive and behavioural strategies are most effective when they are rehearsed and practised each day. Just like learning any new skill, regular practice is the best way forward. Make a plan to do this. Set aside time each day to work on a skill for anxiety management. It is better to do a little bit every day than to do none for days and then do a lot in one day. The good news is that each time you practise the strategies, they will become easier and more natural.

Pace yourself

Too much too soon can trip you up and you can feel overwhelmed. It is better to practise a strategy for longer until it feels more familiar to you before you move on to the next strategy or chapter. It works better if you pace yourself, take longer and work slowly and steadily.

Motivation

Actively keep yourself motivated. Motivation requires some effort. Remind yourself what your immediate focus is. This is all you need to focus on at the moment. Every now and again read Worksheet 1B from Chapter 1 to remind yourself of the benefits of tackling your worry.

Take one step at time.

Ask yourself what you can work on or change today. Remind yourself you are not alone; as you read in Chapter 2, anxiety is a common problem and other people have similar issues as you.

Remind yourself that making changes is not easy but it is possible little by little. Most importantly, be patient with yourself; change takes time for everybody. Focus on your progress. Sometimes when we are trying to make changes we can get caught up with what we have not done, what we still have to do and how hard it is. Making progress in managing anxiety is similar to the process you go through when you decide to improve your fitness. When you first start, it takes considerable effort, planning and motivation. Attaining your fitness goals can seem like a long way off, sometimes almost impossible.

You know that you can't just jump ahead, you need to be patient as you build up your fitness. You know that if you keep doing a bit each day, you will get fitter and many of the exercises that you found difficult initially will gradually get easier and easier. Eventually, if you keep going at a steady pace and don't let setbacks stop you, you will achieve your goals.

Always reward yourself for the small changes. Remember, small steps are very important, as they are what the bigger, more obvious changes are made up of! Think about the things that typically motivate you; how can you use these things to keep you motivated towards tackling your anxiety and reaching your goals of change? Recognize your progress and treat yourself for the effort you have put in.

Look after yourself

In a busy life and when you are feeling anxious or stressed it can be an effort to look after yourself. Of course looking after yourself is always important at any time, but it is particularly so when you are taking up the challenge of making changes. Below are some important ways of taking care of yourself. Add some more ideas about how you already look after yourself or some other things you could do.

- Be kind to yourself; keep your focus on your strengths and the positive aspects of your life.
- Focus your attention on your immediate goals and your plans to achieve these.
- No matter how difficult things get, try to keep a soothing, non-critical, supportive and caring attitude toward yourself. There is plenty of evidence to suggest that being compassionate towards yourself makes you more able to deal with the challenges that life throws up (see Chapter 12).
- Eat well and regularly.
- Get plenty of exercise.
- Get plenty of rest, relaxation and sleep.

● Do something 'potentially' pleasurable or enjoyable every day, even if you don't feel like it. Sometimes when we are anxious or down we don't get pleasure out of things we used to enjoy. But it is important that we still do those things; the pleasure will return. If we sit around waiting until we feel like doing them, it gives worry or anxiety more opportunity to bother us and we can become worse. Pleasurable activities are an important shield against stress, anxiety and low mood. We all need a break! Often when people are busy, stressed or not feeling great they do less enjoyable activities or stop them altogether. They may argue to themselves that they don't have time or energy, or don't deserve it. So remember to look after yourself and schedule potentially pleasurable activities into your day. Use Worksheet 3B to help you come up with ideas.

What other things can you do to look after yourself?
Note them here.

_____

_____

_____

_____

Pleasurable activities record

List all of the potentially pleasurable activities you have done in the past, those you have done recently and those you have not tried yet but think you might enjoy; be as wide-ranging as you can. Write down activities that you can do at home as well as when you are out and about, and activities that will only take a few minutes as well as those that might take an hour or longer. If you have difficulty thinking of activities ask your family and friends what they do, read the examples in the worksheet below, or look at the websites listed in Chapter 15.

Worksheet 3B: My pleasurable activities

Listen to music
Watch a movie
Meet friends for a meal or to play sport
Have a relaxing bath
Do some sort of art
Photography
Gardening
Restore a piece of furniture
Time with pets or animals
Go for a walk in a park, the countryside or
*   on a beach*
Lose myself in a book I enjoy
Play cards or a game with others (board game,
*   chess, pool)*

_____

_____

_____

_____

_____

_____

_____

_____

_____

_____

_____

What to do when you meet roadblocks

You will get stuck at times or even feel like you have gone backwards – everybody does. The key is not to focus on becoming stuck but on what you can do about it. You may not work this out straightaway but there will be a solution. Remember:

- be patient with yourself
- setbacks are normal and not uncommon
- talk with your support people
- why you are putting in all this effort – look back to Worksheet 1B (The benefits of tackling my worry and anxiety) to give yourself extra strength!
- roadblocks can actually be helpful – they can give you a chance to learn and to extend your skills.

Behaviour changing strategy

Because it is more a matter of *when* rather than *if* you hit a roadblock, it can be helpful to think in advance about what you could do. Worksheet 3C has some ideas that can help when you are stuck. Add your own ideas in the blank spaces.

Worksheet 3C: When I get stuck I can …

Let myself off the hook - everyone gets stuck when they are trying to change.

Do something pleasurable.

Spend time with people who care about me.

Talk to my support people.

Make sure I am looking after myself.

Think of someone I know and respect. What would they say or suggest I do?

Talk to my GP.

Be my own best friend. What advice would I give myself?

*Go back one or two steps in the self-help book
and redo them.*
What else could I do ..?

_____

_____

_____

_____

_____

_____

_____

_____

_____

Chapter summary

In this chapter you have:

- learned how a cognitive behavioural approach can help you manage your anxiety.
- identified your support people and talked with them about your plans to work on your anxiety
- learned how to ensure that your efforts to manage your anxiety are successful
- developed and worked through the SMART method to develop your own goals
- learned what you need to do to look after yourself and compiled a list of pleasurable activities to help with this

- planned how you will monitor your progress by updating Worksheet 3A regularly.
- know how to manage roadblocks

Activities for you to do

Before moving on to Chapter 4, make sure you:

- contact the people you have identified who may be able to support you in making progress. Explain to them what you are doing and ask if they are willing to support you.
- write down your SMART goals (Worksheet 3A)
- develop your list of pleasurable activities (Worksheet 3B)
- write down a plan for when you hit a roadblock (Worksheet 3C).

In Part 2 you will learn how to tackle worry. The four chapters in Part 2 focus on beginning to manage your worry and anxiety in different ways to reduce their strength. Chapter 4 begins to unpack your worry and looks at what keeps it going.

Tackle

Get to grips with what you need to do to make a change, and make a start

What keeps worry going?

Overview

In this chapter you will:

- learn about a model (diagram) for understanding worry and anxiety and what keeps it going
- look closely at the parts of your worry, such as underlying thoughts and beliefs, that may have led to worry becoming a problem in your life
- consider the maintaining aspects of your worry, such as emotions, physical responses, beliefs about worry, your attention and your behaviours
- identify your worry triggers, like the stresses in your life. You probably already know what these are!

As we go over these parts of your worry and anxiety, we will coach you in creating your own worry model. This model will be a guide to what you need to tackle in order to decrease worry's ongoing role in your life.

Because it is crucial to develop a model to understand your worry and to guide the cognitive behavioural strategies you'll be using to deal with your worry, this chapter is full of valuable information. We suggest you take your time over this chapter. Don't try to read all of it in one sitting, but take a few days to read it and work through the worksheets so you have time to become familiar with the content.

A model of worry: The worry vicious flower

In recent years, leaders in worry research have developed a number of models to explain worry and generalized anxiety disorder (GAD). International experts in the theory and treatment of worry, such as Thomas Borkovec, Adrian Wells, Michel Dugas and Mark Freeston, among others, have identified and tested the factors that make worry a problem and a cause of distress for many. Based on their findings, we have developed a worry model, which we have called the **worry vicious flower**. This model helps illustrate what causes worry for you and what keeps it going. Figure 4.1 shows the worry vicious flower with some examples of what might go in its various parts.

The main problem of worry is in the centre of the worry vicious flower, surrounded by the petals. These **vicious petals** represent vicious cycles that are driven by the worry and in turn feed and maintain the worry. Examples of these maintaining vicious petals or cycles can include our thinking, behaviours or feelings. For example, if we are worrying and getting anxious, then this anxiety is likely to make us worry more! Of course, there is more than one vicious petal or vicious cycle feeding into the worry and some may have a larger role for you in keeping your worry going.

Just as a flower develops out of the soil it grows in, so worry develops from our biological make-up and our early experiences. The **stem** of the flower represents the unhelpful thinking styles and negative self-talk that has grown over the years, which influences how we perceive ourselves and our experiences. These inner negative thoughts and beliefs colour how we view the world, ourselves and our ability to cope. The underlying early experiences, biology and thinking play a role in whether we experience anxiety, and can act as triggers for worry too.

We are going to describe the parts of the worry vicious flower model next, and later in the chapter you will start to develop your own

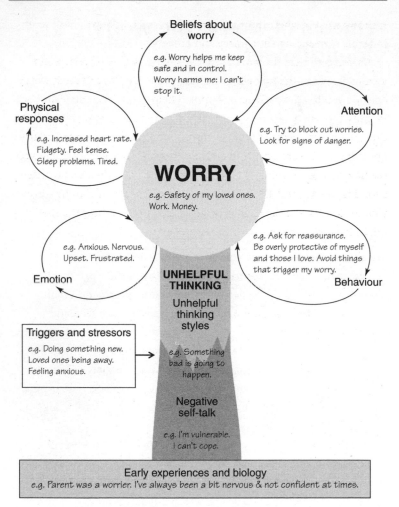

Figure 4.1: The worry vicious flower model

version of the model to help you understand what keeps your worry going. People sometimes wonder why they need to do this because they often know their worry inside out. But having it down on paper helps to give it some structure, can help to make the worry feel more contained and highlights the factors you can target with the strategies in this book. It's like a road map that guides you in tackling your worry.

It shows what is where, how things link up and where you need to go in terms of reducing your worry and anxiety.

As you complete the worksheets for the parts of your own worry vicious flower in the following chapters, try to think of a recent worry episode you have experienced. This will help you to recognize and identify the worry factors we are asking you about. If you worry all the time, use a worry episode that occurred recently that was particularly upsetting. If you are unable to do this, use your worry from today and see how you go, or think of an occasion in the past when you worried a lot. Figures 4.2 and 4.3 show the centres of Luke's and Sarah's worry vicious flowers and the vicious petals, as examples of how the model might look for someone with worry and anxiety.

Beliefs about worry

Worry helps me - If I think things over I'll see all the angles and not miss anything. If I don't worry I'll fail my studies and do poorly at work. Worry helps me.
Worry harms me - I can't turn worry off, it snowballs. Worry means I'm not in control and weak. I can't stop over-thinking things.

Physical responses
Increased heart rate, restless, not hungry, upset stomach, muscle tension, headaches

WORRY

Failing work and studies
Relationship with Amanda ending

Attention
Focus on worries, Try to distract myself playing x-box.

Emotion
Anxious, overwhelmed, irritable, angry.

Behaviour
Drink beer to reduce anxiety, put off work or assignments, check work over and over for mistakes, avoid emails as it will be more work or my boss pulling me up.

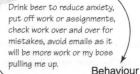

Figure 4.2: Luke's worry vicious flower

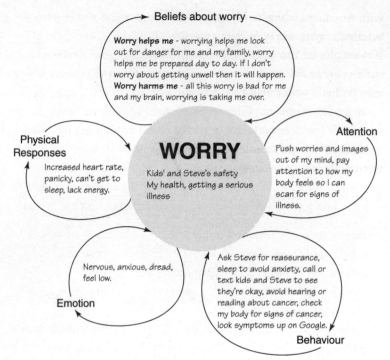

Beliefs about worry

Worry helps me - worrying helps me look out for danger for me and my family, worry helps me be prepared day to day. If I don't worry about getting unwell then it will happen.
Worry harms me - all this worry is bad for me and my brain, worrying is taking me over.

Physical Responses

Increased heart rate, panicky, can't get to sleep, lack energy.

WORRY

Kids' and Steve's safety
My health, getting a serious illness

Attention

Push worries and images out of my mind, pay attention to how my body feels so I can scan for signs of illness.

Nervous, anxious, dread, feel low.

Emotion

Ask Steve for reassurance, sleep to avoid anxiety, call or text kids and Steve to see they're okay, avoid hearing or reading about cancer, check my body for signs of cancer, look symptoms up on Google.

Behaviour

Figure 4.3: Sarah's worry vicious flower

Centre of the worry vicious flower

To tackle worry and the related anxiety, it is helpful to know more about the worry process itself, such as what triggers it or the situations in which it arises, what the worries or anxious thoughts are, what emotions the worry leads to, and what actions or behaviours you did or do once you were worrying. First, we are interested in what your worry themes are, i.e. what are the common types of worry you have, the reoccurring subjects, issues or concerns. These go in the centre of your worry vicious flower. If you look at the vicious flower models of Luke and Sarah, you will see that Luke's worry is centred on failing at work or university and his relationship with Amanda ending; Sarah noted that her husband and childrens' safety was a big worry for her, as well as the fear she would get a serious illness. You might have one worry or a few worry themes such as *my health* or *my family's safety* or *my future is hopeless*. Or you may find you worry about most things.

You are going to start filling in Worksheet 4A. This will help you to identify your worry themes and related unhelpful thinking. The worksheet asks you to note down your thoughts and emotions. Sometimes people struggle to tell the difference between the two.

● An emotion is experienced as a felt sense of something, and it may be felt in certain parts of our body. For example, anger may be experienced as a heaviness in the chest or a sense that our blood is boiling. Anxiety can often be felt in the pit of our stomach. In contrast being happy may feel warm with a lightness to it. An emotion can often be described in a single word, like 'happy', 'sad', 'anxious', 'down', 'excited' etc.

● A thought occurs in our mind, like self-talk or inner mental chatter. Thinking 'I am angry' or 'That person took my parking space' are examples of self-talk. Unlike emotions, thoughts tend to be expressed mentally in more than one word, like a short sentence, or they may occur as a picture or an image. If you think of being happy, you might have a image pass through your mind of a happy memory or see yourself in a place that feels positive to you, like a beach, or with someone who cares about you. So our thoughts can be words in our head or images. Emotions are the feelings we get from these thoughts and they can be pleasant (e.g. happy, content) or unpleasant (e.g. anxious, angry).

The quiz below may help you understand the difference. The words or sentences either describe an emotion or are an example of a thought or a visual thought (like an image in the mind). For each one, decide whether it is an emotion or thought and circle the right word. The answers are at the end of the book.

Quiz: The difference between thoughts and emotions		
1	Sad	Emotion / Thought
2	Angry	Emotion / Thought
3	I am worried about my health	Emotion / Thought
4	An image of me homeless	Emotion / Thought
5	I am really unlikeable	Emotion / Thought
6	Lonely	Emotion / Thought
7	Anxious	Emotion / Thought
8	I am afraid of the worst happening	Emotion / Thought
9	A picture in my mind of my lover walking out the door	Emotion / Thought
10	Frustrated	Emotion / Thought
11	No one at the work function will talk to me	Emotion / Thought
12	Down	Emotion / Thought

Returning to Worksheet 4A, you might be thinking 'I worry all the time so why do I need to keep a diary of it?' This could be true, but often we find that when we know more about something it is easier to deal with it. Also, you might learn that there are patterns to your worry, such as it occurring in certain situations or that you react to it the same way over and over again. Or maybe not. The best thing to do is to monitor the worry and note what happens so that you know.

Self-assessment ✓

Reflect on the themes of your worries and unhelpful thinking over the next few days to help you complete this worksheet.

Worksheet 4A: Worry themes and unhelpful thinking

Date	
Trigger *What situation triggered your worry? What happened to start the worry?*	
Worry theme *What area or part of your life were you worried about?*	
Unhelpful thinking *What was the unhelpful thought that gained your attention? What were your worrying thoughts or images? Sum up what you were thinking.*	
Emotions *What emotions or feelings did you have?*	
Physical response *What did you feel in your body physically?*	
Behaviour *What did you do? How did you behave?*	

Luke and Sarah each used this worksheet for a few days; below are examples of the worry themes and unhelpful thinking from their worksheets.

Luke's version of Worksheet 4A	
Date	Sunday night at 7pm
Trigger *What situation triggered your worry? What happened to start the worry?*	*Was thinking about week ahead at work and assignment due for university*
Worry theme *What area or part of your life were you worried about?*	*Failing at work and university*
Unhelpful thinking *What was the unhelpful thought that gained your attention? What were your worrying thoughts or images? Sum up what you were thinking.*	*This anxiety is going to keep me up all night.* *I just can't cope with this anxiety.* *My performance at work is going to get worse and I'll fail my course.*
Emotions *What emotions or feelings did you have?*	*Anxious* *Nervous* *Down*
Physical response *What did you feel in your body physically?*	*Restless* *Upset stomach* *Tense*
Behaviour *What did you do? How did you behave?*	*Put off working on my assignment.* *Focused on my worries.* *Had a few beers.*

Sarah's version of Worksheet 4A	
Date	Saturday afternoon
Trigger What situation triggered your worry? What happened to start the worry?	Steve's taken Ella to compete in an athletics competition an hour's drive away.
Worry theme What area or part of your life were you worried about?	Kid's safety
Unhelpful thinking What was the unhelpful thought that gained your attention? What were your worrying thoughts or images? Sum up what you were thinking.	They will be in an accident and die. Image in my mind of car smashed up. I'm going to lose Ella.
Emotions What emotions or feelings did you have?	Very anxious
Physical response What did you feel in your body physically?	Sick feeling in my stomach Panicky
Behaviour What did you do? How did you behave?	Kept ringing and texting them to see if they were safe. I paced by front window to look out for them.

Stem of the worry vicious flower

In Chapter 1, we noted that worry can be caused by a combination of factors that includes a biological vulnerability if anxiety runs in your family. Worry can also arise from early experiences in your life that have influenced your beliefs about yourself and your life, or contributed to the belief that you need to worry. This can include parents using worry as a coping strategy so you learned to do the same. Or you may have past experiences of feeling in danger or unable to cope, or experiences that have left you feeling vulnerable, with a sense that you will suffer future harm or threat unless you stay on guard for bad things and worry about them. These experiences shape our thinking and our beliefs about ourselves, often leading to **negative self-talk** and **unhelpful thinking styles**.

Negative self-talk

Because of our past experiences, we start to develop core, or central, beliefs and assumptions about ourselves, others and the world we live in. These beliefs can be experienced as inner self-talk or mental chatter – basically, the messages we give ourselves throughout the day. Such self-talk can be positive or negative; for example, 'I am good' versus 'I am worthless', or 'I never cope' versus 'I can cope'. Negative self-talk tends to be rigid and made up of ingrained beliefs we hold, such as 'The world is a dangerous place' or 'I am vulnerable'. Such negative self-talk leads us to develop rules to protect ourselves from coming to harm. Below are some examples of the typical negative self-talk that someone with excessive worry may have.

Negative self-talk	Consequences
I am vulnerable.	Feel anxious, worried and always on guard or alert.
Something bad is going to happen to me or my loved ones.	Constantly worry about possible danger. Stay at home, or keep loved ones at home, to avoid harm.

I am flawed.	Try to be perfect and feel anxious when I think I can't accomplish this or I don't meet unachievably high standards.
If I try something new, I will fail or mess it up.	Avoid doing new things, or if I do them I am really nervous, which then interferes with how well I do.
I can't cope with anything or any of life's difficulties.	Always feel stressed. Rely on others to do things for me and make my decisions. Have no confidence in myself or my abilities to manage day-to-day challenges.

Unhelpful thinking styles

Because of our past experiences and our negative self-talk, we can develop particular ways and patterns of thinking that are unhelpful; these are known as unhelpful thinking styles. We all experience unhelpful thinking styles from time to time but they tend to be more frequent if we have problems with worry or anxiety. These unhelpful thinking styles act like an anxiety filter, colouring how we view our world and how we respond. Unhelpful thinking styles can both exaggerate our underlying negative self-talk and reinforce it.

There are many different types of unhelpful thinking styles. Some examples are fortune-telling, which occurs when we believe the future is not going to be good, or mind-reading, which occurs when we believe we know what others are thinking about us and assume their thoughts are unkind or critical. In Chapter 6 we will go further into unhelpful thinking styles, but for now keep in mind that unhelpful thinking styles are like negative self-talk – they are learned and become our habitual way of thinking about ourselves.

Negative self-talk is a form of **unhelpful thinking** that make us vulnerable to worry. Unhelpful thinking acts as trigger for anxiety and worry, and also keeps worry going once it starts. In Chapter 6 you will have the opportunity to identify the types of unhelpful thinking you have so that you can tackle them.

Petals of the worry vicious flower

People with worry difficulties or generalized anxiety disorder (GAD) often get caught in thinking processes and behaviours that they feel may prevent the worst from happening to them or their loved ones. These **maintaining cycles** make up the petals of the worry vicious flower, keeping the worry going. Each of the five petals is a vicious cycle in its own right, and all these vicious petals or vicious cycles supercharge your worry! Perhaps not all of them apply to you, but it's likely that most of these vicious cycles are feeding and maintaining your worry. The important thing is that there are strategies that can reduce and weaken these maintaining cycles or vicious petals.

Emotions

We all have an emotional reaction to our thinking and, of course, to our worry. For most of us this will be to feel anxious, nervous or apprehensive. So how do these emotions reinforce our worry?

When we are worried or anxious we often pay attention to the emotion of anxiety and search for a reason why we are feeling this way – as if we believe that because we feel anxious there is something to be anxious or worried about. This is called **emotional reasoning**, and it is a type of unhelpful thinking style. Emotional reasoning is a type of unhelpful thinking style that is strongly tied to our emotions (there is more about this in Chapter 6). It is when we believe our emotions are fact or we misinterpret them as 'evidence' of the 'truth'. We might be giving ourselves the message that 'because I feel anxious, there must be something to be anxious about'. It usually keeps our worry going or makes it worse, when in fact there may be nothing at all to be anxious about.

We may also experience other emotions when we worry, such as irritation or frustration, or feeling low or sad. Possibly we've been worrying so much, we are really frustrated or fed up. Or we may just be worn out from worry and anxiety and are feeling irritable. Sometimes when the worry has been ongoing or particularly strong, we may start to feel down, low, sad or even depressed because we are sick of feeling this way and because worry is having such an overpowering impact on our life. Such emotions can lead people to believe they are overwhelmed with worry and problems, so then they worry more!

So, what emotions do you get when worrying? If you look back at Luke and Sarah's worry vicious flowers, you will see that they both noted feeling anxious on their Emotion vicious petal. Luke also noted feeling overwhelmed, irritable and angry. This had a knock-on effect for Luke as he began to think it meant there must be something to worry about, so he started to worry more! Sarah also noted feeling nervous, a sense of dread and feeling low when she was experiencing worry. She interpreted these feelings as more evidence that something bad was going to happen. Sarah particularly took the feeling of dread to mean danger was not far off in the future.

Worksheet 4B contains an Emotion vicious petal for you to record the type of emotions you get when you are worrying. This worksheet will form part of your worry vicious flower model.

Emotions vicious petal record

Your emotions when you are worrying may be something you know very well but to help you out we've listed below some questions to help you identify your emotions for your Emotions vicious petal.

- When you are worried, what emotions do you experience?
- Do you feel anxious, nervous, apprehensive or afraid?
- Do you experience feelings of frustration or annoyance or feel low?
- Do you feel overwhelmed?

Worksheet 4B: Emotion vicious petal

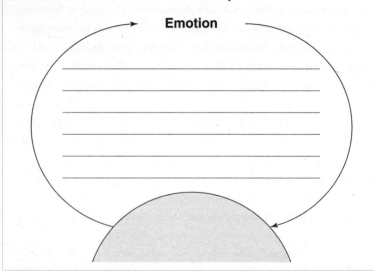

Physical responses

We have already mentioned some of the physical responses you may experience because of your anxious thinking, such as the flight, fight or freeze response. Initial physical reactions can include restlessness, feeling agitated or on edge, muscle tension in the shoulders, neck or chest or a headache. Sometimes you might experience an increased heart-rate or upset stomach. You may start to have trouble falling asleep or staying asleep because of worry or anxiety. In the long term, you may often be tired and experience concentration and memory problems. Sometimes worrying and anxiety can reduce energy levels, sex drive, affect the appetite or worsen physical conditions like irritable bowel syndrome.

All of these physical reactions might be misinterpreted by you as 'something is seriously wrong with me'. Then you might start to worry about these physical sensations, which will only cause more worry! Indeed, when you have both physical and emotional responses to worry, such as feeling shaky and anxious, you are likely to believe things are too overwhelming and this will lead to more worrying.

So, what physical reactions do you get when worrying or when you have an anxious thought? If you look back at Luke and Sarah's worry vicious flowers, you will see that they both wrote on their Physical responses vicious petal that they feel an increased heart rate at times. Luke also added feeling restless, with muscle tension and an upset stomach. Sarah also added experiencing panicky feelings and trouble getting to sleep. When Sarah focused on these physical sensations more, it had the effect of increasing her belief that there was something wrong with her body, like the early signs of a serious illness.

Worksheet 4C contains a Physical responses vicious petal for you to record the type of physical responses you get when you are worrying. This worksheet will form part of your worry vicious flower model.

Physical responses vicious petal record

Think about when you were last worrying and what the effect was on your body. Starting with your head, scan down your body and think about where you usually physically feel worry. It may help to look back at the section on the flight, fight or freeze response in Chapter 1. The questions listed below will also help you to identify your physical responses

- When you are worrying or anxious, what physical sensations do you experience?
- What do you feel in your body?

- Do you have an increased heart rate or a tight chest?
- Do you experience muscle tension, an upset stomach, have trouble breathing or feel hot, restless or shaky?
- Do you feel panicky?
- Do you have trouble sleeping?
- Does the strain of worrying make you feel tired and lacking in energy?

Worksheet 4C: Physical responses vicious petal

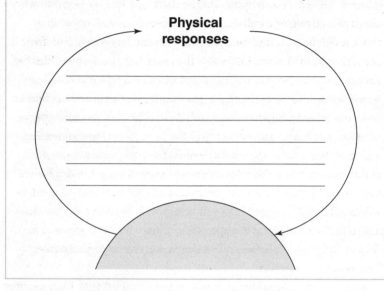

Physical responses

Beliefs about worry

Professor Adrian Wells, a pioneer in worry research and treatment, and others have identified that positive and negative beliefs about worry maintain the worry and generalized anxiety disorder. A positive belief about worry is when we believe worry helps in some way, has advantages, is useful or that it helps to prevent harm or manage distress. We have called these beliefs 'Worry helps me' beliefs. A negative belief is when we believe that worry is harmful in some way. We have called these 'Worry harms me' beliefs.

We will now look at these beliefs about worry and how they keep worry and anxiety going. You will have the chance to write up your Beliefs about worry vicious petal in Chapter 6, but for now just work through the section below as we help you to identify what beliefs about worry you might hold.

Worry helps me

Given that worry is a problem for you, it may seem odd to suggest that you see worry as helpful. On the surface, when we begin to worry about something or dwell on it, this may seem useful, or we may think it will help us find an answer or prevent something bad from occurring in the future. But is this the case? Just think about this for a moment. Why do you worry? What would happen if you did not worry? People often think that if they don't worry, something bad or unfortunate will happen to them or those they care about. Or they believe if they don't worry they will not be prepared for something and they won't cope. Do you believe you need to worry about your children, parents or other loved ones to protect them? If you have a task like a big project at work or an exam, do you think you need to worry about it to do well? Do you believe you need to worry to find a solution to a problem? If so, it is likely that you have beliefs that 'Worry helps me' and you have adopted worry as a coping strategy. This is not uncommon.

People sometimes think that worry helps to show they care, i.e. they believe that the act of worrying means that others know that they care and are concerned about them. Also, they believe worrying means they are looking out for others and that this will protect others from harm. They may be reluctant to let go of worrying or the belief it helps for fear that it will mean that they are not concerned or 'worried' about their loved ones' wellbeing.

Many people that experience worry have difficulty tolerating uncertainty, which can mean they worry about situations or issues they think might go wrong. If you experience this, it may mean you have difficulty making decisions because of stress about not making the 'right' choice. You might also use safety-seeking behaviours, discussed later in this chapter, such as not making decisions (avoidance), getting others to make a decision for you, or avoiding situations or choices where you aren't guaranteed a specific, safe or definite outcome. Situations that seem uncertain may trigger a worry episode. Once the worry starts, this reinforces fears and feelings of uncertainty and thoughts of not being in control. We then start to feel more anxious and this anxiety signals to us that there may be a possible threat … so we worry more because we believe 'Worry helps me' and will prevent uncertainty! We end up going over all the possible things that could go wrong, which creates more uncertainty and leads to ongoing doubt, worry and anxiety. Does this sound at all familiar?

The problem with finding uncertainty difficult to tolerate and believing that worry helps to prevent uncertainty is that life itself, the world we live in and our futures, have many uncertainties. We can't avoid it! Trying to rid our lives of uncertainty through worrying will only cause exhaustion and distress as you strive to protect yourself and those around you from uncertain futures. To enjoy life more and be less worried about all that can go wrong. we need to develop our ability to tolerate uncertainty and rethink our belief that 'Worry helps me'.

We tackle these 'Worry helps me' beliefs more in Chapters 6 and 8, but in this chapter we would like you to start to become more aware of your 'Worry helps me' beliefs using Worksheet 4D. To help you fill in the worksheet, it might be useful to look back at the 'Worry helps me' beliefs on Luke's and Sarah's worry vicious flowers. Luke noted that he believes worry helps him to see problems from all angles, to be in control and to get things done, and that it prevents him from failing. Sarah believes that worry prevents danger to her and her family, and protects her from developing a serious illness. These beliefs mean that both Luke and Sarah end up worrying more.

Self-assessment ✓

What are the 'Worry helps me' beliefs that you hold? Put a tick in the box next to them. In Chapter 6, you will copy the ones you ticked onto Worksheet 6B, which contains the Beliefs about worry vicious petal.

Worksheet 4D: Beliefs that 'Worry helps me'

Worry helps me to be prepared. ☐
Worry helps me to overcome uncertainty. ☐
Worry helps me to cope. ☐
Worrying prevents bad things happening to me or my loved ones. ☐
Worrying helps to prevent harm to myself or those I love. ☐
Worry helps me to find answers or solutions to problems. ☐
Worry helps me to remember things or get things done. ☐
Worry helps me to be a caring person. ☐
Worry helps me to be a responsible person. ☐
If I don't worry about things, no one in my family will. ☐

Other 'Worry helps me' beliefs

Answer the question below to see if you hold any other 'Worry helps me' beliefs. (In Chapter 6 you will also write these beliefs onto Worksheet 6B.)

What are the advantages of worry?

_____

_____

_____

_____

Worry harms me

Just as we can have beliefs that worry is helpful, we can also have beliefs about the harmfulness of worry, i.e. that worrying is dangerous in some way or can't be turned off. These 'Worry harms me' beliefs tend to be triggered when we are worrying, along with feeling anxious or apprehensive. Once worry has kicked in, it is common for people to think that the worry will cause harm in some way, e.g. stop us from ever being able to get to sleep, make us go crazy, or cause us to lose control of our thoughts or ourselves. We may believe that worrying will cause us to develop a physical illness or that the worrying just will not stop.

What happens when these 'Worry harms me' beliefs take hold is that we start to worry about our worrying! This **worry about worry** supersizes our worrying, leading to more anxiety, further physical responses, more doubt and feelings of uncertainty, and then more worry … and on and on it goes!

If you look at Luke's and Sarah's worry vicious flowers earlier in the chapter, you will see that they both listed 'Worry harms me' beliefs on their models. Luke noted that he believes he can't turn the worry off and that worrying so much means he is weak. Sarah believes worrying is bad for her brain and is taking her over. Such beliefs create worry about worry for both of them and more anxiety!

If we start to question these 'Worry harms me' beliefs, we will learn that worry is not as uncontrollable or harmful as we may believe. The first step is to pinpoint your 'Worry harms me' beliefs using Worksheet 4E.

Self-assessment ✓

What are the 'Worry harms me' beliefs that you hold? Put a tick in the box next to them. In Chapter 6, you will copy the ones you ticked onto Worksheet 6B, which contains the Beliefs about worry vicious petal.

Worksheet 4E: Beliefs that 'Worry harms me'

Worry will make me go mad or have a breakdown. ☐
My worrying is uncontrollable. ☐
I can't stop worrying. ☐
Worrying will make me lose control. ☐
Worry will harm me physically. ☐
Worry will stop me functioning at home, work or in other activities. ☐
Worrying all the time means I'm weak or a failure. ☐
If I don't stop my worry, it will harm me. ☐

Other 'Worry harms me' beliefs

Answer the question below to see if you hold any other 'Worry harms me' beliefs. (In Chapter 6 you will also write these beliefs onto Worksheet 6B.)

What are the disadvantages of worry?

_____

_____

_____

_____

Attention

Now we turn to the part that attention plays in worry and anxiety difficulties. You will have the opportunity to develop and work on your Attention vicious petal in Chapter 7. For now, we want you just to extend your understanding of attention's part in worry and anxiety difficulties.

Attention plays an important role in determining where we direct our mental focus. Attention can be adaptive in that it helps us to concentrate on home, work and social activities when we need to. Our attention works for us in situations where there is the possibility of harm, such as crossing the road or walking at night in an unlit or dark street. However, sometimes our attention can be unhelpful, e.g. if it is on high alert when it does not need to be, or when it gets stuck focusing on the same thing over and over again, e.g. if it is always monitoring our bodies and minds for signs of anxiety or worry.

There are several ways in which attention can backfire on us. First, there is **threat monitoring**, which is when we are always scanning for potential danger. Secondly, because we want to try and change the focus of our attention, we might use strategies that are unhelpful, such as **pushing thoughts away** and **distraction**. We will look at these now.

Threat monitoring

If you have difficulty tolerating uncertainty, are concerned about bad things happening or are worried about worry itself, it is very likely that you will be on the lookout for threat and find your attention is frequently searching for anything you believe to be harmful. You are likely to always be on guard for danger or any sort of perceived threat; basically you will be overly vigilant. Because you are always scanning for possible dangers, you may also perceive things to be more of a threat than they really are. This overestimation of danger is understandable given that you believe that things are going to turn out for the worst. For example, if you worry that your child may be involved in an accident, it may seem as if news stories about children in accidents jump out at you from the television or internet, and you may take this as evidence that your child is more at risk of an accident. So every time your child travels in a car you might be plagued by images of the car being in an accident and your child being seriously injured. Or if you fear getting a terminal illness, you might continually monitor your body for any sensations or signs that you believe are symptoms of cancer. If you have beliefs that 'Worry harms me', you might monitor your mind for any sign of 'worry' or that your thoughts are 'out of control' (which of course leads to more worry about worry!).

While there are no guarantees in life, the fact is that risk, or the chance of something happening, is unlikely to be reduced by worrying about something occurring or by paying more attention to it through threat monitoring. What can be guaranteed is that monitoring for threat and paying excessive attention to such things will increase your worry and anxiety. In Chapters 7 and 9, we will show you how to retrain your attention to reduce threat monitoring and therefore reduce your worry and related anxiety.

Pushing thoughts away and distraction

Another way that attention can maintain our worry and anxiety is when we try to turn off our attention to anxious images, thoughts or worries, when we mentally try to push away, distract ourselves from or ignore anxious thoughts or worry. If a thought, mental image or worry is upsetting you or if you have beliefs that worry is harmful, it is understandable that you want to banish it from your mind. But trying to push worries or upsetting images from your mind, or to replace them with a less upsetting thought or even with a positive thought, will only give the original anxious thought or image more attention than it deserves. Indeed, research has found that trying to distract yourself from or push away worry, upsetting thoughts or images can cause these thoughts to be more present in your head when you are trying to not think about them; thus it can lead to the thoughts or worries bouncing back into your mind more over the following hours and days. Let's test this out by trying to push some non-anxious thoughts or images away and see what happens. Do the two-minute exercise below

Reviewing behaviour

Pushing thoughts away exercise

This is a timed exercise, so you will need a timer, the stopwatch on your smartphone or someone else to tell you when two minutes is up.

1. When you are ready, start your timer and then close your eyes gently. Try hard not to think of your favourite animal that is coloured yellow.
2. Work at pushing thoughts or images of this animal out of your mind for two minutes. Each time your coloured animal comes into your mind, try to banish it from your mind.

What did you notice as you were doing this exercise? Was it difficult to push the coloured animal out of your mind? Often, when we try not to think about something, it stays in our head! You may have found you were able to not think about the animal briefly but then it popped up again in one form or another. This is true of worry and anxious thoughts. It is how our minds work. The more you try to push away or get rid of anxiety images, thoughts or worries, the more likely it is that the very opposite will happen. In the past, you may have tried to not think of a worry or told yourself 'Don't be so silly', but unfortunately the strategy of pushing thoughts away, telling yourself not to think about it or not to worry, or trying to distract yourself just keeps the worry bouncing back.

If the exercise had no or little effect on you, it may be that on this occasion you were able to not think this thought because it was not too anxiety-provoking, but with worries this is generally not the case; they are usually more resistant to being blocked out because we are concerned about the issue they relate to.

Pushing thoughts away and distraction may seem like useful ways of dealing with worry and our attention being focused on negative things, but this is not the case. Occasionally it may provide a brief respite, but in reality pushing thoughts away and distraction just keeps worry and anxiety active in your mind. For example, at times Luke focused more attention on his worries, leading to more anxiety and worry. Sarah would try to push away her worries or push out the upsetting images she would have of her children being hurt in an accident of some sort, but this ended up making the worries and images stronger and causing her more distress.

So the attention strategies of threat monitoring and pushing thoughts away and distraction feed your worry. We need to recognize if our attention is strengthening the persistence of worry and anxiety and then modify how we use our attention so it's more flexible and we can shift our attention away from monitoring threats or trying to block or push thoughts away. There is more about this in Chapter 7, where you will complete your Attention vicious petal.

Behaviour

The remaining maintaining factor, or vicious petal, is behaviour. As mentioned earlier in the book, our thinking leads to responses, including emotional and physical responses; the actions we then do or don't do is our behaviour. When we experience worry and anxiety this can lead to behaviours that in turn keep our worry and anxiety going. As you read more about behaviours here, you may recognize some of your own behaviours that keep worry going. Write these down on Worksheet 4F.

Behaviours vicious petal record

Think about when you were last worrying and what the effect was on your behaviour.

Worksheet 4F: Behaviours vicious petal

Behaviour

Avoidance and safety behaviours

Understandably, those who worry try to avoid situations that trigger their worrying. Avoidance is when you avoid anything that you believe may trigger your worry and anxiety or make it worse.

In addition to directly avoiding something, there are several other things that people with worry do to stop the worst from happening.

Professor Paul Salkovskis (1991) identified the important role of **safety-seeking behaviours**, or **safety behaviours** as they are often called, in maintaining anxiety problems. Safety behaviours are actions or strategies that people take to prevent or reduce their feared consequences from happening or to reduce their levels of anxiety and worry. Safety behaviours can be very ordinary and not obvious to others or even to you, but they are powerful encouragers of worry. The trap with safety behaviours is that they may give a brief escape or relief from worry and anxiety, but this relief is often fleeting. In the long term, these behaviours, which we assume keep us safe, have a habit of keeping worry going.

A tale of safety behaviours

Young Alex believed monsters lurked in his bedroom, which led to worry and anxiety for him every night. He was convinced that the monsters hid under his bed, waiting for him to fall asleep so they could grab him, or that they hid in his wardrobe waiting for him to open the door so they could pounce. Alex was so convinced the monsters existed that he would repeatedly check under his bed before getting into bed to make sure they weren't there. Or he would run into his room and jump onto his bed so the monsters could not grab him by his feet. Alex would also get one of his parents to look in his wardrobe to make sure it was safe. Sometimes he would avoid his room altogether and sleep in his parents' bed. Alex's parents had tried to convince him that these monsters didn't exist. They pointed out that they had checked his room for him many times and no monsters were there because they didn't exist. However, Alex did not believe this; he just thought that the monsters hadn't been there on the occasion his parents checked or that his parents had scared them away.

Checking under his bed and in the wardrobe, jumping onto the bed, avoiding his bedroom and reassurance from his parents were safety behaviours for Alex and they kept his monster worries and the related anxiety strong. They meant that Alex never got to find out that monsters were not in his room and the belief remained convincing.

Alex's parents worked out that Alex needed to let go of these safety behaviours so he could learn that his beliefs and fears were unfounded. Alex was scared at first but gradually he began to reduce his reliance on his safety behaviours by not checking, not jumping onto his bed and by sleeping in his own bed every night. Alex learned that he was okay and, indeed, no monsters appeared or attacked him. As his use of safety behaviours lessened, his belief in the monsters and his worry that something bad was going to happen to him weakened. His worry and anxiety faded, and eventually he didn't think about monsters at all when he went to bed.

Alex's story illustrates the unhelpful nature of safety behaviours and avoidance. In the tables below a number of avoidance and safety behaviours are listed, along with the consequences of using them. Read through the list and decide if any apply to you. Also, look back at Luke and Sarah's worry vicious flowers. Luke noted that he avoided opening work emails, which meant that he missed important messages and colleagues got frustrated with him, and this caused him unnecessary stress, anxiety and more worry! It also meant that he did not learn that his emails were not all 'bad news' for him and that maybe he could cope with whatever the email asked of him.

Self-assessment ✓

Read through the lists of avoidance and safety behaviours. If any apply to you, put a tick in the end column and then write them on your Worksheet 4F (Behaviours vicious petal).

Common avoidance behaviours

Behaviour	Example	Consequence of behaviour	Tick if it applies
Avoid new situations.	Don't go anywhere new or that you don't know well.	Fail to learn you might be fine and could cope.	

Behaviour	Example	Consequence of behaviour	Tick if it applies
Avoid making decisions.	You get others to solve problems for you or make decisions	Never learn that maybe you can problem-solve or make a good decision, so your confidence in yourself never gets a chance to grow.	
Avoid responsibility.	Avoid taking on a new position or task at work or taking a course as you believe you'll get it all wrong.	Get stuck in a rut and don't learn to have confidence in yourself or see you do have the abilities to achieve things in life.	
Delay doing things, procrastinating to avoid anxiety or worry.	Things don't get done, or when it comes to the crunch it seems too hard or the original issue has become a bigger task or problem.	Annoys others and you get frustrated with yourself because you don't achieve as well as you would like.	
Sleeping too much to avoid anxiety and worry.	Going to bed early, sleeping later than normal or napping in the day.	You end up overly tired and don't learn you might be able to cope better than you think.	

Don't watch TV or read newspapers; avoid anything you believe will trigger worry.	Avoid TV in case you hear something about an illness you worry about having, or hear about a car accident because you think your family will be in one.	You can't avoid day-to-day information all the time and trying to do so keeps you preoccupied with avoiding the very thing you are trying not to see, hear or think about. If you do by chance see something, it leads to worry, anxiety and beliefs you won't cope, or to superstitious thinking that this is a sign the 'bad thing' will happen.	

Common safety behaviours

Behaviour	Example	Consequence of behaviour	Tick if it applies
Be overly protective of loved ones, not letting them go out or do much.	Not taking your kids to the beach or local pool in case they drown.	Family frustrated with you and you don't see that they may actually be okay. Can lead to those around you (children) becoming anxious about the world too.	

Behaviour	Example	Consequence of behaviour	Tick if it applies
Be overly cautious to stop mistakes from happening or try to do things perfectly.	Being overly slow and careful when writing an email or doing your work.	Takes you forever to do things. Don't learn that you don't need to be excessively cautious all the time and that you might be more capable than you think. Trying too hard to be perfect is exhausting and you'll feel down when you don't meet your overly high and unrealistic standards.	
Use alcohol or food or misuse drugs to avoid or reduce feelings of anxiety or worry.	Drinking most evenings to shut down the worry.	Substances usually make worry and anxiety worse when they wear off and also they are not good for your mood, weight or physical health.	
Over-use the internet, shopping or gambling as a means of escape or distraction.	Spending too much time on the internet or shopping.	This costs you time and money, and may lead to feelings of guilt and a reliance on these unhelpful coping strategies. You then worry about what you've been doing too!	

Use lists excessively.	Having lots of 'To do' lists.	The lists never end and you don't learn that you can rely on yourself to get things done without writing everything down.	
Plan excessively to reduce uncertainty.	When going away or doing anything new, you spend hours on the internet finding out all the details and trying to be certain you've covered all the bases.	Lose time and you will probably get very anxious if you feel things aren't going to plan. You don't learn that a little planning is okay and that maybe you will cope with whatever comes your way!	

Using avoidance and safety behaviours means you don't see that the worst may not happen or that you can cope with some anxiety and uncertainty. You deprive yourself of opportunities to learn to have more confidence in yourself and in the choices you make.

Checking and reassurance-seeking

Checking and reassurance-seeking are types of safety behaviours, and common factors in maintaining worry and anxiety. If you worry about things and continually feel uncertain, or if you believe that something dreadful might happen or may have happened, then it makes perfect sense for you to check on whether it has occurred or to seek reassurance from others that it won't happen. Why wouldn't you do this if it makes you feel better? However, these worry-related behaviours are unhelpful.

When people struggle with worry and anxiety they often seek reassurance from others as a way of reducing their distress or apprehension. Such reassurance-seeking is generally done to reduce uncertainty. It may be that if you have to make a decision you will always tend to ask others for their thoughts to reduce your own doubts or anxiety. But the problem is that while someone may tell you everything is going to be all right, after a brief respite from worry you might find that the worry and anxiety slowly starts to seep back in and you start to doubt what they've said to you, so the worry grows again. You may seek more reassurance, which again provides a brief respite, but then the doubt creeps back in and the cycle is repeated again.

In the table below a number of checking and reassurance-seeking behaviours are listed, along with the consequences of using them. Read over the list and if any apply to you, put a tick in the end column and write them on your Worksheet 4F. Also, look back at Luke and Sarah's worry vicious flowers to see if that helps you to identify any behaviours. For example, Sarah wrote that she continually asked Steve for reassurance about her worries, but his replies only gave her short-term relief and then the doubt would creep back in and she would ask him again and again. Eventually, she started to wonder if he was just saying things to keep her quiet and this increased her uncertainty and left her feeling stuck.

Self-assessment ✓

Read through the lists of avoidance and safety behaviours below. If any apply to you, put a tick in the end column and then write them on your Worksheet 4F (Behaviours vicious petal).

Common checking and reassurance-seeking behaviours

Behaviour	Example	Consequence of behaviour	Tick if it applies
Repeatedly check on your loved ones because you think danger is just around the corner.	Keep texting or calling a loved one to check they are safe when they are out.	Breeds doubt because it keeps you preoccupied with the worry that if you don't check, something bad has happened or will happen. It's frustrating for them to have to respond to you each time. Repeatedly checking won't make someone any safer, and if you can't get hold of them your anxiety will sky-rocket!	
Repeatedly check a task or your work to ensure there are no mistakes.	At work you go over things repeatedly or at home you monitor yourself and everything you do for errors.	Slows your performance down. Can irritate you and others. Don't get to learn that checking once is enough.	

Behaviour	Example	Consequence of behaviour	Tick if it applies
Search the internet for information on serious illnesses.	Find online information about symptoms to see if the sensations you are having are okay or not.	You're flooded with misleading information. You will always find something that feeds into your beliefs that you have a serious illness. This rapidly increases your worry and anxiety!	
Check your body repeatedly for signs of a serious illness.	Prodding or feeling your body for lumps or signs of a serious illness, e.g. cancer.	Prodding will only irritate your skin, leaving soreness and redness which you might interpret as symptoms of a serious illness, e.g. cancer.	
Ask others repeatedly for reassurance about your worries.	Keep asking someone if you will be okay or for their reassurance about your decisions.	Asking once for someone's opinion is okay but more than that and you fail to gain confidence in yourself, your ability to make decisions or your ability to believe in yourself.	

		Keeps you preoccupied with your worries and anxious if you don't get the answers you want. Stops you learning to cope with uncertainty. Can frustrate others too.	

Triggers of your worry and anxiety

So far we have looked at how you may have had developed negative self-talk and unhelpful thinking styles, and the maintaining factors of worry, such as emotions, physical responses, beliefs about worry, attention and behaviours. Apart from behaviours, these are all thinking and attention processes, physical sensations and feelings that generally occur within us (internal triggers), and each of these can trigger your worry and make it persist, as Figure 4.4 shows.

We also know that our behaviours (avoidance and safety behaviours) can trigger worry and keep it going. Sometimes, though, there can be triggers outside ourselves that set off our worry (external triggers). We refer to these triggers as **stressors**. Stressors may be things that happen in your home, work or in your social life. For example, your workload may be becoming too much for you, or you may have a disagreement with a partner, friend or family member, or you may experience an accident or upsetting event. Perhaps it is something you hear about from others or something you see or hear on the news or the internet that sets off your unhelpful thinking or

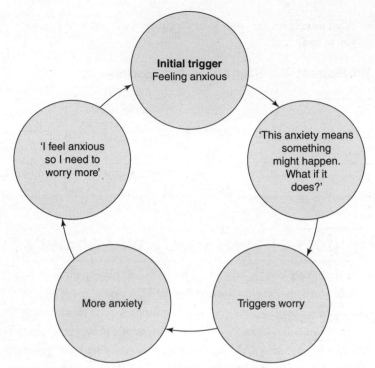

Figure 4.4: What triggers our worry and keeps it going

worry. Chapter 11 looks at how to manage such stressors, but the first step is to identify what your triggers and stressors are. Use Worksheet 4G to list any triggers or stressors you are aware of.

Triggers and stressors record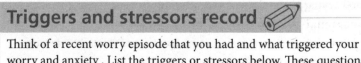

Think of a recent worry episode that you had and what triggered your worry and anxiety . List the triggers or stressors below. These questions may help you to identify some of your triggers.

- The last time you were worrying or anxious, what triggered it?
- Are there places or situations that tend to trigger your worry, e.g. at work, at home, watching TV, doing a certain task or activity or your loved ones being away or late home?

- What usually triggers your worry? (Think of a recent worry episode you've had)

Worksheet 4G: Triggers and stressors

_____

_____

_____

_____

_____

_____

Chapter summary

In this chapter you learned about:

- the worry vicious flower model that explains what feeds into and maintains worry and anxiety
- the roles of negative self-talk and unhelpful thinking styles and how they influence your worry and anxiety
- the maintaining factors and how they produce vicious cycles that keep your worry and anxiety going
- how trying not to think about something keeps it popping back into your mind
- identifying your own maintaining factors and started to develop your own worry vicious flower.

We have now looked at all the parts of the worry vicious flower and you have completed the vicious petals for emotions, physical responses and behaviour, the triggers and stressors section. In Chapters 6 and 7 you will complete the stem of the vicious flowers and the rest of your vicious petals, and you will bring all of the parts of your worry vicious flower together in Chapter 7.

Well done on getting through this chapter and its worksheets – it's a lot of effort on your part! It's important that you keep working on Worksheet 4A as we will come back to what you record on this worksheet in Chapter 6.

In Chapter 5 you will learn about and get started on some strategies that will lessen your worry and anxiety. We are going to start to tackle the Physical responses vicious petal.

Physiological strategies

Overview

This chapter targets the Physical responses vicious petal of your worry vicious flower, and in this chapter you will learn strategies to help improve your wellbeing and so reduce your stress and anxiety. These strategies include:

- physical exercise
- progressive muscle relaxation
- slow breathing
- pleasurable activities

In Chapter 1 we described how anxiety can affect our bodies, especially when our worry and anxiety goes on for extended periods of time. These effects include muscle tension and feeling restless or on edge, all of which are common symptoms associated with worry and generalized anxiety disorder (GAD). Being in a stressed state for very long periods of time can lead to increased activation of our body – increased heart rate and blood pressure, as well as an increase in cortisol production – which in the long term can be unhealthy for our bodies. Some people with GAD also have tenser muscles than those who do not worry excessively. Relaxation, slow breathing techniques and physical exercise are common stress management strategies and we encourage you to use these skills as a way of building your resilience to stress and mental health problems.

The strategies in this chapter are not intended to be single treatments for worry and anxiety, but rather to be used in combination with each other and the other strategies covered in the book. At the end of this chapter we look again at pleasurable activities, touched on in Chapter 3, like socializing and doing things you might enjoy. It is important to make sure there are a reasonable number of pleasurable activities in our day-to-day lives as these also reduce stress, anxiety and negative emotions.

Physical exercise

We all know that physical activity and exercise has many benefits, such as improving health, improving the immune system and reducing the risks of dying younger. Exercise appears to balance out naturally occurring body and brain chemicals, which can reduce anxiety. Plus exercise helps to reduce the level of stress hormones in our bodies. But did you know that exercise is an effective way to increase emotional wellbeing and that it can act as a defence against stress? Regular exercise can reduce feelings of depression and levels of irritability. Most importantly, exercise protects against anxiety and helps to reduce anxiety symptoms. Exercise can reduce worry symptoms and other problems that you may experience with worry or GAD, such as low mood, tiredness, low energy and muscle tension, and improves concentration and sleeping problems.

Exercise helps with our self-esteem and how good we feel about ourselves. It helps us to feel that we are achieving something. If you can increase your sense of mastering activities by doing some exercise, you can strengthen your belief that you can achieve things! For example, exercise, no matter how much or how little, gives us concrete evidence that we can do things, which we can develop into supportive self-talk statements such as 'I can do difficult things' and 'There are things I can do to manage my stress and anxiety'. This sense of achievement and productive coping can increase feelings of hope. In addition, exercise might be helpful if you also have a chronic illness as well as your anxiety. For example, if you suffer with cardiovascular problems, multiple sclerosis or another ongoing medical condition, anxiety may be present too and exercise can also be beneficial in these circumstances.

Another important way that exercise may help is that when you exercise your body is physically activated, so that you experience physical sensations like an increased heart-rate, feeling hot, sweating and other normal physical experiences that accompany exercise. People with anxiety are often anxious about the physical sensations of anxiety and you might notice that the sensations you experience when exercising feel similar to some of the sensations you feel when you are anxious. You may have been trying to avoid these sensations. By exposing yourself to these physical sensations through exercise, you are giving yourself the opportunity to learn that these sensations are not harmful or dangerous. Exercising will help you discover that these are just the physical sensations your body has when it is physically activated. Doing exercise helps to reduce your sensitivity to these physical sensations, and so it lessens your anxiety responses to normal bodily reactions and processes. You may also find that exercising more means that you are engaging in an adaptive and helpful way of dealing with stress, and that other unhelpful ways of dealing with stress and negative emotions, like worrying, will be used less.

What do I do?

Exercising twice a week is beneficial, but is more effective when done three to four times a week for 20–30 or more minutes of moderate intensity. There are different types of exercise. **Resistance training** includes exercises that involve some degree of exerting force against a weight, for example using free weights or using exercise equipment or machines. **Aerobic exercise** tends to be continual in nature or of a longer duration (20 minutes or more), and of moderate to vigorous intensity, such as running, swimming and aerobics classes.

Aim to exercise three or more times a week for 20–45 minutes at 50–85 per cent of your maximum heart rate. It can be confusing to know what your maximum heart rate is and how to track this.

Chapter 15 lists websites that will help with this. Otherwise, use the table below to work out your level of intensity.

Intensity	Activities and effect	Target
Light	Includes activities that take little energy and effort. You should be able to hold a conversation without much difficulty while doing these. Examples: household chores, mowing the lawn, slow walking.	
Moderate	Includes activities that lead to a noticeable increase in your breathing and heart rate. You can still hold a conversation but you will need to pause for breath at times. Examples: brisk walking, moderate cycling.	30 minutes, four or more days a week.
Vigorous	Includes activities that leave you out of breath. You would not be able to hold a conversation while doing these. Examples: swimming, running, some team sports, aerobics classes.	75 minutes a week if you are not doing other exercise.

Tips for success and dealing with obstacles

- If you haven't exercised before or for a while, or you have any health concerns, check with your doctor before starting regular exercise.
- Start with small steps, then gradually increase your exercise over time.
- Remember to warm up and cool down. Do some stretching too.

- Wear appropriate exercise clothes and footwear.
- Drink water before, during and after exercising.
- Don't eat a heavy meal directly before exercising.
- Don't exercise too close to bedtime as this may make it difficult to get to sleep.
- If you are just starting out and the amount of exercise each time feels too hard, you can break it up, e.g. 10 minutes of moderate intensity exercise, three times during the day.
- If you believe you already have plenty of physical exertion or exercise in your life or as part of your job, aim to keep it up and ensure you build in some of the pleasurable activities discussed in Chapter 3 and later in this chapter.
- Stop exercising if you experience any pain and see your doctor.

To keep you on track, it can be motivating to exercise with someone. Is there someone who could do some exercise with you each week? Look back over the support people you listed in Chapter 3. Could one of them exercise with you at a regular time? Perhaps they could go for a brisk walk or cycle ride with you, kick a ball about in the park with you or go to a gym class with you?

Bear in mind that exercising is rather like taking prescribed medicines for psychological difficulties, i.e. it can take a little time for mood improvement and anxiety-reducing effects to be noticeable. It may take a few weeks to notice stable changes in your overall anxiety, mood and irritability, but other things start to improve sooner, such as gaining a sense of achievement, sleeping better, and feeling more positive emotions immediately after exercising. Use Worksheet 5A to write down the short- and long-term benefits of exercising. Keep these benefits on a wallet-sized piece of card you can look at often, on a memo in your phone or in some other way that you can use to jog your memory of why you are exercising!

Benefits of exercise record ✏️

Write down the benefits of exercise and increased physical activity. Think about the benefits for you that there may be immediately after exercising through the following weeks, months and longer. Some examples are given in the worksheet.

Worksheet 5A: The benefits of exercise

Short-term benefits (today, this week)

Lifts my mood

Reduces stress, tension and anxiety

Helps with my sleep

I've done something to make me feel different today

I've achieved something!

I've taken steps to break the physical factors that feed worry and anxiety

_____

_____

_____

_____

_____

_____

_____

_____

_____

_____

Long-term benefits (next few weeks and onwards)

Helps increase wellbeing

Good for my weight and physical health

Reduces risk of stroke, diabetes and heart disease.

Lowers blood pressure

Decreases anxiety and depression symptoms

Improves energy, concentration and sex drive

Increases sense of self-worth

_____

_____

_____

_____

_____

_____

_____

_____

_____

_____

_____

_____

_____

_____

_____

Luke and Sarah wrote down some of the benefits of exercising for them.

Luke's benefits of exercise worksheet

Short-term benefits (today, this week)

Be less stressed and have less muscle tension

Work off some of my anxiety and stress
Sleep better at night if I exercise in the day

It's doing something for myself

Can do my activities with Amanda or a friend,
  so that would be good for me socially too

Long-term benefits (next few weeks and onwards)

Reduce my overall anxiety and be more resilient to anxiety and being cranky

Improve my health and fitness

Good for my weight and physical health

More energy

Might help me relax more too if I am more physically active

Sarah's benefits of exercise worksheet

Short-term benefits (today, this week)

Takes a bit of time but can work it into my day and it helps me to have something to focus on other than Steve and the kids, plus will be good for my anxiety and worry.

Sleep better.

If I do swimming, I enjoy being in the water - it's calming for me.

I like being outside too, so walking would tick that box.

Every time I exercise it gives me the chance to get used to some of the physical sensations I'm frightened of, like an increased heart rate, and learn they're not signs of impending doom. This will definitely make me less anxious.

> ## Long-term benefits (next few weeks and onwards)
>
> *Doing exercise increases energy levels and that is a goal for me. Will mean I don't feel so drained and will have more energy for playing with the kids.*
>
> *Good way to feel more on top of my anxiety, rather than the other way round.*
>
> *I'm always worried about my health so it's odd I don't do much exercise. This would be a helpful way to be healthy rather than worrying about it all the time!*
>
> *Can have some time with friends walking or swimming, which would be great.*
>
> *More relaxed.*

Luke and Sarah can use these benefits to help motivate themselves to start doing exercise at times when they are feeling like they can't be bothered, or when they're feeling too anxious or stressed to exercise.

If at any point you are feeling stuck about starting to exercise or unmotivated to do physical activity, use some of these **exercise barrier busters** to give you that extra push.

Exercise barrier busters

- Schedule your exercise time on your calendar or phone.
- Find an exercise or activity you might enjoy.
- Keep your exercise gear or bag by the door, in the car or in your office – somewhere it's always handy.
- Use music to get you 'pumped'.
- You don't have to go to a gym. You can do exercise at home or in the neighbourhood, e.g. walking, running, cycling – this doesn't cost money either.
- Try exercise with an added enjoyable element to it, however small! Such as walking or cycling in a park or where there is pleasant scenery, or get a friend to walk or cycle with you. Find a walking or cycling trail you like.

- Try water sports, like swimming or even surfing. Anything that gets your exertion level up.
- Try sports that involve others, like touch rugby, netball, squash or basketball. These can be fun social events and it can be motivating to be part of a team.
- Sign up for an exercise class at your local gym or community centre.
- Mix up your physical activities and exercises so you don't get bored.
- If you are pushed for time some days, then make exercise part of your day, e.g. walking upstairs, walking the kids to school and jogging home, during a break at work going for a brisk walk, run or swim, taking the dog for a walk. Try walking faster to the bus stop or train station, or getting off your bus or train a stop early for extra walking.
- Starting your exercise activity is often the biggest hurdle. Once you're in to it, it's less difficult. Try it for five minutes or so and see how you go.
- Remember the sense of achievement and the boost to your wellbeing that you felt after the last time you exercised? Remind yourself of this when you're struggling to do your exercise for the day.
- If you miss doing an exercise activity, don't beat yourself up about it; this happens. Problem-solve it by doing it the next day or by thinking about what you could do instead.
- If you are concerned about being judged while exercising or if you have concerns about your body image, try exercise at home or near your home. You don't have to go to a gym or pool if that creates a barrier for you.
- Look over your Worksheet 5A on the benefits of exercise for you.
- Use a phone, iPad or computer app to monitor and track your exercise progress.

Worksheet 5B can be used to develop some physical activity goals and record your progress. Remember, if you get stuck, to challenge your barriers or problems by using the pointers above or getting someone to exercise with you.

Exercise activities planner and record

Write down your physical activity goals for the next 10 weeks. Use the SMART goals method from Chapter 3 to help make your goals specific, measurable, achievable, realistic and time-related. Each week, make a note of how you did.

Remember to use the exercise barrier busters if you are finding it hard to motivate yourself.

Worksheet 5B: Exercise activities planner

LONG-TERM GOAL
What exercise activities do you want to be doing in 3–6 months' time?
e.g. going to the gym three times a week for 45 minutes, or swimming three times a week

GOALS FOR THIS WEEK (WEEK 1)
What are your physical activities goals for this week?
e.g. walking briskly three times for 20 minutes each time

What I'd like to do –	What I did –

GOALS FOR WEEK 2
What are your physical activities goals for week 2?
e.g. walking briskly once for 30 minutes and swimming twice for 20–30 minutes

What I'd like to do –	What I did –

GOALS FOR WEEK 3 ONWARDS
What are your exercise and physical activities goals for the following weeks?

	What I'd like to do	What I did
Week 3		
Week 4		
Week 5		
Week 6		
Week 7		
Week 8		
Week 9		
Week 10		

After week 10, you can start this process again with new physical activity goals!

Below is Sarah's exercise worksheet for the first few weeks, showing how she slowly increased her exercise activities. She had to make some adjustments to her weekly goals from week to week. Sarah had a few minor setbacks, but this happens, so she looked over her benefits of exercise worksheet again to motivate herself and she focused on how she could problem-solve her setbacks by changing her exercise activities to be more achievable. She kept working away at her weekly goals.

Sarah's exercise activities planner

LONG-TERM GOAL
What exercise activities do you want to be doing in 3–6 months' time?
e.g. going to the gym three times a week for 45 minutes, or swimming three times a week

In 3 months be able to do 3 brisk walks a week for 40 minutes each and a swim for 30 minutes.

GOALS FOR THIS WEEK (WEEK 1)
What are your physical activities goals for this week?
e.g. walking briskly three times for 20 minutes each time

What I'd like to do –	What I did –
3 brisk walks of 30 minutes	*Only managed 2 brisks walks of 20 minutes each. But have organized to do more next week by going swimming with a friend.*

GOALS FOR WEEK 2
What are your physical activities goals for week 2?
e.g. walking briskly once for 30 minutes and swimming twice for 20–30 minutes

What I'd like to do –	What I did –
3 brisk walks of 20 minutes *1 swim for 20 minutes*	*Did 2 walks. Will aim to do this next week too, until I get fitness up a bit for 3 walks.* *Did a 10 minute swim and rest of time paddling as was too tired! But did make a start.*

GOALS FOR WEEK 3 ONWARDS What are your exercise and physical activities goals for the following weeks?		
	What I'd like to do	**What I did**
Week 3	2 walks (20 mins) + 1 swim for 15 mins	2 walks (20 mins) + 1 swim for 15 mins
Week 4	2 walks (20 mins) + 1 swim for 15 mins	2 walks (20 mins) + 1 swim for 15 mins
Week 5	2 walks (20 mins)1 swim for 20 mins this week	

Remember, exercise may be more helpful and effective at reducing anxiety over time when you combine it with some of the other strategies in this book that work with your thinking and other behaviours.

Relaxation

Relaxation produces a state that is the opposite of the physical arousal associated with anxiety and stress, increasing our wellbeing, reducing stress and lessening anxiety. Learning relaxation techniques has a number of health benefits, such as lowering blood pressure and the heart rate, reducing levels of cortisol and tiredness, and improving sleep patterns. Reducing our overall physical and muscle tension and anxiety makes us less likely to react as often and as intensely to what triggers our worry or anxiety.

Muscle relaxation techniques as a treatment approach for anxiety have been used since the 1930s, when physician Edmund Jacobson developed progressive muscle relaxation (PMR), based on the belief that relaxed muscles contribute to a relaxed mind. Since then, relaxation techniques and procedures within therapy have evolved into various forms. PMR involves the tensing and relaxing of muscles throughout the body in an ordered way. For example, you might start with your hands and move towards your head and then down towards your feet, contracting and releasing the muscles in each part of your body in turn.

Relaxation strategies like PMR are likely to be more effective if you practise them while also trying not to engage with worry. Practising PMR not only reduces your general physical tension and feelings of being keyed-up, but gives you the opportunity to practise and develop your ability to not engage with worry. The relaxation and slow-breathing strategies in this chapter are a way of anchoring yourself to the present moment. So while you are doing PMR you may learn that you can have worries without having to react to or engage with them. You can practise directing your attention elsewhere, perhaps on the relaxation process itself, rather than getting stuck in your worries.

Switching of your attention away from your worries in this way is different from distraction. Practising PMR and learning that worried thoughts can come and go as you do this can strengthen your ability to focus on the present moment rather than focusing on worries. This may lessen habitual worrying. It may sound difficult to you, but this is something you can make progress towards by following the strategies and tips outlined in this book.

Sometimes people with worry problems unintentionally avoid experiencing emotions and physical sensations in their bodies because they are caught up in worry. Doing PMR and slow-breathing exercises gives us the opportunity to experience these physical and emotional feelings and learn that they are not dangerous and that they do come and go; they pass.

What do I do?

Initially, aim to practise PMR once or twice a day. Each practice can take 15–20 minutes. Relaxation is a skill and regular practice will help you develop this skill. Read through the instructions below and then try the technique or use the audio version available online. PMR and slow-breathing exercises (outlined later in this chapter) are often easier if you can listen to someone guiding you through them. PMR exercises are also available on the website associated with this book.

If you suffer with any injuries or pain, check with your doctor before using PMR.

Progressive muscle relaxation technique (PMR)

1. Make sure you are somewhere where you won't be interrupted or distracted, preferably somewhere quiet.
2. You can either sit or lie down.
3. Get into a comfortable position. Loosen tight clothing and take off your shoes.
4. Work through each muscle group, in the sequence shown below. Tense each muscle for 5–7 seconds and then relax it for 15 seconds. Then repeat, so that each muscle group is tensed and relaxed twice.
5. When you tense your muscles, tense firmly but not so hard that you are straining. Pay attention to how the tension feels.
6. When you relax the muscles, pay attention to the sensation of the muscles being relaxed.
7. If you get distracted or your attention wanders, gently bring it back to the muscles you are tensing and relaxing at that moment.
8. Follow the sequence below. Remember to notice the feelings of tension and relaxation as you go, close your eyes if you are able to.

● Right hand – make a clenched fist, tense it, then relax. Repeat.
● Left hand – make a clenched fist, tense, then relax. Repeat.
● Forearms – tense both forearms and hands, bend both hands back, then relax. Repeat.
● Biceps – clench the fists and bring both fists up to your shoulder in a bicep curl, tense your bicep, then relax. Repeat.

- Shoulders – shrug your shoulders up towards your ears and tense, the relax. Repeat.
- Forehead – wrinkle and tense your forehead, raise your eyebrows, hold, then relax. Repeat.
- Eyes – close your eyes tightly and tense them and your cheeks, then relax. Repeat.
- Mouth – close your mouth, grimace and push your lips together tightly, then relax. Repeat.
- Jaw – bring your back teeth firmly together but don't clench them. Hold firm, then relax. Repeat.
- Tongue – press your tongue firmly to the roof of your mouth, then relax. Repeat.
- Neck – press your head *gently* against your chair or pillow, then relax. Repeat.
- Shoulder blades – push your shoulder blades back towards each other as you push your chest slightly forward, tense, hold, then relax. Repeat.
- Chest – breathe in and fill your lungs, hold the breath for 5–10 seconds and tense the chest muscles, then relax as you breathe out. Repeat.
- Stomach – tighten the abdomen muscles, make them hard, hold, then relax. Repeat.
- Buttocks – squeeze your buttocks together, tense, hold, then relax. Repeat.
- Right leg – straighten your right leg, raise your foot slightly off the floor and tense your thigh muscle, hold, then relax. Repeat.
- Left leg – straighten your left leg, raise your foot slightly off the floor and tense your thigh muscle, hold, then relax. Repeat.
- Lower legs – with both feet or the backs of the legs resting on the floor, slowly bring your toes towards your head, stretch the calf muscle, then relax. Repeat.
- Toes – scrunch up the toes of both feet and hold, then relax. Repeat.

Then give yourself a few minutes to become aware of your surroundings again and to adjust to a more alert state. Gently open your eyes when you're ready.

Slow breathing

When we are anxious or feeling stressed, our breathing tends to become faster or shallower. You may be breathing from the upper lungs or chest area rather than from your lower lungs and stomach area (diaphragm). This over-breathing and hyperventilation are not necessarily dangerous, but continuing to breathe in this manner can contribute to tiredness and feelings of being keyed up and nervous.

Slow breathing can reduce stress and anxiety. While slow-breathing techniques are not effective for all anxiety disorders, they are effective for those with chronic worrying or GAD who are prone to over-breathing and ongoing hyperventilation. Improving skills in slow breathing or diaphragmatic breathing (breathing from your lungs more fully and in a slowed manner) contributes to a state of general relaxation. Slow breathing is a routine strategy intended to be regularly practised, just like physical exercise, for a reduction in your general stress and overall levels of anxiety, rather than as a direct strategy for decreasing worry when you are worrying or in response to an anxiety trigger.

If we practise slow breathing regularly, it becomes habitual. So we are aiming to retrain the way we breathe to be more evenly paced and healthy and to give us some protection from stress and anxiety.

What do I do?

Practise the slow-breathing technique twice a day for 10 minutes each time. It might be helpful to do it before or after your PMR practice. Try it at home or during a break at work.

Slow breathing technique

1. Make sure you are somewhere where you won't be interrupted or distracted, preferably somewhere quiet.
2. Get into a comfortable position. You can either sit or lie down.
3. At first, place one of your hands on your stomach and the other on your chest.
4. Take a slow and deep breath, through your nose if you can. Pull the air down to your lower stomach. As you do this, feel your hand on your lower stomach; your belly should expand out and your hand should rise. The hand on your chest should rise much less.
5. Slowly exhale through your nose or mouth (whichever is most comfortable to you), letting the breath flow out of you. You should now see and feel your hand and stomach drop gently down to where it started from.
6. Count to three as you breathe in and to four as you breathe out: 'In, two, three. Out, two, three, four'. Inhale and exhale at a slow, even pace. Exhale for a second or two longer. (After practising for a few weeks, work towards counting to four as you breathe in and five as you breathe out.)
7. Now place your hands gently at your side.
8. Feel free to close your eyes and continue to breathe in and out slowly for 10 minutes.

People sometimes struggle with learning to breathe from their stomach (diaphragm). If you're having difficulties with the technique, lie down on the floor with one hand on your chest and one on your stomach. As you slowly breathe in, try to focus on expanding your stomach out as if it's a balloon. You want the hand on your lower stomach to rise more than the one on your chest as you breath in. Keep practising – you'll get there!

An important point!

Relaxation and slow-breathing techniques are beneficial for coping with stress and general anxiety. They are intended to be practised routinely during the week, just like exercising. But if these strategies are being used to prevent or escape a feared catastrophe, avoid feared physical sensations or a panic attack, this can be unhelpful and their use can become a **safety behaviour** (see Chapter 4). Do not use the relaxation or slow-breathing techniques if you are having a panic attack and think your physical sensations will harm you or are dangerous to you. For example, if you think, 'I need to slow my breathing down or I'll have a heart attack' or 'I will not be able to breathe' and then use slow breathing, this stops you from learning that these beliefs are unfounded and untrue. Instead, let the panic sensations run their course. Scary as this might seem, remember it's just the flight, fight or freeze response kicking in! These are just physical sensations.

Tips for success and dealing with obstacles

- Don't do these activities straight after eating or vigorous exercise.
- Makes sure you practise in a room that is comfortable, especially in temperature, and free from distractions.
- Don't monitor or judge how you are doing. If this starts to happen, refocus your attention on what you are doing (your breath or the muscles you are focusing on). It's about practising the technique, not how well you do it.
- If worries or other thoughts are distracting you while you are practising PMR or slow breathing, just observe that the thoughts are there and then gently bring your attention back to your breath or the muscles you are working on. Thoughts will come and go – that's what they do.
- Sometimes while practising PMR or breathing you might feel uncomfortable. If you are normally used to worrying or being anxious, then being relaxed can feel strange or even wrong. In such situations, relaxation or slow breathing can sometimes trigger an increase in anxiety. If this happens, gradually build up the time

you spend doing these exercises until you get used to the feeling of being relaxed and learn that it is not harmful or something to be frightened of.

● While doing slow breathing you might sometimes feel light-headed, which can be caused by over-breathing or shallow breathing. This won't harm you, but check that you are breathing at the right pace and in the right way as described earlier.

● When practising slow breathing, don't take big, deep gasps. It's important to keep your breaths slow-paced and smooth.

● Sometimes you won't feel relaxed after you do PMR. The goal is to reduce your stress generally and increase your overall relaxation. If this doesn't happen on occasion, that's okay – it will with time. Keep practising regularly.

● Try to practise both PMR and slow breathing in the daytime to avoid falling asleep –you won't learn the techniques or finish the training if you aren't awake! An exception would be if you are having trouble getting to sleep at night; it's fine to use PMR to help you, but make sure you also practise PMR during the day too (not on your bed and stay awake).

● Try to practise at a regular time each day if you can, as this establishes a good routine. You may find it helpful to keep a record of when you have practised, as a way of reminding yourself to do it and to keep yourself on track with regular practice. There are a number of apps available that help you do this.

Pleasurable activities

In Chapter 3 we talked about looking after yourself and suggested you consider using pleasurable activities as a way of doing this. Pleasurable activities are also a good way to target the Physical responses vicious petal because these activities are about getting us activated! So pleasurable activities are a strong tool against anxiety because they help you to look after yourself and they often reduce the physical responses that can maintain worry and anxiety.

In Chapter 3, you filled in Worksheet 3B with a list of pleasurable activities you could do. Feel free to add to the worksheet some of the strategies from this chapter, like relaxation or exercise. When doing pleasurable activities, watch out for negative thoughts or self-talk trying to sabotage your efforts to do things for yourself. Think about and behave towards yourself as you would towards a friend who is worn out or not doing anything enjoyable. This is not about being selfish; it's about focusing on yourself to build up your wellbeing, so that you are less anxious and stressed, more able to function in day-to-day life and more engaged with others, rather than being consumed by worry or anxiety. It's okay to do pleasurable things for yourself!

During your pleasurable activities try to focus on the present moment and what you are doing, watching or participating in. If worries are trying to bother you, just notice them and then bring your attention back to what you are doing. It's time to claim your life back from worry and anxiety! Make time this week for a couple of these activities. It's okay to be good to yourself, especially when you are working hard to overcome worry and anxiety.

Below are Sarah and Luke's progress with the strategies in this chapter.

Luke

Luke knew that exercise was good for him and had always tried to go to the gym or run regularly. In fact, he enjoyed it when he got into it, but with work and university workloads stacking up he had let these things go. He wondered who had time for exercise, let alone relaxation techniques! Luke also thought, 'What is the point in doing pleasurable activities' because he felt so stressed that he believed he would not enjoy them and would be worried about not doing his work or study.

Luke realized he was not doing himself any favours by reading about these strategies and not putting them into practice. He also recognized that his unhelpful thoughts about the strategies being time-consuming and not a quick fix were sabotaging any chance he had of giving these strategies a decent go. He talked this through with Amanda and between them they worked out that he could cycle to work a couple of days a week and at university he could park his car a 15-minutes walk from his lecture room, giving him 30 minutes walking on lecture days. This would give him plenty of physical activity. Plus his mate Mark was keen to do something with him once a week, such as play a game of squash or go surfing. This was good because as well as giving more physical activity, these activities were enjoyable for Luke too. Luke and Amanda also decided that they would go out somewhere for a meal every few weeks or if money was tight they'd watch a movie and cook a meal at home, maybe having friends over.

Luke struggled most with the PMR but he knew it would help with his sleep and would be good for tackling his anxiety. He found it rather hard to talk himself through the PMR exercise so he used an online version. He also loaded it onto his phone so he could practise it each night before bed. Luke grasped the slow-breathing technique quite well and he used a 10-minute timer on his phone so that he could practise in work breaks and at home sitting in the back garden. He noticed that during both PMR and slow breathing, some worries kept popping into his head and he had thoughts that he should be doing his work. Luke just noticed these thoughts but then refocused his attention on his breath or the muscles he was targeting. Sometimes this was easier to do than he predicted it might be, and other times harder, but over time he became able to engage more in these wellbeing strategies than engage with his worries.

Sarah

Sarah did not like physical exercise at all and it raised unpleasant memories of physical education classes at high school. She was tempted not to pay much attention to this recommended strategy for anxiety. However, as she had heard, several times, that exercise was a good way to overcome anxiety and feeling low, she decided she needed to try to work it into her life. Her decision to exercise was helped by noting down the benefits of exercise for her on Worksheet 5A. As the kids were at school during the day, she started going for brisk walks, slowly building up the pace and amount of time she walked. Having music playing on her headphones helped greatly. Her friend Maria was keen to go to the local pool to swim once a week too. This was good because it was cheap and they could go even when it rained. Sarah was rather surprised that she was, at times, enjoying her walks and swimming.

Sarah began practising both the PMR and slow-breathing techniques together in the afternoon and sometimes in the evenings as well. A couple of times she felt uncomfortable feeling relaxed and she figured it may be because she wasn't used to it. After a few practices she worked out that this was the case. She realized she needed to learn that it was just a difference in physical sensations and it was being without the anxiety that she had to get used to; over time she found out it was fine. Once Sarah got into PMR regularly she started to feel less stressed overall. She and Steve also worked on doing more together, and with the kids and some of their friends, as a way of increasing the pleasurable activities in their lives.

Chapter summary

This chapter reviewed four ways in which you can tackle the Physical responses vicious petal: exercise, progressive muscle relaxation, slow breathing and pleasurable activities. These strategies take time, but they are an investment in your wellbeing and are strong tools for dealing with anxiety.

In this chapter you have learned:

- some strategies for tackling the physical factors involved in your worry
- how powerful physical activity and exercise can be in combating anxiety and increasing your wellbeing
- progressive muscle relaxation and slow-breathing techniques, useful tools for increasing general relaxation and decreasing stress and anxiety
- the importance of pleasurable activities and that having a regular amount of these in our life is an important way to vaccinate us against anxiety and stress.

Activities for you to do

In this chapter you have completed worksheets related to the physical strategies we have covered. Below are some activities to keep working on.

● Work on exercising regularly using the exercise activity planner (Worksheet 5B).
● Put your benefits of exercise list (Worksheet 5A) somewhere you will see it often!
● Find time each day for your relaxation and slow breathing practice.
● Ensure you have some pleasurable activities scheduled too. (Pick activities from your list of pleasurable activities in Worksheet 3B).

In Chapter 6 we focus on your thinking, looking at unhelpful thinking from the stem of the worry vicious flower and working on the Beliefs about worry vicious petal.

Working with your thinking

Overview

Earlier in this book we talked about how your thinking can contribute to the development of worry and anxiety, and also how your thinking keeps the worry and anxiety going, including in Chapter 4 when we looked at the stem of the worry vicious flower which contains unhelpful thinking. In this chapter you will learn:

- to identify the types of unhelpful thinking you may use
- to understand and to start to work on other types of thinking, i.e. your beliefs about worry, which also feed and maintain your worry and anxiety
- to develop your Beliefs about worry vicious petal.

In later chapters it will be important to know what your unhelpful thinking and beliefs about worry are; becoming more aware of your unhelpful thinking will make it easier to learn how use strategies for thinking differently (see Chapter 8) to tackle your worry and anxiety.

Unhelpful thinking

Chapters 1 and 4 touched on how early experiences in your life can influence your beliefs about yourself and your life, and establish the belief or rule that you need to worry. Other experiences – like having parents who are worriers, feeling unable to cope or past experiences of feeling vulnerable – may mean you have developed certain unhelpful ways of thinking. While you might have had good reasons for developing these beliefs or thoughts in the past, they are probably no longer beneficial or constructive beliefs in your adult life. In the here-and-now they only serve to activate anxiety and worry. Look at the worry vicious flower at the beginning of Chapter 4 to remind yourself where unhelpful thinking fits in to feeding your worry.

To tackle unhelpful thinking, you need to identify what your unhelpful thinking is, i.e. what forms of negative self-talk and unhelpful thinking styles do you experience or get caught up in? In Chapter 4 you completed vicious petals for emotions, physical responses and behaviours; now it is time to complete the stem of your worry vicious flower by adding your negative self-talk and unhelpful thinking styles.

Negative self-talk

In Chapter 4, we talked about our past experiences influencing the beliefs we have about ourselves, others, and life in general. Such beliefs can be positive and not cause you difficulties later in life, but some of these beliefs can be negative. The negative beliefs and assumptions people hold (e.g. 'I'm a failure', 'I can't cope', 'I attract misfortune') become the internal negative self-talk that can have several consequences, such as leading to anxiety and the triggering of worry, as well as activating the use of unhelpful behaviours such as avoidance and safety behaviours.

An important point about negative self-talk is that people often develop these beliefs when they are young and before they have developed the ability to question whether the beliefs are true or not. This negative self-talk may have been based on reasonable grounds at the time, such as someone telling you that you couldn't cope or wouldn't achieve anything. Perhaps you had experiences when you were young that understandably lead to the development of internal, self-protective beliefs and self-talk that harm is likely to happen to you, meaning that you must avoid it and worry about it. But as people move into adulthood they often don't reflect on their negative self-talk or question whether or not it's still valid or whether it was even factual in the first

Unhelpful thinking vicious flower stem record

On the lines on the stem below, note down:

- any negative self-talk that you experience; these are negative messages you tell yourself. Some common examples that might help you are listed in the bullet points following this worksheet.
- after reading through the section 'Unhelpful thinking styles', add any unhelpful thinking styles you have identified that you use.

Worksheet 6A: Negative self-talk and unhelpful thinking styles

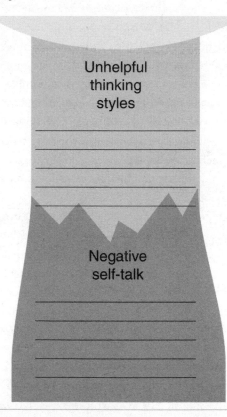

place. It has always just been there and its accuracy or helpfulness goes unquestioned; it is taken as truth. The good news is that negative self-talk is just our thoughts, not fact, and we can chose to think differently about what this talk is telling us. This first step, though, is to identify what you are dealing with so that you can tackle it.

Thinking back, what early or past experiences in your life may have influenced the development of worry and anxiety as a problem for you?

- Is there a history of anxiety or difficulties with mental health problems in your family that may have led to a vulnerability to anxiety?
- Were there upsetting experiences when you were a child, teenager or young adult that might have contributed to worry? These might include accidents, family or relationship problems, or others harming you in some way?
- Did others question your ability to cope?
- Did others question your ability to do well at home, school, etc?
- Was there frequent uncertainty in the family home?
- Did anyone in your family have difficulty managing worry?

Based on these experiences or what you know about yourself, what strongly held unhelpful beliefs or negative self-talk might you have about yourself as a person, about your future or about life in general? Write down any negative self-talk you might experience on Worksheet 6A (just the negative self-talk; you will add unhelpful thinking styles on the same worksheet later in the chapter). Examples of negative self-talk are:

- I'm vulnerable.
- I'm flawed.
- I can't cope.
- I'm weak.
- Something bad is going to happen to me.
- Something bad is going to happen to those I love.
- I'll fail.

- Others are better than me.
- Others are in control of their lives.
- Everything is too much for me.

If you are having difficulty identifying your negative self-talk, you could ask one of your support people if they can help you, if you feel comfortable doing so.

Unhelpful thinking styles

As you know, our thoughts influence our emotions and behaviours. Sometimes, particularly if we are feeling anxious, low or irritable, our thoughts can be distorted or negatively shaded. This does not necessarily mean that our thoughts are wrong in these situations, but often when people feel anxious or experience a negative mood they are more likely to experience unhelpful (distorted) thoughts or images. Indeed, most of us experience unhelpful thinking styles at various times across the day, but it is when we buy into these thoughts that they trigger or feed worry and anxiety. Also, because of underlying negative self-talk, people are often prone to experiencing unhelpful thinking styles in their day-to-day life. Believing or paying attention to these unhelpful thinking styles can then reinforce or feed underlying negative self-talk beliefs too.

Types of unhelpful thinking styles

There are common types of unhelpful thinking styles that people experience or engage in, which can increase anxiety and set off worry. These are described below. Read through each description and reflect on your own thinking. Which styles do you experience? You may experience only one or two of these styles or you may experience several. This does not matter. We all have different histories that have contributed to how we perceive things and how we think about day-to-day situations and experiences. As with any thoughts, unhelpful thinking styles are learned, which means they can be unlearned too!

If you are having difficulty in identifying your unhelpful thinking styles, you could ask one of your support people if they can help you. It might also be helpful to observe your mental chatter for a few days and see which styles occur. Write down the styles you notice on Worksheet 6A under Unhelpful thinking styles.

Fortune-telling

This unhelpful thinking style is a huge factor in worry! Basically, it's seeing the future as bleak or believing something bad will occur. Examples of this thinking are: 'Something bad is going to happen', 'I'll never have a good life', 'I'll mess up' or 'I'll never be happy'. When people accept these messages, they end up worrying about their future as if these predictions are true. But none of us can predict the future.

Catastrophizing

This is an exaggerated version of fortune-telling, expecting the worst will happen; it's about jumping to dreadful conclusions. It is believing that the worst possible outcome will occur to us or those we care about. Examples of this thinking are: 'My children will be killed or kidnapped', 'This upset stomach is a sign of cancer', 'My loved one is flying today and the plane will crash' or 'If I get fired I'll never get another job again and I'll end up bankrupt'. If we believe such distortions, which are not based on fact, we are likely to be overwhelmed by anxiety and worry.

Over-generalizing

This occurs when we believe that because something has happened once, this will always be the case. This style of thinking often arises when something has happened and we then relate it to everything else, including events that have not even taken place yet. An example would be if someone does not do as well as they would have liked in an exam and then thinks, 'I always get things wrong' or 'I never do well at things and I never will', so that they are left feeling hopeless and apprehensive.

Black-and-white thinking

Viewing something from one extreme or another, with no in-between, is black-and-white or all-or-nothing thinking. This type of thinking allows for no flexibility in viewpoints at all. Experiences, situations and people are perceived as falling at one extreme or the other with no areas of grey. Examples of this thinking are: 'If I don't do this completely right, I'm a failure', 'That person is all bad', 'I need to be in complete control of my life or something bad will happen', or 'You're either my best friend or not a friend at all'.

Discounting the positive

This occurs when we discard good things that have happened by discounting or ignoring them. Examples of this thinking are: 'I only did well that day because of luck' or 'People are only nice to me because they feel sorry for me'.

Negative filter

Sometimes people perceive things through a negative filter to the point where they only focus on the negative or downside of past, present and future experiences. Examples of this thinking are: 'No one at work likes me' or 'Last week was awful and all bad'.

Magnifying or minimizing

This includes magnifying or exaggerating your faults; for example 'I am the worst in my workplace at keeping on top of things' or 'I am the worst partner'. Or you might tend to minimize your strengths or positive characteristics or abilities; for example 'I could never have achieved that on my own, it's only because people were helping me that I was able to do it'. This unhelpful thinking style has the effect of undermining your beliefs that you can achieve things or cope with situations. It eats away at your confidence, leading to worry and anxiety, particularly about new situations.

Emotional reasoning

In Chapter 4 we talked about emotional reasoning's role in the Emotion vicious petal, and this unhelpful thinking style is strongly linked to worry and anxiety. Simply put, emotional reasoning is believing that your feelings or emotions are fact, i.e. whatever negative emotion you are experiencing you take to be evidence supporting the truth of the thought you are thinking. Examples of this thinking are: 'I've been worried and anxious about something bad happening all morning, therefore it must be going to happen', 'I feel anxious about my health, which means I must have cancer', 'I feel that something terrible is going to happen to my daughter; this must be a sign that it will', or 'I feel like a failure; this means I must be one'. Emotional reasoning can happen with emotions besides anxiety too. Examples of this thinking are: 'I feel worthless, which means I must be' or 'I feel angry with my wife; this feeling means she must have done me wrong and that justifies my rude behaviour towards her'.

Blame and personalization

Blame or personalization occurs when you place the responsibility for events or occurrences entirely on someone else or yourself without considering whether the responsibility might have been shared. An example would be if someone blames their partner or a family member entirely for an argument ('It's all your fault'), when in fact both of them were responsible, not just one or the other. The same thinking occurs when we accept the full blame for something but in fact other people have contributed to the problem, or the event was beyond our control. Examples of this thinking are: 'My relationship is in a bad state all because of me', or 'My employer went bankrupt because I didn't sell enough products – it's all my fault'.

Labelling

Labelling is when you make sweeping, general statements based on something that may have only happened once or in one setting. Examples of this thinking are: 'I'm a failure because they did not get back to me', or 'I'm a reject because I don't have Facebook friends'.

People also label others; for example, if a person at work or in a social setting is short with you, you may label them an 'idiot' or a 'terrible person' when in fact the problem is their behaviour, not necessarily the person as a whole. The person themselves may be okay, but it's their actions that are a problem. The same goes for you too. Sometimes you may make a mistake or not behave as well as you could have done, but this does not mean you are worthless or a bad person; it simply means there are some behaviours you can work on and change.

Negatively labelling ourselves or others means that we block any opportunities for change or a second chance.

'Should' and 'must' thinking

This thinking occurs when you hold on tightly to ideas about the way things should or should not be, either with regard to yourself or to others. Examples of this are: 'I *should* always get things right' or 'I *must* be the best partner'. Another example of this style of thinking are beliefs that you *must* be in complete control of your life and future, or beliefs that you *should* be strong and not ask others for help. 'Should' and 'must' thinking puts in place standards that are often unrealistic, unachievable and create anxiety.

People place these demands on others too; for example, 'My children *must* do well in sport and at school' or 'Others *should* always accept my opinion'. These unrealistic standards, which are unlikely to be met, can leave you feeling on edge and anxious when trying to meet them, and down if you believe you haven't reached your goals. When others don't meet our 'should' and 'must' expectations, we are often left feeling hurt, upset or angry.

Beliefs about fairness

Many people hold beliefs or assumptions that life should be fair. Unfortunately, because other people, the world and life tend not to operate according to the same beliefs or rules, such assumptions set people up to be let down when their expectations are not met. This results in a sense of injustice and feeling hurt, upset and angry.

Mind-reading

This unhelpful thinking style can be a real trap! It is believing that you know what others are thinking without evidence to support this assumption. From time to time you may be right, but in reality we do not know for sure what those around us are thinking, just as they cannot read our minds. The problem is not only assuming you know what someone is thinking but also behaving according to that assumption. If you are wrong, this can lead to negative outcomes for you and negative responses from others. For example, if you meet someone new and think 'They don't like me' or 'They think I'm an idiot', you may not be friendly, so they might respond to that lack of warmth by not talking much, which can be interpreted as evidence that 'They do not like me', when that may have never been the case at all. Another example would be talking to someone who seemed distracted and believing it was because they're not interested in what you're saying or that they think you are 'boring', when in fact it may be that they are tired or concerned about something else. Engaging in mind-reading by predicting that others are thinking negatively about you is a sure way to create worry and anxiety!

Now that you have read through the unhelpful thinking styles, did any relate to you? If you haven't already done so, write down on Worksheet 6A the styles you believe you might engage in. You might have noticed that most of the time negative self-talk is also likely to be distorted with unhelpful thinking styles. For example, telling yourself 'I'll fail' or 'I can't cope' are forms of fortune-telling and you are also labelling yourself as a failure. Saying 'I am weak' is labelling too. Having the thought 'Others are better than me' is minimizing yourself and your abilities. You might have also noticed that sometimes the unhelpful thoughts we experience can fall into more than one of the types of unhelpful thinking styles. If this happens, don't get too caught up in deciding which unhelpful thinking style it is; the important thing is to recognize that the thought is unhelpful!

Beliefs about worry

In Chapter 4 we introduced you to beliefs about worry and their role in maintaining worry and anxiety. There are two types of beliefs about worry: 'Worry helps me' and 'Worry harms me'. We also asked you to become more aware of your beliefs about worry by completing Worksheets 4D and 4E to identify your 'Worry helps me' and 'Worry harms me' beliefs. Now, we want you to transfer the 'Worry helps me' and 'Worry harms me' beliefs you identified from these worksheets onto Worksheet 6B below.

It is important to know that 'Worry helps me' beliefs are similar to unhelpful thinking. These beliefs direct how you respond to any triggers, thoughts or images that have even the slightest hint that you or those you care about may experience harm or future problems. Basically, 'Worry helps me' beliefs may be telling you to worry about many of the thoughts that cross your mind. Holding on to beliefs that worry helps means that whenever a 'What if …?' question pops into your head, you automatically start to worry as a way to cope with or prevent the worst from happening. 'Worry helps me' beliefs escalate a trigger or a 'What if …?' thought into a full-on worry episode. The good news is that by tackling 'Worry helps me' beliefs you can reduce your worry and anxiety.

Start with writing down your beliefs that 'Worry helps me' on Worksheet 6B below. Go back to your Worksheet 4D on beliefs that 'Worry helps me', look over any of the examples you ticked off and any you wrote down yourself. Now write them on your Beliefs about worry vicious petal where is says 'Beliefs that worry helps me'.

On the other hand, 'Worry harms me' beliefs kick in when you are starting to feel anxious and believe that your worry won't stop or will harm you in some way. Examples include beliefs that you will go crazy from worrying or that the worrying simply won't stop. It might help you to look back at Luke and Sarah's worry vicious flowers in Chapter 4.

Beliefs about worry vicious petal record

Look back at Worksheet 4D, at any examples you ticked and any beliefs you wrote down, and write them on the petal where it says 'Beliefs that worry helps me'.

Look back at Worksheet 4E, at any examples you ticked and any beliefs you wrote down, and write them on the petal where it says 'Beliefs that worry harms me'

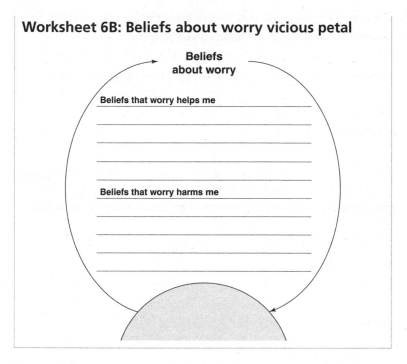

Worksheet 6B: Beliefs about worry vicious petal

Beliefs about worry

Beliefs that worry helps me

Beliefs that worry harms me

You might be starting to see that beliefs about worry can have a large role in keeping your worrying and anxiety active and continuous. One of the most important things to remember about beliefs about worry is that they are at odds with each other: **they clash!** If on the one hand someone believes that 'Worry helps me' but on the other hand they think that 'Worry harms me', they are setting themselves up to feel stuck. They think they should worry, but when they do, they then worry that it's going to overwhelm and harm them – it's easy to see why worry takes hold and persists. These opposing beliefs about worry get you into a catch-22 situation that it is difficult to escape.

These beliefs about worry are like a potent fertilizer that causes your worry to thrive. But there is a way out! Changing your attitude to worry, by learning that worry is not helpful and it won't harm you, decreases the hold that worry has on you. We target these beliefs in the following chapters. However, the first step in weakening these beliefs about worry is for you to notice when they are operating and to start to doubt what these beliefs are telling you.

Identifying unhelpful thinking and beliefs about worry

In order to think differently you first need to be able to recognize when unhelpful thinking, including negative self-talk, unhelpful thinking styles and beliefs about worry, are present. Remember our beliefs about worry are just thoughts about our thinking or thoughts about our worrying. So it is important to begin to notice these types of unhelpful thinking so that you can approach them in a way that does not result in anxiety or more worry!

Identifying and tackling unhelpful thinking

We are training you to tackle your unhelpful thinking. Over the next few chapters you will learn and put into practice the following steps.

1. Monitor your mental chatter, then ask yourself, 'What thoughts or beliefs are going through my mind?'
2. If you experience an unpleasant emotional change, ask yourself 'What thoughts or beliefs are going through my mind?'
3. Once you have identified the thoughts going through your mind, ask yourself 'Is this thinking *unhelpful* for me?'
4. If the answer is yes, then identify what type of unhelpful thinking it is:
   - negative self-talk
   - an unhelpful thinking style
   - a belief about worry ('Worry helps me' or 'Worry harms me')
5. When you know what sort of unhelpful thinking it is, use the 'thinking differently' strategies to deal with it (Chapters 6 and 8).

Learning to notice different types of unhelpful thinking or beliefs about worry is a skill that we can learn with practice. In fact, you are already developing this skill by gaining a better understanding about your thinking and reflecting on it as you read through this book. Knowing what type of unhelpful thinking or belief about worry you are dealing with will help you to tackle it using the approaches in the following chapters. This is like frequently feeling unwell because of something you've eaten; unless you work out which food is affecting you, it's going to be difficult to feel better. Just as some foods are nutritious and good for us, so some thoughts good for us. Conversely, some foods and thoughts don't agree with us, even some that may have been okay in the past. But before you can tackle these thoughts you need to identify which ones lead to you feeling unwell, which ones are unhelpful.

In Chapter 4, you completed Worksheet 4A, on worry themes and unhelpful thinking, which asked you to note the different parts of your thinking. Now, start to work on Worksheet 6C, a modified version of Worksheet 4A, to help you record and further develop your ability to recognize the different types of unhelpful thinking that you experience.

Self-assessment ✓

Spend a few days working on this worksheet. When you notice anxiety has been triggered or an unhelpful thought is occurring.

- Write down the date, trigger and the worry theme; examples of a worry theme might be home, work, health, money, relationships, a loved one's safety, my future, etc..
- In the 'Unhelpful thinking' row, write down the unhelpful thinking that caught your attention (e.g. 'Something bad will happen to me', 'I'll never get this right').
- In the next three rows record the emotions (e.g. anxious, sad, nervous, frustrated), physical sensations (e.g. fast heartbeat, hot, tense) and behaviours (e.g. avoided going out, repeatedly checked on my kids' safety) that occurred.
- Now reflect on the thinking you wrote down in the 'Unhelpful thinking' row and work out which category or type of unhelpful thinking styles might be present (e.g. black-and-white thinking, mind-reading, fortune-telling, etc.), writing these in the 'Type of unhelpful thinking'

row. If you notice that it is a belief about worry ('Worry harms me' or 'Worry helps me'), then put this down too.

Worksheet 6C: Types of unhelpful thinking

Date and Trigger	
Worry theme *What area or part of your life were you worried about?*	
Unhelpful thinking *What was the unhelpful thought that gained your attention?* *What were your worrying thoughts or images? Sum up what you were thinking.*	
Emotions *What emotions or feelings did you have?*	
Physical response *What did you feel in your body physically?*	
Behaviour *What did you do? How did you behave?*	
Type of unhelpful thinking *Which unhelpful thinking style or belief about worry is this thought?*	

Luke and Sarah each used this worksheet for a few days; look at their worksheets for ideas about how to complete your worksheet.

Luke's version of Worksheet 6C		
Date and Trigger	1 Monday morning at work, feeling anxious about task	2 Argument with Amanda on Wednesday night about her not wanting to stay over
Worry theme What area or part of your life were you worried about?	Failing at work	Relationship
Unhelpful thinking What was the unhelpful thought that gained your attention? What were your worrying thoughts or images? Sum up what you were thinking.	I'm going to screw this up and my boss is going to be on my case. I'm useless. I need to keep thinking about what I need to do.	She's going to leave me. I'm a crap boyfriend. I feel she is going to dump me. She thinks little of me. Can't stop worrying about it.
Emotions What emotions or feelings did you have?	Anxious, irritable	Anxious, felt low
Physical response What did you feel in your body physically?	Increased heart rate, upset stomach	Increased heart rate, restless
Behaviour What did you do? How did you behave?	Worried about it. Put off starting because it felt too hard.	Had a few beers to calm down. Texted her repeatedly afterwards to see if she still wanted to be with me.

Luke's version of Worksheet 6C

Type of unhelpful thinking *Which unhelpful thinking style or belief about worry is this thought?*	*Fortune-telling* *Minimizing, labelling* *Beliefs worry helps me*	*Fortune-telling* *Black-and-white thinking* *Emotional reasoning* *Mind-reading* *Worry harms me*

Sarah's version of Worksheet 6C

Date and Trigger	1 *Saturday -Ella going on a sleep-over*	2 *Sunday night - felt a bit of a pain on the side of my leg, started rubbing the spot where it was a lot.*	3 *Constant worry - Jacob's wellbeing*
Worry theme *What area or part of your life were you worried about?*	*Kid's safety*	*My health*	*Kid's safety and wellbeing*
Unhelpful thinking *What was the unhelpful thought that gained your attention? What were your worrying thoughts or images? Sum up what you were thinking.*	*Something will happen to her.* *I need to think this over a few times to make sure she's going to be safe.* *The house will burn down where she's staying.*	*It's cancer, I'm going to die from this.* *Worrying about it will help me be prepared for the worst.* *Worrying about it is going to trigger the cancer off.*	*He won't make friends at school.* *If I don't worry about him then I'm not a good mum.*

Emotions What emotions or feelings did you have?	Anxious, upset	Anxious, dread	Nervous, bit upset
Physical response What did you feel in your body physically?	Panicky, upset	Increased heart rate, panicky, can't sleep	On my mind, trouble sleeping, tiring too
Behaviour What did you do? How did you behave?	Keep worrying about it. Don't let her go in the end.	Asked Steve for reassurance until he told me to stop. Went on the internet to look up cancer. Kept rubbing the spot it was at	Keep asking him how he is. Just keep focusing on it.
Type of unhelpful thinking Which unhelpful thinking style or belief about worry is this thought?	Fortune-telling Worry helps me Catastrophizing	Catastrophizing Worry helps me Worry harms me	Fortune-telling Blame, personalization, labelling, a worry helps me belief too!

Chapter summary

In this chapter you have:

- learned about the different types of unhelpful thinking styles and how they can negatively bias your thinking, leading to anxiety and worry
- worked on identifying your unhelpful thinking, including negative self-talk and unhelpful thinking styles, and completed the stem of your worry vicious flower
- worked on identifying your unhelpful beliefs about worry, including 'Worry helps me' and 'Worry harms me' beliefs, and completed your Beliefs about worry vicious petal

Activities for you to do

Before moving on to Chapter 7, make sure you have:

- identified the types of unhelpful thinking you use (Worksheet 6C)
- kept up your activities from Chapter 5, including physical exercise and regular practice of PMR and slow breathing.

In Chapter 7, you learn more about attention and being flexible in your thinking, and you will complete the last part of your worry vicious flower model, the Attention vicious petal, and put your complete worry vicious flower together. You will also start to learn strategies to help you manage your attention and to start detaching from worry.

Cognitive flexibility, attention and your thinking

Overview

Earlier chapters have explained how your thinking contributes to keeping your worry and anxiety going, and in Chapter 6 you started to identify the unhelpful thinking styles, negative self-talk and beliefs about worry that cause and maintain *your* anxiety. In this chapter you will learn:

- how your attention contributes to maintaining your worry and anxiety
- strategies you can use to manage worry by increasing the flexibility of your attention.

Attention and cognitive inflexibility

By 'attention' we mean how we actively focus on and process information. According to William James, a well-known psychologist and philosopher, focusing attention is 'the taking possession by the mind, in a clear and vivid form, of one out of what seem several simultaneously possible objects or trains of thoughts'.

It is common for people with anxiety to have great difficulty not giving their worry attention. Or to have difficulty switching attention to other thoughts or problems; that is, to refocus their attention away from worry. Anxiety causes us to become self-focused; our attention becomes narrow, rigid and directed inwards onto perceived threats and our responses. We become preoccupied with what is going on in our head (worry), emotions and body, and with monitoring for possible threats and danger.

A number of brain-imaging studies show that excessive verbalization (our internal mental chatter – worry) is a major factor in maintaining generalized anxiety disorder (GAD). These studies show excessive activity in the left inferior frontal cortex and the speech area of the brain in people with GAD (Nitschke et al., 1997). When your attention is focused on your own busy internal mental chatter or worries, it can be very difficult to focus on any other activity, to recall or remember things and to problem-solve. This leads to the chronic internal narrow focus of your attention on worry, creating an inflexible and rigid thinking style, meaning that your attention is often fixated on worry. This worsens and maintains worry, anxiety and distress.

How attention feeds worry

By 'giving your worry attention' we mean how much worries are in the forefront of your mind or what your attention is focused on. As you know from Chapter 4, our thoughts are not as important as they would have us believe! When these unhelpful thoughts swarm into worry or become worry chains, they can seem louder, pressing or urgent, *but* these are just thoughts, just worry. By focusing attention on your worry, more meaning is attributed to the worry's themes (e.g. threats, your or your family's safety or wellbeing) than they deserve.

Our focused attention is used for many things; it is how we get the most out of or experience the moment. We learn and encode new tasks by using our focused attention to keep going over and rehearsing things in our mind. But sometimes our focused attention is where worry and rumination get rehearsed and practised, and then they dominate our experience, making us feel anxious and distressed. It is hard for us to concentrate on anything else when worry dominates our focused attention.

When your attention is focused on worry, you are being robbed of experiencing the moment you are in currently. If your attention is being used up by worry and rumination, and the associated distress and anxiety, there is not much attention left for anything else. This is why it is harder to problem-solve, learn and remember things, concentrate or think clearly. Everything else falls to the 'back of your mind' as worry takes over and fills up your attention.

To understand more about how our attention works, think about the process you need to go through when you first start to learn another language, play a musical instrument or develop any new skill. Also, think about meeting new people and how you try to remember their name. In the beginning you need to give the new task a lot of focused attention, thinking considerably about what you are doing, and the new task can feel effortful and complicated. We know that if we persist most of the aspects of the new task will eventually become automatic for us and we will no longer need to give the task all of our focused attention. We do not have to think hard about how to speak French or play the cello once we have become proficient. Our continued rehearsal or information processing contributes to that activity being more automatic or natural.

A similar process occurs with our worry. When we give focused attention to our worry, it grows stronger, as if we are rehearsing it or practicing it. Our worry starts to 'feel' like it is more than just worry or a chain of thoughts. The worry starts to dominate how we feel because we have practised and rehearsed it so much; the worry becomes stronger, habitual and can seem out of our control.

The good news

The good news is that you can have more control or flexibility over your attention and, therefore, your worry and rumination than you might currently realize. Think again about learning a new task: what happens if you don't keep practising the cello or your French? Initially it might not matter very much but the less the focused attention you give to any task (e.g. the less you practise), the more you start to forget how to do the task. The skills you developed start to fade into the background. This is exactly what happens to worry if it is starved of attention.

Think also about the times when worry is not in your focused attention at present – that is, when your worries are still there in your mind but more in the back of your mind, such as when you are asleep, when your attention is absorbed (even if briefly) by something you are doing or when you are talking to someone about something that really interests you – or the times when something has distracted you from your worry; the worry fades to the back of your mind. Imagine if you could take those small times when your attention is not focused on worry or ruminating and stretch that time out or increase the frequency of the times when worry is more in the back of your mind rather than in the forefront, grabbing all your attention.

Let's now start to complete the last part of your worry vicious flower, by filling in your Attention vicious petal. Write down your answers on Worksheet 7A. It might help you to look back at Luke's and Sarah's worry vicious flowers in Chapter 4.

Attention vicious petal record 🖉

Take some time to work out where you focus your attention when you are anxious and when worrying. The following questions may help you.

- When you are worried or anxious, what is your attention on?
- What are you often on the lookout for?
- What are you on guard or alert for?
- Is your attention focused on things you believe to be signs of danger? Such as scanning or being vigilant for what you believe may be

harmful to you, your health, your finances, your career or your loved ones' wellbeing, or even attention on worry itself in your head or the anxiety sensations you are experiencing?

Worksheet 7A: Attention vicious petal

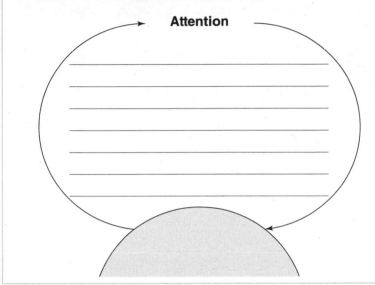

Developing flexible control over attention and thinking

A number of strategies have been developed to help people with worry and anxiety gain better control over their attention. These strategies help people learn how to sustain their attention on the here and now, and how to broaden and distribute their attention, thereby increasing their cognitive flexibility. Cognitive flexibility allows us to choose what we focus our attention on. The strategies that have been shown to be effective for managing worry and anxiety are mindfulness, attention training and detached mindfulness.

Mindfulness

Mindfulness is a meditation skill that has been around for thousands of years and has been taught in many religions, especially Buddhism. Classical mindfulness involves the combination of calmly concentrating on one's direct experience (*samatha*) and insight (*vipassana*) through concentration. In Buddhism, mindfulness is characterized as the ability to achieve direct experience of an object of our attention. Dr Jon Kabat-Zinn, who introduced non-religious mindfulness skills for people experiencing chronic pain in the 1980s, says that mindfulness is 'paying attention in a particular way, on purpose, in the present moment and non-judgmentally'. Since the 1980s, mindfulness has been modified, adapted and integrated into many forms of therapy for mental health problems (including anxiety), such as dialectal behaviour therapy, mindfulness-based cognitive behavioural therapy, acceptance and commitment therapy, mindfulness-based stressed reduction, and metacognitive therapy.

Mindfulness is a skill to help you refocus your attention or reorientate yourself. It involves training your awareness so that you broaden your attention into a more open and flexible state so that new ways of managing worry are possible. Mindfulness skills can help you experience your feelings, thought processes and worry in a way that is not overwhelming.

Giving mindful attention and developing a more accepting or non-judgmental approach to the present moment are helpful strategies because they allow us to let go of inflexible, habitual thinking (like worry and rumination) and reactions to current experiences, and instead choose more helpful ways of responding. There is growing evidence from studies in this area that mindfulness has positive implications for both psychological and physical health (Cavanagh et al., 2014). Mindfulness has also been used to enhance sports competitors' performances; enhancing awareness of the present moment is a critical component in peak sports performance as it helps to create a state of complete focus on the task or event while minimizing external distractions. So improving your mindfulness skills can not only reduce worry but also benefit you in many aspects of your wellbeing.

Attention training and detached mindfulness

Professor Adrian Wells and colleagues have developed detached mindfulness, a form of mindfulness which, when practised along with attention training exercises, is very useful for managing anxiety. Detached mindfulness and attention training are two of the main therapeutic techniques in metacognitive therapy, an effective therapy for anxiety developed by Professor Wells at the Metacognitive Therapy Institute (Wells 1999).

A key principle underlying Professor Wells' approach to worry and anxiety is that the problem is not that you are having worries, but the way you are responding to or attending to those worries. Worries are just worries; they are not always important but we tend to respond to them as if they always are.

As mentioned previously, the thoughts that pop into our minds are often automatic and can be associated with distress and anxiety. Worry often starts in response to one of these distressing thoughts or events occurring in our minds, i.e. our unhelpful thinking or negative self-talk. The worry or excessive thinking, at least initially, is a person's attempt to cope and to problem-solve. Examples of such thinking include:

- 'Thinking about this will help me sort things out.'
- 'If I keep thinking and monitoring things I can prevent this from occurring again.'
- 'Keeping thinking about this will keep me prepared so I can cope.'

In Luke's case, this often happened when thoughts about work or study entered his mind. He might not have been thinking intentionally about work but such thoughts would automatically occur. This would then activate his beliefs that 'Worry helps me' and he would focus his attention on his work concerns. A chain of worry would start: 'This work is too much … I'm going to screw up … My boss will be annoyed with me … I'll lose my job … This worry is making me anxious … I can't stop it'. For Luke, his worry and his attention on the worry meant he had little attention to spare for real problem-solving about his difficulties at work and left him feeling worn out and anxious.

Of course, this not the end of the story with worry. Worry seems to take on a life of its own and can seem difficult, if not impossible, to control at times. For many people who experience anxiety, the magnitude of their worry can lead them to start worrying that all this worrying is going to cause them physical or emotional harm in some way. The anxiety symptoms are often misinterpreted as indications of harm. As Professor Wells has said (2009), people start to worry *about* worry. He calls the beliefs that people have about the benefits or disadvantages of worry 'metacognitions' (which is why the therapy he developed is called metacognitive therapy). We talked about these beliefs about worry in Chapter 4.

To prevent possible harm, people often try to control, suppress or push away the worry, which might seem like a helpful strategy but in fact just gives the worry more attention and makes things worse. Our minds become caught up in an exhausting inflexible cycle of worrying about our problems or potential threats, worrying that the worry is out of control and going to cause us harm, and worrying about how to avoid or resolve problems. Focusing our attention on this worrying causes our attention to become more and more inflexible so it becomes difficult to switch off from our fixation on worry – it's a vicious cycle.

Attention training

Attention training is a technique developed by Wells to help people unlock their inflexible attention style and increase awareness of their attentional control. Attention training can strengthen your ability to focus externally (rather than focusing internally on worries) so that you develop new ways to relate to your worry and be more flexible! The attention training developed by Wells involves actively listening to and focusing attention on different sounds, first on one sound at a time, then quickly switching attention between different sounds and then dividing your attention to try to attend to as many sounds as possible at the same time. The aim in practising attention training is to actively focus on the different sounds irrespective of what else might be going on in your mind and around you. This trains your attention, like a 'muscle', to be more flexible and able to switch away from worry. Audio recordings of attention training exercises are available free online with this book.

Detached mindfulness

Detached mindfulness is a state of awareness in which someone is aware of the thoughts or worry that are occurring in the mind, but they do not respond or evaluate the worries in any way. As the name implied it consists of two components.

- **Mindfulness** is the state you are in when you are aware of your internal mental activities (thoughts, images, worries) and also aware that worries are merely worries, rather than facts.
- **Detached** refers to stopping or postponing giving any focused attention to worry, other than observing that it's occurring. Not giving your worry your focused attention is achieved by not reacting, judging or evaluating the worry, not searching for signs of danger, and choosing not to dwell on the worry; in essence, 'not responding' to the worry.

So detached mindfulness is accepting that worry is there and will come and go from the back of your mind into your focused attention. Your task is to try to refocus your attention on whatever you are doing. The aim of attention training and detached mindfulness is not to avoid, suppress or push away worry or feelings. On the contrary, worry or worrying images are allowed to be in your mind, it is only your attention and where your attention is focused that you need to be concerned with.

Both attention training and detached mindfulness require practice each day, as both are skills that you can learn and have beneficial effects that develop with practice.

Key messages

- Worry is just thoughts.
- Worry and feelings cannot control you.
- Worry and feelings cannot harm you.
- Just because you worry about or feel something does not make it true or mean it will happen.
- Worry feeds on your focused attention.
- Focusing on worry keeps it going.
- Worry takes you away from experiencing the moment.
- Worry and feelings can only dominate your experience if they are given your attention.

Practise observing your worries

For a few minutes, be still and practise being consciously aware of your thought processes. If possible, first try doing this when your worry is not at its worst. Observe your thoughts or worries but don't do anything in response to them. Try to take a step back in your mind to view the worries. Concentrate on being an observer of the activity in your mind. Let that activity occur freely and go wherever it goes. Be aware but don't try to engage or interact with the worries.

Practise regularly being the observer of your own thought processes or worry. Allow your mind to wander and notice where it wanders to. This can seem strange and difficult to do when you first start, but with practice it will become easier.

Suppression versus mindfulness

It is important to know the difference between detached mindfulness and trying not to think about worry or trying to suppress it. One of the most common but unhelpful ways to manage anxiety is to try to distract yourself from or suppress worries. Paradoxically, trying not to worry is a form of actively engaging with the worry because you are trying to push it away, but the worry gets more attention *because* you are purposefully trying to not think about it. Even if you succeed in suppressing your worries for a while, they will always bounce back at some point.

Returning now to Worksheet 7A, read through the following questions about suppressing worry. If you answer yes to any of them, add the methods you use to try to suppress your worries to your Attention vicious petal.

- What do you do to fight off worries, chains of unhelpful thoughts or worry images in your mind?
- Do you try purposefully to push worry away?
- Do you try to argue with the worries to get rid of them?
- How do you purposefully try to not think about worry or distract yourself? Do you tell the worry to go away?
- Do you tell yourself 'Don't think about this'?
- Do you tell yourself 'Stop worrying'?
- If a worry keeps coming back, do you tell yourself that 'I'm losing control', or 'I must try harder to not think about this'?
- Do you use work, television or other ways of trying to distract yourself?

Luke's Attention vicious petal

Luke realized that worry felt like a habit but he also realized that his beliefs that worry was helpful made him direct his attention even more to the worry in his head. So he put down on his Attention vicious petal 'focus on worries'. Luke recognized that when worry started to bother him, he would try to ignore it or distract himself from it, e.g. he would go on Xbox or the internet, or just try to push the worries away. But he remembered that this often didn't work, leaving him more anxious and frustrated. Sometimes he tried having a few beers to dampen down the worry. This didn't really work either, and it left him feeling rubbish the next day as well as anxious. Luke hadn't really thought much before about the role of his attention on his worry and anxiety. It was promising to know that he could train his attention to be more flexible.

Sarah's Attention vicious petal

Sarah realized that she fell into all the traps with her attention and worry. She would try to push worries away, and also try to push away worry-related images of bad things happening to her and her family. But nine times out of ten the worries came back into her mind. Sarah also understood that she was good at using her attention to look for threats, such as scanning her body for signs of illness or noticing and becoming preoccupied with news stories about things happening to children. Sarah wished she wasn't so good at this, as it left her feeling alert and anxious. She worked out too that because she had 'Worry harms me' beliefs she often found herself worrying about her worry, which meant she directed her attention to look for worry in her mind. This just seemed really senseless to her. She noted these things down on her Attention vicious petal.

Sarah had some hope, though, because it seemed there were some things she could do to get greater control or flexibility over what her attention was focused on. Sarah also started to notice that when doing her relaxation exercises she was able, at times, to unhook herself and her attention from worry when it began to form in her mind. This gave her some evidence that her attention could become more flexible.

Attention flexibility activities

Chapter 9 outlines strategies for developing more helpful responses to your worry and rumination, but first it is important to practise some attention exercises so you start to develop more flexible control over what your focused attention directed on. Some call this brain gym! As with any new task, starting with small steps and repeatedly practising those steps will make it easier to apply your skills in tougher or more challenging situations.

The following exercises will give you practice in shifting your attention from one thing to another so that it will be easier to apply your new attention skills to shifting your attention away from worry and rumination.

Attention training exercises

Walk

Go for a short walk. As you are walking, focus your attention on what you see, hear and notice about your body. Take time to focus on everything that you can hear, both close by and at a distance. Take time to look around, really focusing your attention on the details of what you see. For example, notice whether the trees are moving in response to wind; look at the different shades of greens in the trees – how many different colours can you see? Can you see any animals or people? Is it cold? What are people wearing? Can you see people wearing hats? How many people have glasses on? Remember, your task is to observe, not to make judgments in any way. Whatever you see just *is*; it is neither good nor bad. Focus on what you can feel physically on the outside of your body. Can you feel the wind on your face as you walk? Can you feel your clothes on your body? Notice the feel of your feet on the ground as you walk. Once you have focused your attention on what you see, hear and physically note, practise shifting your attention between these senses as quickly as possible from one to the other. Then try to broaden your attention as much as possible and give your attention to all that you see, hear and observe physically at once. Accept that worries and thoughts about other things will come into your focused attention; when this happens, just gently redirect your attention back to your walk observations.

Music

Put on some music that has two or three different instruments playing (but music without a singer, as you don't want to be distracted by the meaning of the words). In the same way as for the walk, practise focusing your attention on each instrument one at a time. Listen as hard you can to the tone of each instrument, the rhythm it is playing, does the volume change, is it always playing or are there times when it rests? Do this for each instrument one at a time. Once you have done this, try to shift your attention rapidly from one instrument to another; then broaden your attention so that you listen to the sound all of the instruments make together. When worries or any other thoughts or images not related to the music drift or jump into your focused attention, gently redirect your attention back to the music.

Give your attention to something you enjoy doing

The next time you are doing something you enjoy, e.g. sport, cooking, playing with children, a craft, repairing or creating something, then try to give this activity all of your focused attention. Absorb every aspect of the activity with all of your senses. What do you see when you focus all of your attention on the activity you are doing? Is there any noise associated with that activity? What do you notice when touching the activity? Be as much in the present moment with the activity as you can. As worries, or any other thoughts not related to the activity you are doing, drift or jump into your focused attention, gently redirect your attention back to the activity.

It's important that attention training is practised regularly, daily if possible, for at least four to six weeks. Some people may find it helpful to have someone guiding them through their attention training exercises until they are able to do these by themselves. The app accompanying this book includes attention training exercises, and Chapter 15 lists websites where you can download other attention training exercises.

Worry vicious flower record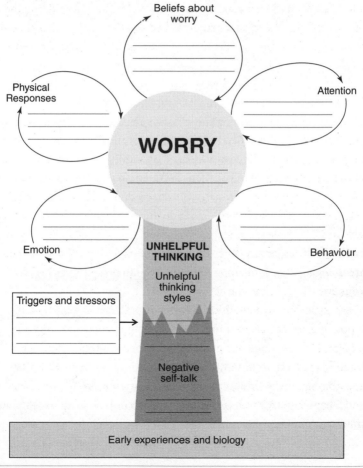

Copy what you have written in each of the vicious petals –Emotion, Physical responses, Behaviour, Beliefs about worry, Attention – onto the worry vicious flower below. Fill in too the stem of the flower with Unhelpful thinking, i.e. Negative self-talk and Unhelpful thinking styles, and your triggers.

Worksheet 7B: Worry vicious flower

Beliefs about worry

Physical Responses

Attention

WORRY

Emotion

Behaviour

UNHELPFUL THINKING

Unhelpful thinking styles

Triggers and stressors

Negative self-talk

Early experiences and biology

Putting the worry vicious flower together

By working through the chapters up to here, you will have completed all of the petals of the worry vicious flower model and in Chapter 5 you started using strategies to weaken the Physical responses vicious petal. Now, it's important to take a moment before you go on to Chapter 8 to copy what you have written in each of the vicious petals and on the stem of the flower onto Worksheet 7B above.

Chapter summary

In this chapter you have learned about:

- the link between attention and worry, and how focused attention on worry makes the worry stronger and more problematic
- why attention training and mindfulness can help you manage worry
- the difference between mindfulness and suppression.
- using strategies including detached mindfulness (Chapter 9 will have more details) to alleviate your worry and rumination.

You have completed your Attention vicious petal and also put together your whole worry vicious flower. If you haven't done this, give it a go now.

Activities for you to do

Before moving on to Chapter 8, make sure you keep practising regularly:

- the observing your worries exercises
- the attention training exercises.

In Part 3, Escape, you will continue to learn how to weaken the parts of your worry vicious flower, to escape from the anxiety and worry it generates. The chapters in Part 3 cover how to manage the unhelpful thinking and beliefs that trigger and maintain your anxiety, and how to use attention and mindfulness strategies to manage worry.

Escape

Deal with negative thoughts and behaviours and begin to replace them with new ones. Increase your attention's flexibility too.

CHAPTER 8

Thinking differently

Overview

For many years cognitive behavioural therapy has been an effective approach to helping people overcome and manage negative thinking, anxiety and other mental health difficulties. This chapter will focus on the unhelpful thinking and beliefs about worry that trigger and maintain your worry and anxiety. You will learn:

- how you can escape from unhelpful thinking by thinking differently, i.e. approach your thinking in more adaptive ways that lessen the occurrence of distress, anxiety or worry
- how to respond differently, in a way that doesn't trigger or feed worry, once you notice unhelpful thinking is occurring
- how to think differently about the 'Worry helps me' and 'Worry harms me' beliefs, so they don't maintain your worry or anxiety.

Unhelpful versus helpful thinking

Given that most of us experience unhelpful thoughts, why do some people appear not to struggle with anxiety or other upsetting emotions? What is it they are doing or not doing with these thoughts? There may have been times in your life when you've had unhelpful thoughts and they have not led to further unhelpful thinking or activated worry, anxiety or feelings of being upset. Why is this?

The way we *respond* to our thoughts is the key. At times, you may have unhelpful thoughts but you don't pay them much attention so they don't take hold and trigger worry and cause an emotional reaction. Perhaps you notice the thought but are able to take the power away from it by recognizing that it is unhelpful thinking and re-evaluating what the thought or image is trying to tell to you.

In essence, the key is to take a step back from your thinking and determine whether the thinking is helpful or unhelpful. If the thinking is helpful or constructive in some way, that is fine. But if it is unhelpful thinking – an unhelpful thinking style or negative self-talk – it is necessary to determine whether such thoughts can be re-evaluated to become more realistic or adaptive.

So how do you know if your thinking is unhelpful? The table below shows some of the key differences between helpful types of thinking, like reflection and solving a problem or issues that can be resolved, versus unhelpful thinking, such as unhelpful thinking styles and negative self-talk.

Key differences between unhelpful and helpful thinking

Unhelpful thoughts or images	Helpful thoughts or images
Are unrealistic.	Are realistic.
Create negative emotional states.	Are more likely to produce a sense of relief.
Maintain or increase anxiety and distress.	May increase anxiety, but is temporary.
Are critical, biased or prejudiced towards yourself, others or your future.	Are unbiased towards yourself and others; it is fair self-reflection.
Never seem to resolve the problem.	Lead to problem-solving or constructive solutions.
Are repetitious; they go around and around in your mind, like a cycle.	Are not repetitious and result in you 'working the problem out' – constructively working towards a solution.
Are paralysing and keep you stuck, so you can't seem to move forward.	Make it more likely a solution will be found and that the solution is productive.
Are energy zapping; they leave you feeling exhausted and tense.	Make you feel less exhausted and like you're making progress with an issue or unhelpful thought.
Lead you to worry.	Are associated with a decrease in worry or don't activate worry.

Strategies for tackling unhelpful thinking

When a thought comes to your attention, ask yourself: 'Is this *helpful* or *unhelpful* thinking?' Use the key differences table above to help you determine this. Ask yourself how does this thought lead you to feel emotionally and physically? Does this thought lead you to behave in helpful and productive ways or unhelpful ways that maintain anxiety?

- If the thinking is *helpful* and *realistic*, e.g. thinking about an issue in a constructive way, being non-critical of yourself or solving a problem that has a solution (see also Chapter 12, steps for problem-solving), you can continue with this line of thinking.
- If the thinking is *unhelpful* or *unrealistic*, deal with the unhelpful thoughts using the strategies for unhelpful thinking styles, negative self-talk and beliefs about worry outlined in this chapter..

Working with unhelpful thinking styles to think differently

In Chapter 6 you worked on identifying the unhelpful thinking – unhelpful thinking styles and negative self-talk – that trigger and feed your anxiety and worry (the stem of your worry vicious flower).

You might be wondering why we are asking you to work on your unhelpful thinking before the underlying negative self-talk. Basically, unhelpful thinking styles often maintain negative self-talk, so by starting with unhelpful thinking styles, you will also begin to weaken negative self-talk too.

Tackling unhelpful thinking styles

At the end of Chapter 6 you used Worksheet 6C to identify your unhelpful thinking and beliefs about worry. In the last row you were asked to note any unhelpful thinking styles and beliefs about worry that you had observed in your thinking after reading Chapter 6. Now read over the pointers below for thinking differently when you notice that unhelpful thinking is occurring. Take some time to reflect on the unhelpful thinking styles you tend to use, based on your Worksheet 6C, and the styles you know you are inclined to experience, and use the thinking differently tips to tackle these unhelpful thoughts.

Fortune-telling

As you might remember from Chapter 6's introduction of unhelpful thinking styles, fortune-telling is about believing you can see into the future. Consider how many times in your life you have engaged in fortune-telling that has resulted in worry and anxiety? Was this fortune-telling actually true? If humans can't really tell the future, is it helpful for you to keep on trying? Moreover, is the anxiety and worry generated from fortune-telling helpful? Did it actually do anything to stop bad things from happening?

Catastrophizing

This thinking style is believing the worst possible thing could happen. Anxiety is primarily related to people overestimating threat or danger. When a catastrophizing thought or image comes to your attention, try to step back from this thought objectively. Think of others who are not feeling anxious; would they see this thought in the same light? Would they predict the worst outcome also? Remember, it is just a thought, not a fact. Just because you think it, it does not mean it will happen.

Over-generalizing

Over-generalizing is thinking that because something has happened once things will always be that way. If you notice that you are over-generalizing, review your evidence for the sweeping generalization or conclusions you are making. For example, is it completely true that you *always* get things wrong *all* of the time? Is it 100 per cent accurate that you *never* have things work out in your favour?

A simple way of avoiding giving yourself over-generalized and negative thoughts or inner statements is to practise using words such as 'sometimes', 'might', 'may', 'regularly' and 'often' instead of words like 'always' or 'never'. For example, thinking or saying 'I never get things right' leads to possibly feeling low about yourself and worried about getting things wrong in the future. Whereas if you say to yourself, 'I sometimes make mistakes but sometimes I do well', this is likely to lead to less intense negative feelings and potentially a sense that there is an opportunity to do well or to achieve, leading to feelings of hope.

Black-and-white thinking

Black-and-white thinking is about viewing things as all or nothing, one thing or another. If you notice you are doing this, question whether what you are thinking about definitely is one way or another? Try to look at the thought or issue on a continuum rather than being black or white. Is there any middle ground, any grey areas? Try to think in parts or percentages; for example, 'Eighty per cent of the time I do well in my studies and the other 20 per cent I do okay' or 'Most of the time I am a pretty good friend but occasionally I let others down or might be a bit unsociable'.

Discounting the positive

This is about ignoring, playing down or lessening positive things that have happened or good things about yourself. It may be that you find it difficult to acknowledge positives about yourself because it's something that you're just not used to doing. You may also feel uncomfortable taking notice of or thinking about good aspects of yourself or your achievements. If a friend or loved one was discounting the positives about themselves, what might you suggest to them? How might you bring their attention to some of the good things about themselves or help them accept that they are okay and good at some things? So why not do the same for yourself! Think about some of the positive things those who know you well would say about you. Remind yourself about those positives regularly. This isn't about being vain or thinking too much of yourself, it's about being fair-minded and non-critical in the views you have of yourself or things you have achieved or experienced.

Negative filter

Using a negative filter is like viewing all we see through negatively tainted, dark lenses. This is a common trap with anxiety, worry and being self-critical. One way to manage this type of unhelpful thinking is to shift your attention away from a focus on the negative points and refocus on points or aspects of yourself or a situation that are positive or constructive. If you are using words loaded with negativity such as 'awful', 'terrible' or 'horrific', notice this and work towards dropping these expressions that only fuel negativity and pessimism.

Magnifying or minimizing

Rather than minimizing your strengths and abilities and magnifying your flaws, notice when you are doing this and think about what the impact is on you of using this unhelpful thinking style. Would you want people you care about to magnify their faults or minimize their good points? So why do it to yourself? Acknowledge your abilities and be reasonable in the judgement of your flaws; no one is faultless. Be realistic towards yourself, not rigid and relentless.

Emotional reasoning

Emotional reasoning is believing or deeming your emotions to be fact, i.e. when we base our thoughts and beliefs on what we feel, but the key thing is that emotions are *not* fact! They are real and we feel them, but they may not be accurate reflections of how things really are. It is likely that there have been many times in your life when your emotions, gut reactions or intuition were mistaken. This does not mean we should ignore our emotions but it does mean we should consider them in a way that acknowledges they may not be completely valid or predictors of the truth. Remember, our emotions are only a part of us, they are not what define us and you are not your emotion. Feeling bad does not mean you are bad, and feeling anxious is not concrete evidence that something awful is going to happen or has happened.

Blame and personalization

If you are inclined to negatively personalize experiences or your interactions with others or tend to blame yourself, then consider what your evidence is for the issue that you are taking responsibility for. Is there any evidence against this? Is there evidence that you are not fully responsible for the matter you're blaming yourself for?

With blame, look at what you are blaming yourself for. Was it completely your responsibility and fully within your control? Recognize what responsibility you hold in the situation and then problem-solve this. If you made a mistake, so be it; what can you do to remedy it? Remember you are only human. But don't blame or criticize yourself for things that are not within your control.

Labelling

Labelling is when we brand ourselves or others with critical or belittling names or labels. Be careful not to buy into your negative self-talk. If you have done something wrong or acted in a way you're not happy with, then recognize that these are behaviours or actions that you can become more aware of and work towards changing. Remind yourself you are only human; no one is flawless. It doesn't mean you are a 'failure' or 'bad' if you get something wrong. Would you want someone you care about labelling themselves with harsh and critical negative self-talk? What impact would it have on them? Just as we want others to be compassionate towards themselves, try to be compassionate towards yourself.

'Should' and 'must' thinking

This thinking style about having strict and inflexible rules about how you or things *should* or *must* be. We all have different rules and values depending on our backgrounds, our culture and other influences. Because of this, it is unrealistic and unachievable that everyone on the planet would operate according to the same rules or values. If we hold on to the belief that we should or must do something 'right' or a certain way or that others should do so, we are going to be let down and disheartened frequently. People and life will disappoint us at times. The degree to which this impacts on us depends on how strongly we needlessly hold onto 'should' and 'must' thinking. When we don't meet our self-imposed 'shoulds' (e.g. 'I *should* be a perfect parent', 'I *must* never let anyone down'), we will probably feel anxious or low. If we hold others to the same rigid rules (e.g. 'Others *should* be nice to me', 'Others *must* listen to my opinion') and these expectations are not met, we are likely to end up feeling hurt or angry.

Instead, we can try to be more flexible about what we expect of ourselves and others. This does not mean we need to lower our standards or allow ourselves to be poorly treated by others. Rather, it's about recognizing that sometimes there are reasons why we or others can't achieve set standards. It's about giving yourself a break, because no one is perfect. If others don't meet your rules, consider that they have different ways and try not to focus on what you probably can't change.

Beliefs about fairness

This is about holding on tightly to beliefs that life and the world should be fair. Unfortunately, the world is not fair. Fairness in life, or beliefs that karma will restore some sort of equality or justice in how people's lives play out, are myths. Holding onto this unhelpful thinking style is a magnet for feeling wronged or hurt. It is okay to reflect on whether we have been treated inappropriately and then to try to address it if we have. However, sometimes we simply cannot do anything to rectify situations or have our needs or rights honoured by others. If this is the case, it is better to look after yourself, ride out your hurt or frustration, than to keep focusing on it and turning it into something you worry about. Notice when this thinking style is in play and then let go of trying to hold on to fairness myths; focus your energy on more constructive activities or tasks in your life or on engaging with supportive people.

Mind-reading

This occurs when you believe you know what others are thinking. If you notice you are mind-reading, rather than pondering on what someone else is thinking or assuming you know what is going on in their mind, operate on the rule that we are never guaranteed we will be right so don't give these thoughts the time of day. Suspend the belief that you know what others are thinking. If necessary, you can ask the person what they are thinking or what's on their mind rather than assuming it is related to you or that it is negative.

What do I do?

Here is an exercise for tackling your unhelpful thinking styles and trying to think about these types of thoughts differently.

Reviewing behaviour

Look back at the unhelpful thinking styles you recorded on Worksheet 6C or think about which unhelpful thinking styles you have experienced most over the past week or two.

- Pick the three most common unhelpful thinking styles for you and write them in the first column on Worksheet 8A.

- In the second column, write down how you might rework this thought so it is not distorted, i.e. so the unhelpful thinking style is not present; use some of the tips above to help you think differently. For example, you could remember that 'This is just black-and-white thinking', or 'I can think of the situation as on a continuum or in percentages instead'. Or see it for the unhelpful thinking it is; for example, 'There goes that mind-reading again, telling me people don't like me', or 'That's a good an example of catastrophizing my anxiety is telling me, but that's all it is, because it's not fact!'

Take one type of unhelpful thinking style and practise thinking differently about it for a few days; then try the same with the next style, and so on.

Worksheet 8A: Unhelpful thinking styles

Unhelpful thinking style	Thinking differently
1	
2	
3	

It can also be helpful when you notice an unhelpful thinking style to note this yourself just before you try to rework the thought to be more helpful and realistic. Recognizing an unhelpful thinking style as just that may be enough to remind you that you don't need to occupy yourself with it, as in these examples:

- 'There goes fortune-telling again! Which only ends up triggering my anxiety.'
- 'That's a good example of me doing black-and-white thinking, which just increases my anxiety.'
- 'I have just spent time trying to read his mind, I don't know how to read minds and trying to just makes me anxious.'

Look at Luke and Sarah's worksheets showing their common unhelpful thinking styles and their new ways of thinking differently.

Luke's Worksheet 8A

Unhelpful thinking style	Thinking differently
1 Mind-reading	Rather than thinking and believing that Amanda and my boss are thinking negatively about me, or even that they are thinking about me at all, I need to remember that mind-reading is a trap. I have predicted Amanda has been thinking negative thoughts about me before and when I've asked, I've been wrong. She is still with me and my boss still employs me and says positive things about me. When mind-reading happens I can remember it's a skill I really don't have.
2 Magnifying and minimizing	Instead of magnifying my problems and the things I'm not so good at and minimizing my strengths I need to flip this. Bring my attention on to what I am good at and acknowledge this, with less focus on the negatives. If I do recognize something I am struggling with, then I can think about what steps I can take to improve my skills with this difficulty or problem-solve the issue.

3 Black-and-white thinking	Yes, I am very black and white with myself and with how I view others. I can try to think about things more on a continuum or using percentages. So I might be good at 85% of my work tasks and 90% of the time I do well on my assignment tasks. No one can be 100% good at everything all of the time and trying to only burns me, makes me anxious and triggers anxiety and worry.

Sarah's Worksheet 8A

Unhelpful thinking style	Thinking differently
1 Fortune-telling	Hundreds of times, if not more, I have predicted that something will go wrong or something bad will happen. It never really does. I can't see into the future, otherwise I would've won the lottery by now! I am going to stop trying to predict the future.
2 Catastrophizing	I don't know how things will turn out and many times I've thought something disastrous would happen and it hasn't. Worrying about these things won't affect the chance of it happening. Catastrophizing is just my anxiety talking, it's trying to protect me from harm but really is giving me false messages and making things worse.
3 Blame and personalization	This is a habit for me, I seem to blame myself or take things personally without even thinking about it. I need to take a step back and pause before doing this. Ask myself, 'Is this situation fully within my control or fully my responsibility?' Would I want my kids blaming themselves and personalizing every negative experience they come across? So why do it to myself!

Tackling negative self-talk

You can approach your negative self-talk in a similar way to your unhelpful thinking styles. First, look at how negative self-talk can affect your emotions, physical responses and behaviours using Worksheet 8B. Then you can use Worksheet 8C to develop some ways to tackle this negative self-talk.

Reviewing behaviour

In the first column of Worksheet 8B, write next to the numbers your negative self-talk from Worksheet 6A, or the negative self-talk statements that you are aware you use.

Next, think about and write down the consequences of these thoughts for you, i.e. your emotions, physical response and behaviour.

In the last column, write down why negative self-talk is unhelpful. The table includes some examples to help you.

Worksheet 8B: Negative self-talk's impact on me

Negative self-talk	Emotions	Physical responses	Behaviour	Why this negative self-talk is unhelpful
e.g. I can't cope	Anxious	Panicky, increased heart rate	Avoid most things	Don't try new things, get anxious every time something new happens.
e.g. I'm a failure	Low, anxious	Restless, sleep problems	Check over and over for mistakes I've made. Focus on what I'll get wrong.	Makes me worry, I focus more on my shortcomings.

Negative self-talk	Emotions	Physical responses	Behaviour	Why this negative self-talk is unhelpful
1				
2				
3				
4				
5				

Now on Worksheet 8C, next to the corresponding number, write down the negative self-talk from Worksheet 8B. Do this one at a time. As you do this, look over the unhelpful thinking styles from earlier in this chapter and see which style fits with each of your own negative self-talk statements and write this down. Use the same approaches that you used for unhelpful thinking styles to deal with this negative self-talk. Finally, in the last column write down more realistic or helpful thoughts. To help you with this column, there are some tips on how to tackle negative self-talk below. To help develop more helpful and realistic ways of thinking differently, ask yourself:

- What type of unhelpful thinking style is this thought?
- Is this thought based on feelings and not fact; am I using emotional reasoning?
- Am I fortune-telling?
- Am I blaming myself for things not fully within my control?
- Am I setting myself unrealistic, unreasonable or perfectionist standards?
- What would I tell a friend who had this thought?
- Would I want a family member or friend to think this way? What might I say to them to help them be less hard on themselves? What would I get them to direct their attention to instead (maybe good things about themselves or that they're only human).
- What are the consequences of this thought; how does it make me feel?
- What are the disadvantages of believing this negative self-talk; how does it affect my emotions, behaviour, and my self-worth?
- How would things be if I did not have this belief or unhelpful thinking?

Behaviour changing strategy ♘

Write down your negative self-talk statements from your Worksheet 8B in Worksheet 8C below, next to the corresponding number (e.g., the negative self-talk statement from row 1 of Worksheet 8B should go in row 1 of Worksheet 8C). Then work out what unhelpful thinking style your negative self-talk is and put that in the second column. Finally, in the third column note down any ways you could think differently about this.

Worksheet 8C: Tackling negative self-talk

Negative self-talk	Unhelpful thinking style	What is a more helpful way of thinking? What can I do differently in response to this thought instead of worrying or focusing on it?
e.g. I can't cope	Fortune-telling	I can't predict the future.
	Minimizing my abilities	I'd help a friend think about how they might cope, like problem-solving, looking after themselves with exercise. I could do this for myself too.
	Over-generalizing	I've coped before when I believed I couldn't.
e.g. I'm a failure	Labelling	I am not perfect but I'm okay, I am only human.
		I can't be good at everything, it's not realistic.
		This thought makes me feel low and anxious, it's not doing me any favours.
		I wouldn't want my children to think this about themselves. So why give myself this message!

Negative self-talk	Unhelpful thinking style	What is a more helpful way of thinking? What can I do differently in response to this thought instead of worrying or focusing on it?
1		
2		
3		
4		
5		

Here are some other helpful ways to respond to negative self-talk.

- Remind yourself: 'I'm only human, with strengths and flaws. No one is perfect.'
- Remind yourself: 'If I make a mistake it's an opportunity to learn and to improve my confidence. We all make mistakes!'
- Think about someone you know who doesn't worry; what would they do with this thought? Try doing what they might do if it's an adaptive strategy.
- *Act as if* the negative self-talk is not completely true (remember, it's just a thought). For example, if your negative self-talk is telling you not to do something because you'll fail, then act is if the thought was saying 'I could do this'. If the thought is saying 'I won't cope', act as if 'I might cope' and think about what steps you need to take to act this way. Perhaps set it up as a behavioural experiment (see Chapter 10).
- On a wallet-sized piece of cardboard, create a 'thinking differently prompt card' as a reminder of how to think differently, or develop an electronic version as a memo on your smartphone, computer or other electronic device. On this 'prompt card' write down two or three 'thinking differently' statements, including:
  - your main ways of thinking differently from the unhelpful thinking styles you've been using (from Worksheet 8A)
  - the helpful thoughts you developed to combat your negative self-talk (from Worksheet 8C).

  Keep the prompt card somewhere private but visible to you (e.g. in your wallet/purse, on the bathroom mirror) so you can use the card as a reminder of how to think differently. Also, seeing these 'thinking differently' thoughts regularly will strengthen them so they can compete with the old ways of unhelpful thinking.

Chapter 13 has more guidance on developing healthy self-talk. Also, if you want more guidance or support with working on self-talk or low self-esteem, see *How to Deal with Low Self-esteem*, another title in this series.

Luke and Sarah both filled in the worksheets on negative self-talk. On Worksheet 8B, Luke noted that his negative self-talk was 'I'm a failure', and he wrote that this negative self-talk was unhelpful because it made him feel low but also very anxious about anything he did because he predicted he would get it wrong. Using Worksheet 8C, he reflected on his negative self-talk of 'I'm a failure' and realized this was labelling himself, minimizing his abilities and magnifying any problems he had or errors he made so that they took up his full attention, leaving no room for recognizing what he was able to do well. Luke also thought labelling himself as a failure was quite black and white as it left no room for recognizing that he was not failing at everything, all of the time. He developed more helpful ways of thinking differently, such as acknowledging to himself what he could do and directing his thinking into problem-solving any issues he had at work or with his studies. If he did identify something he was having difficulties with, Luke thought he could focus on how to improve this skill, such as getting someone at work to help him learn to do something better or joining a study group at university if he was falling behind on something. He was going to try to remember that he was only human and then act *as if* he was competent at what he did. Luke created a 'thinking differently' prompt card on his smartphone to remind himself of ways of thinking differently.

Sarah was aware that negative self-talk about vulnerability and harm were her strongest inner messages. 'I'm vulnerable' and 'My kids are vulnerable' were what she jotted down on Worksheet 8B. Sarah then wrote down that this was unhelpful because it meant that every time she felt a sensation in her body she interpreted it as a symptom of a deadly illness rather than just a normal physical sensation. It also meant that every time the kids left the house she felt panicky and was consumed by the belief that she needed to worry about them. Using

Worksheet 8C, Sarah categorized her thinking that she was vulnerable as forms of fortune-telling and catastrophizing, realizing that she had no way of seeing into the future and also that she often coped better than she expected when difficulties in life arose. Recognizing this negative self-talk as an unhelpful thinking style gave her time to see the thoughts for what they were: her anxiety talking! This helped her to step back from vulnerability-related thoughts before they became a chain of worry. Sarah created a 'thinking differently' prompt card for her purse; that way it was handy and she would see it often to help strengthen her thinking differently skills.

Working with beliefs about worry to think differently

Chapters 4 and 6 looked at beliefs about worry, including 'Worry harms me' and 'Worry helps me', and how these beliefs are unhelpful and maintain worry and anxiety. Just as you worked on thinking differently about your unhelpful thinking styles and negative self-talk, you can re-evaluate and think differently about your beliefs about worry.

Tackling 'Worry harms me' beliefs

'Worry harms me' beliefs occur when worry has kicked in and you believe it is uncontrollable or even harmful to you. But is this the case? One of the ways to start to think differently about your beliefs is to question these beliefs or rules you have about worry. Let's rethink these 'Worry harms me' beliefs.

Reviewing behaviour

Look at Worksheet 6B to remind yourself of your 'Worry harms me' beliefs and then read the 'Worry harms me' beliefs in the table below.

Next, ask yourself each of the questions in the right-hand column, about your beliefs and your own experience with worry. Are your 'Worry harms me' beliefs truthful and realistic?

Can you think differently about your 'Worry harms me' beliefs? Remember, just because we think something – even if we have believed it for a long time – that does not make it true. Even when we feel strongly about one of our beliefs, it does not make it correct. A thought is just a thought.

'Worry harms me' beliefs	Questions to help you think differently
My worrying is uncontrollable. I can't stop worrying. Worry will stop me functioning at home, work and in other activities.	Have there been times when you have been worrying about something and you've been interrupted or distracted by something else, like a phone call, receiving a text or someone talking to you? What happened to the worry? Did it stop, even for a short period of time? If so, then is it true that worry is unstoppable?
	Have you noticed that when you engage in some of the strategies in this book, such as slow breathing, progressive muscle relaxation or attention training exercises, your worry fades from your awareness? If so, does this provide evidence that worry does stop at times, even if only briefly?

Worrying will make me lose control. Worry will make me go mad or have a breakdown. If I don't stop my worry, it will harm me. Worry will harm me physically.	Have there been times when you thought your worry was going to make you lose control mentally or go insane? Did this happen? Why not? Was your worrying interrupted because you were distracted by someone or something? If so, is it possible that being interrupted or distracted would really prevent you from going insane? Worrying has not led to masses of people ending up in hospital. If it was seriously bad or life threatening, wouldn't there be warnings in the media about worry leading to serious harm? There are reasonable numbers of people in the community with worry problems and GAD, but there aren't multiple inpatient units dedicated to worriers in every suburb. What does this say about worry being harmful?
Worrying all the time means I'm weak or a failure?	Worry is common; so does this mean every person who worries is weak or a failure? Do you have friends or people you know who worry? Does this mean they're weak or a failure?

After reflecting on your 'Worry harms me' beliefs, you may have recognized that worry is not uncontrollable all of the time and that it does not lead to insanity. The *belief* that worry will harm you is the real problem, rather than worry itself presenting any danger to you. Use this information to help you start to think differently about worry.

Behaviour changing strategy ♘

Read through the table below. Pay attention to the 'Worry harms me' beliefs that you hold, and then consider the *disadvantages* of holding those beliefs. You will notice the beliefs have been grouped according to common misconceptions people have about worry's uncontrollability, losing control or experiencing serious harm due to worry, or worrying being a sign of failure.

Now, read through the examples of thinking differently about 'Worry harms me' beliefs. Pick some thinking differently statements from the last column that apply to you or add any others you can think of for yourself on the lines provided at the end of the columns. Work on bringing these statements to mind every time you find that your 'Worry harms me' beliefs are triggered or active.

'Worry harms me' beliefs	Disadvantages of holding 'Worry harms me' beliefs	Thinking differently about 'Worry harms me' beliefs
My worrying is uncontrollable. I can't stop worrying. Worry will stop me functioning at home, work or in other activities.	Worrying about my worry being uncontrollable makes me worry about worrying, leading to more anxiety and worry. It's a vicious cycle!	Yes, in the past worry appeared unstoppable. Possibly the way I was reacting to it was keeping it going. I now know that while it's unpleasant, worry comes and goes.

| | Believing that worry is uncontrollable keeps my attention focused on it, and monitoring the worry prolongs it – which is exactly what I don't want!

This belief makes me fearful of worry and leads to problems like feeling anxious, tense and restless and having sleep problems. | I am able at times to pay less attention to worry, so it's not uncontrollable.

Using the strategies in this book, such as detached mindfulness, allows me to tune out from worry more. Worry does not completely control my mind.

I can still function and achieve things. Worry doesn't prevent me functioning.

Add your own 'thinking differently' thoughts here:

_____

_____

_____

_____

_____

_____ |

'Worry harms me' beliefs	Disadvantages of holding 'Worry harms me' beliefs	Thinking differently about 'Worry harms me' beliefs
Worrying will make me lose control. Worry will make me go mad or have a breakdown. If I don't stop my worry it will harm me. Worry will harm me physically.	Worrying about my worry being harmful makes me worry about worrying! Which feeds my worry more and can make me think this is a sign of madness, rather than recognizing it is just worry or anxiety that is being sustained and worsened by my attention being focused on it. Sometimes 'Worry harms me' beliefs lead to feeling panicky, which I might then believe to be a sign my body is being harmed. In fact, it is just a normal flight, fight or freeze reaction. My body reacts the same way when I have had a fright or when doing physical exercise. 'Worry harms me' beliefs lead me to misinterpret normal physical sensations	I've never gone mad or insane from worry. Yes, worry can feed my anxiety, but it will not make me go insane, that's just catastrophizing, which is an unhelpful thinking style. Worry and anxiety are common human experiences; it's okay to let worry run its course rather than trying to push it away or focus on it. *Add your own 'thinking differently' thoughts here:* _____ _____ _____ _____ _____ _____ _____

	as dangerous or believe that the worry will seriously hurt me.	
Worrying all the time means I'm weak or a failure.	This leads to me being very self-critical, which makes me feel bad and can lead to low mood. Holding this belief is demoralizing and diminishes my self-worth. This belief undermines my confidence in my ability to cope and it makes me anxious about my future.	Having worry or anxiety does not mean I am weak. Many people I know worry and I would not see them as being weak, so I should not view myself as weak either. I'm only human. Lots of people have mental health issues and manage to go about their day-to-day life or overcome them. This is evidence of strength, not weakness. *Add your own 'thinking differently' thoughts here:* _____ _____ _____ _____ _____ _____

Reflecting on the points in the table above and your own experiences of worry being interrupted or fading away at times, how accurate is it that worry harms you? Practise reminding yourself *every day* about the 'thinking differently' statements about worry in the last column of the table. This will help you to tackle those unhelpful 'Worry harms me' beliefs when they get triggered!

Tackling 'Worry helps me' beliefs

You may wonder why you should give up or think differently about the beliefs that 'Worry helps me'. But if you hold on to these beliefs, your worry will continue to be driven by an underlying belief or rule that worry is useful. This makes it more likely that you will keep using worry as a coping strategy or as a form of protection against unfortunate or bad things happening. But remember, worry is a *faulty* coping strategy that is pretending to be a protective and effective way of dealing with life. 'Worry helps me' beliefs are misguided and deceptive thoughts that only serve to power your worry. Worrying does not have to occur for you to care about your or your loved ones' safety or wellbeing, or your achievements at home or work.

Reviewing behaviour

Look at Worksheet 6B to remind yourself of your 'Worry helps me' beliefs and then read the 'Worry helps me' beliefs in the table below.

Next, ask yourself each of the questions in the right-hand column, about your beliefs and your own experience with worry. Are your 'Worry helps me' beliefs truthful and realistic?

Can you think differently about your 'Worry helps me' beliefs?

'Worry helps me' beliefs	Questions to help you think differently
Worrying prevents bad things happening to me or my loved ones. Worrying helps me avoid harm to myself or those I love. Worry helps me overcome uncertainty.	Worry can't stop unfortunate things from happening. So is it helpful for you to worry about things you can't change? Have there been times in the past when you have worried and got very anxious only to learn the worry was false? How can worrying and feeling anxious make you more certain? If someone asked you what steps they would need to take to be more certain about something, would you suggest worrying about the issue to them as a strategy to make them feel more certain? Why not?
Worry helps me be prepared. Worry helps me cope.	If something unfortunate or upsetting occurs, worrying in advance does not make people more prepared – only anxious. What is the advantage in worrying when it does not prepare you and just makes you feel more anxious? Are there times you've done things without needing to worry and it has all been fine? Was worry needed or was it throwing up worry stories that may never happen?

'Worry helps me' beliefs	Questions to help you think differently
	Can you think of people you know who cope without having to worry? What does this say about worry as a coping strategy? Worry is a flawed coping strategy that people may have learned. It actually encourages anxiety and doubt. How does this anxiety and doubt help with coping?
Worry helps me find answers or solutions to problems. Worry helps me to remember things or get things done. Worry helps me be a responsible person.	Worry does not successfully lead to solutions, just more worry and anxiety. Is this good problem-solving? Worry can interfere with concentration and focus, and it leads to distress! People typically find it harder to think or remember things if they are anxious due to worrying. How does this distress impact on your ability to get things done or find solutions? If worry helps, why don't people with worry have all their problems sorted?
Worry helps me be a caring person.	Sometimes others may view worrying as caring. But sometimes it can frustrate others or strain relationships. Is this helpful?

	There are more compelling ways to show you care. Are there others who you know who are caring and who don't worry? How do they show they care? Can you adopt the ways they show they care rather than using worry? If a friend asked you how they could be more caring of others, would you recommend to them, or coach them in, worrying?

After reflecting on your 'Worry helps me' beliefs, you may have recognized that worry does not prevent bad things from happening, it does not help you be prepared, it does not help you find answers and it is not necessary to show you are a caring person. Use this information to think differently about your 'Worry helps me' beliefs and to change your view of worry.

Behaviour changing strategy

Read through the table below. Pay attention to the 'Worry helps me' beliefs that you hold, and then consider the *disadvantages* of holding those beliefs. You will notice the beliefs have been grouped according to common misconceptions people have about worry's ability to prevent bad things from happening, to prepare people or help them cope, to help solve problems or to show they care.

Now, read through the examples of thinking differently about 'Worry harms me' beliefs. Pick some thinking differently statements from the last column that apply to you or add any others you can think of for yourself on the lines provided at the end of the columns. Work on bringing these statements to mind every time you find that your 'Worry helps me' beliefs are triggered or active.

'Worry helps me' beliefs	Disadvantages of 'Worry helps me' beliefs	Thinking differently about 'Worry helps me' beliefs
Worrying prevents bad things happening to me or my loved ones. Worrying helps me avoid harm to myself or those I love. Worry helps me overcome uncertainty.	These beliefs give me a false sense of security as worrying about something negative or bad happening doesn't make it less likely to happen. Worrying makes me anxious. People might have worried about something bad happening before and it still did, so worrying doesn't prepare me or prevent events from occurring. Worry does not help me, it just keeps me awake. Worry doesn't reduce uncertainty; it usually increases doubt and floods me with infinite possibilities of what could go wrong or happen ... it supercharges my anxiety.	Worry does not have a special mechanism to stop things from happening. So I need to detach from it. Trying to control future events through worrying is like trying to control the ocean's currents with my mind ... it's a useless strategy. Remember that worrying increases my levels of doubt and uncertainty. Worrying becomes a magnet for thoughts and images of terrible events happening to me or my loved ones. It only serves to make me distressed. I need to remember to **think differently** about the belief that worry is helpful and detach from worries when they visit me.

		Add your own 'thinking differently' thoughts here:
		_____
		_____
		_____
		_____
		_____
		_____
Worry helps me be prepared. Worry helps me cope.	Worry does not lead me to healthy coping; it only makes me distressed, anxious, doubting, irritable, causes poor sleep and leads to relentless thoughts of grave things happening and beliefs about not being able to manage. There is no way I can be certain and prepared for everything that may happen to me, so worrying is a flawed coping strategy and will only lead me to	Having 'Worry helps me' beliefs may make me think things will be okay, but worry isn't a useful coping strategy because it just makes me more worried and upset. I end up torturing myself with distressing images or doom-filled worry stories. Engaging in worry only guarantees me anxiety and doubt, not constructive coping. I need to use problem-solving instead if I can; otherwise I need to

'Worry helps me' beliefs	Disadvantages of 'Worry helps me' beliefs	Thinking differently about 'Worry helps me' beliefs
	feel exhausted and anxious.	see worry for what it is and use detached mindfulness! Constructive coping involves looking after myself by reducing stress, using exercise, thinking differently and mindfulness. *Add your own 'thinking differently' thoughts here:* _____ _____ _____ _____ _____
Worry helps me find answers or solutions to problems. Worry helps me to remember things or get things done. Worry helps me be a responsible person.	Worry does not help me problem-solve; instead I end up going over the same thing repeatedly and not getting anywhere.	If worry was useful, I'd have no problems to be concerned about. Instead it's misleading for me to believe it helps me. If anything, it hinders me getting problems sorted.

	Worrying makes me anxious and means I question myself more rather than solve my problems.	I can drop worrying as a coping strategy and use problem-solving steps for actual concrete difficulties that occur.
	Worrying keeps me preoccupied with unhelpful thoughts rather than focusing on other aspects of my life.	Add your own 'thinking differently' thoughts here: _____
	Worrying usually distracts me and typically does not help me remember things.	_____
	Worrying is tiring and time-consuming.	_____
		_____
		_____
		_____
		_____
Worry helps me be a caring person.	Worrying doesn't make me more caring, it just makes me a worrier. Worrying to show I care could be frustrating to others at times. There are other characteristics I have	There are different ways I can express to others that I care about them rather than voicing my worries to them. Expressing my worries can just end up making people anxious or annoyed.

'Worry helps me' beliefs	Disadvantages of 'Worry helps me' beliefs	Thinking differently about 'Worry helps me' beliefs
	or different ways I can act towards others that show I care and don't lead to anxiety for me and annoyance to others.	I can show my loved ones I care by telling them directly, doing nice things for them, helping them problem-solve an issue or just give them encouraging words or affection instead! Add your own 'thinking differently' thoughts here: _____ _____ _____ _____ _____

Reflecting on the points in the table above and elsewhere in this book, how accurate are your beliefs that worry helps you? Is there now a different way to think? Is it possible that although worry may seem helpful on the surface, it's actually keeping your anxiety going and is not a productive way of coping or solving problems? Remind yourself of your 'thinking differently about worry' statements as often as you can. When you are aware that your 'Worry helps me' beliefs have been triggered or are active, try to answer back with your 'thinking differently about worry' statements. With practice you will come to see much more clearly that worry is a fruitless process, rather than it being useful. So think differently about worry and detach from it.

'Worry helps me' beliefs are like the urge to scratch

Buying into 'Worry helps me' beliefs is like having an insect bite that's itchy and believing that scratching it will help. While it may seem right to scratch the itch, this only aggravates the bite and makes it flare up. The same is true for believing you need to worry about something, believing that worry will help. This only makes you focus on the worry more and leads to getting caught up in it ... the worry flares up!

Just as it is better to direct our attention away from an itch, so the same is true for worry. See your 'Worry helps me' beliefs for what they are! Think differently about them and then detach from the worry.

You are now going to use Worksheet 8D to develop statements for a 'prompt card' for beliefs about worry similar to the earlier 'prompt card' for tackling unhelpful thinking. Refer to these cards when you notice 'Worry helps me' or 'Worry harms me' beliefs are active and driving your worry as a reminder of how you can respond differently.

Behaviour changing strategy

Now you are going to develop your own 'prompt card' for tackling beliefs about worry, by filling in Worksheet 8D. To help you do this, you will need to refer back to the last two Reviewing behaviour boxes and the last two Behaviour changing strategy boxes, in which you considered your 'Worry harms me' and 'Worry helps me' beliefs.

Worksheet 8D: Tackling beliefs about worry

'Worry harms me' beliefs are *not* truthful or realistic because:
(*Add any thoughts prompted by doing the 'Questions to help you think differently' column in the Reviewing behaviour box about 'Worry harms me' beliefs, plus your statements from the 'Thinking differently about 'Worry harms me' beliefs' column with evidence that worry does **not** harm you.*)

_____

_____

_____

_____

The disadvantages of holding this belief are:
(*Use information from the 'Disadvantages of Holding this Belief' column in the Behaviour changing strategy box about 'Worry harms me' beliefs.*)

_____

_____

_____

_____

'Worry helps me' beliefs are not truthful or realistic because:
(*Add any thoughts prompted by doing the 'Questions to help you think differently' column in the Reviewing behaviour box about 'Worry helps me' beliefs, plus your statements from the 'Thinking differently about*

'Worry helps me' beliefs' column with evidence that worry does **not** help you.)

_____

_____

_____

_____

The disadvantages of holding this belief are:
(*Use information from the 'Disadvantages of Holding this Belief' column in the Behaviour changing strategy box about 'Worry helps me' beliefs.*)

_____

_____

_____

_____

Instead of buying into beliefs about worry, I can think differently and can do the following:
(*Add some of your 'Thinking differently' about worry thoughts from the last two Behaviour changing strategy boxes. Also add any actions you can take when unhelpful beliefs about worry emerge, e.g. reminding yourself worry is not helpful or harmful, problem-solving the issues that you can, using mindfulness.*)

_____

_____

_____

_____

Chapter summary

In this chapter you have learned:

- the difference between helpful and unhelpful thinking, and how to identify when your thinking is unhelpful
- more about unhelpful thinking, including identifying your unhelpful thinking styles, and strategies for how to tackle these and think differently
- more about negative self-talk, and you have some strategies to try, such as noticing what type of unhelpful thinking style is dominating your thought processes and questioning how helpful this is for you
- more about beliefs about worry, the disadvantages of holding these beliefs and how to think about them differently.

Activities for you to do

Before moving on to Chapter 9, make sure you keep on:

- using the unhelpful thinking styles exercise (Worksheet 8A) to help you think differently when unhelpful thinking occurs
- using the tackling negative self-talk exercise (Worksheet 8C) to help you think differently when negative self-talk occurs, and the prompt card you created to tackle negative thinking
- reminding yourself why beliefs about worry are unhelpful (Worksheet 8D), and using your prompt card to guide and remind you about what to do instead.

The prompt cards you developed in this chapter will help to remind you how to deal with unhelpful thinking styles and beliefs about worry. Use both your prompt cards regularly to strengthen your 'thinking differently' thoughts. These new beliefs and ways of thinking need nurturing by you to grow strong and to be able to compete with the old unhelpful thinking and beliefs about worry.

In Chapter 7, you learned about the role of attention and how it feeds worry. In Chapter 9 you will develop your attention flexibility skills using different types of mindfulness, and you will learn how to use these strategies to manage worry and anxiety.

Using mindfulness strategies

Overview

In this chapter you will learn how to use:

- classical mindfulness
- detached mindfulness.

As Chapter 7 explained, the aim of mindfulness is to be fully mindful of the present moment, i.e. focusing your attention so you are aware of your emotions, thoughts, physical sensations and actions in the present moment, without judging, criticizing or attributing meaning to any internal events.

Mindfulness is a valuable skill to practise even when your mind is not full of worries. It can contribute to a fuller life experience, increase our ability to respond to our own internal processes in more helpful ways and broaden our world and experiences. Mindfulness is a good practice to build into your everyday life. Although it can be challenging to learn initially, with regular practice you will develop skills that are useful in dealing with our busy, fast-paced world bombarded by external stimuli as well as our own internal mental chatter such as worry.

Key points about mindfulness

It might help you to read Chapter 7 again before you begin the exercises in this chapter. If you have not practised the attention training exercises recently, we suggest you spend a few days doing the brief attention training exercise from Chapter 7 to activate your attention flexibility.

The most important point to remember is that no matter how distressing they are, *our worries are merely worries*. Many of us, particularly when the worries are associated with anxiety, can forget this and focus our attention on the worries. But remember that it is your response to your own negative mental activity that increases and prolongs the distress and anxiety; the more attention our worry gets, the more problematic it becomes.

No matter how 'true' a worry seems or feels, worries are just chains of thoughts, just the mental chatter that goes through your mind. Your task is to take a step back and be an observer of the mental chatter, notice the worry. The exercises that follow help you to do this. As you will see, mindfulness involves accepting the presence of your mental chatter, letting the worries and worrying images come and go freely, without judgment and with a sense of distance from them.

Detached mindfulness

Some people with anxiety find it easier to develop their skills with a detached mindfulness exercise before they begin the classical or general mindfulness practice.

Detached mindfulness is slightly different from classical mindfulness in that the goal is not self-awareness, but to focus specifically on detaching or disconnecting from any response to worries, and to develop a strong sense of being separate from those worries. Detached mindfulness is a state of awareness in which one is aware of the worries but one doesn't respond to or evaluate them in anyway. Detached mindfulness is similar to classical mindfulness in that regular practice enables you to achieve distance from your worries so you can be more present in your daily life rather than being distracted by worries or related images.

Detached mindfulness metaphors

There are many metaphors, or ways of viewing thinking processes such as worries, that illustrate the skill of detached mindfulness. Using metaphors to represent your worries can give you a different perspective on your own unhelpful mental chatter and enable you to develop some distance and objectivity.

Professor Wells has developed a variety of metaphors (examples or tales to symbolize or represent something) as ways to practise detaching from your worries, some of which follow (Wells, 2006). Once you have tried the detached mindfulness metaphors, we encourage you to develop your own metaphors to represent your worries and then to practise detaching from them. Remember that your attention will wander as you practise; that is not important. When your mind does wander, gently bring it back to focus mindfully on the metaphor you are engaging with.

Misbehaving child

Dealing with worries or worrying images is similar to how you might deal with a misbehaving child. Imagine your worries are like a stubborn, misbehaving, attention-seeking child. The more you respond to the child (your worries), the more they will demand of you and your attention. The more you try to turn your back on them and ignore them, the more they will try to get your attention. The best strategy is to simply watch them without reacting. Don't fight with them, as that will keep them going for longer. Keep a passive watch over the worries. Be aware of their attention-seeking behaviour but focus your attention on the present, on whatever it is you are doing in the here and now.

Stories

Remind yourself that your mind likes to tell you lots of different stories, and some of these stories make you feel anxious and distressed. The problem is not that your mind tells you stories, because this is what minds do; rather, the problem is the attention you give to those stories. Remind yourself that your mental chatter or worries are just your mind creating stories, and that you can be aware of these but don't need to focus your attention on them. Be aware, take a step back in your mind and just observe or passively watch the story. Just because this is a story you have been telling yourself for years does not mean it is true. Just because it 'feels' true does not mean it is true. Don't do anything in response to the story. You can choose which stories you give your attention to and which you choose not to focus on and leave in the back of your mind.

Luke's stories

When Luke read about the concept of stories and detached mindfulness, he related completely to it. He had two main stories that his mind repeatedly told him. They were his worry themes, and were often presented to him by his mind in graphic detail. Both stories were like short films running in his head, but they were more than 3D; they were images and feelings too. The first story was of him arguing with Amanda and her storming off out the front door, leaving him. This image was like a kick in the stomach, complete with anxiety. The story went on and on in his mind, with him seeing himself heartbroken and tearful.

The other story that repeatedly ran through his mind was of his boss reprimanding him for doing a poor job. He had seen his boss angry before and somehow this had morphed into a story in his mind of being in the firing line and his job going down the toilet. He was not surprised he felt anxious and overwhelmed when these stories played out … worry in pictures! Luke knew it wasn't going to be easy to resist getting tangled in these stories and their images, but he understood the notion of catching these stories early and seeing them as stories, or worries, rather than truth or fact. Luke was going to try and work on letting these stories run like old films in the background of his mind and not pay attention to them.

Sarah's stories

Sarah had plenty of stories; she recognized frequent ones, like images of being in hospital with cancer, hooked up to a drip and fading away, or images of her kids stolen from her and crying for her. These stories caused her tremendous anxiety, dread and panic sensations. There were other stories too; for example, her husband Steve having a car accident or seeing herself not coping with some issue or another. These stories were often similar in nature. Every now and then a new story would arrive, usually if she was going to do something new or go somewhere she hadn't been before. The story then flooded her with ideas of something going bad or images of the worst happening. While the words and pictures changed, the storyline was always the same … catastrophizing, and the gravest outcome happening. Sarah started to realize these were just stories. They were worries and images of fiction. They had not occurred.

Sarah started to notice when these stories arrived in her awareness trying to absorb her attention. When she noticed them, she practised detaching from them by observing them and seeing them as something her mind just does. At times she was successful with this, particularly with the stories that were less distressing, but she had more difficulty with the stories about her health or something happening to her kids. This was not surprising given how long these stories had been on high rotation in her mind. But she realized that with practice, it would become easier to let these stories pass, much like observing clouds in the sky. Sarah decided that for her, paying attention to these stories was like noticing adverts that sometimes appeared in the corner of her computer screen. They often tried to catch her attention with flashy words, moving images, sounds or colours, but it was up to her how much attention she paid them. This made sense to her because when she paid attention to the adverts or clicked on them, they sucked her in and they seemed to become more frequent on the various webpages she visited. This was much like her worries or stories; the more she gave them attention, the more regular they became. Over time Sarah found giving these stories less attention and approaching them like adverts in the background of her mind meant that she was more able to step back and detach from them.

Clouds passing by

Imagine your worries are clouds passing by. Clouds are always passing but each one is transient, and as they move, they change and take on different forms and naturally drift away. Just as it is futile to try to push the clouds away and to try to control them, so it is pointless to fight with your thoughts and try to control them. Instead, just watch your worries as they float by in the distance; let them exist as a cloud and watch them drift by.

Leaves on a stream

Imagine yourself sitting quietly next to a gentle, babbling stream. Watch the leaves float past you one by one, drifting down the stream. As you notice your worries, place them on a leaf and watch the worries float away. Let the worries come into your stream image and let them glide away again. If they return, as worries can, let them flow by again and again.

Driving a car with noisy children in the back

View your worries as some children in the back of your car. You know they are there; they are chatting, laughing and generally making quite a lot of noise. However, although you are aware of them, you do not give all your attention to them. You choose not to engage with them as your attention is on the road on which you are driving. No matter how distracting they are, you know you need to focus your attention on the road in front of you, the traffic, pedestrians and potential hazards so that you and the children get safely to your destination. Like the children in the back of the car, you know your worries are there but while you are passively aware of them, most of your attention is focused on what you are doing in the present moment. You are aware of the worries in the back of your mind but you choose to direct your attention to the activity you are doing right now.

Tips for detached mindfulness

- No matter how distressing the worry, remind yourself that thoughts are just thoughts, worries are just worries.
- Regularly practise shifting your focused attention.
- Keep the metaphors you create for detached mindfulness simple. Practise them regularly.
- Remind yourself that everybody finds it hard to direct their attention and it will get easier with practice.

Classical mindfulness

Classical mindfulness, like any other new skill, takes time to learn and requires regular practice. These exercises start with easier ones and move on to more difficult ones to help you to develop your skills in this area.

Sustained external mindfulness exercises

Observe a painting, photograph or view from a window

Sit quietly where you won't be disturbed and focus all of your attention on a painting, a photograph or the view from the window. What do you see? Focus your attention on the whole image for a moment; observe the different shapes and colours. Now gradually focus your attention on each section of the image and on the details in the image. Observe the different gradations of colour, notice textures and look at where the light and shadows fall. Is there more than one colour? If so, choose one colour and focus on it for a minute, then turn your attention to a different colour or pattern or texture in the image or view you are observing.

Can you see movement in the image or out of the window? Notice this movement. If you are observing a still image, focus on how movement is represented. Focus on all aspects of the image in front of you as if you have never seen it before. If a thought or worry comes into your mind, observe this and redirect your attention back to the part of the image you were focusing on.

Do the same attention activity for other objects; for example, observe in as much detail as you can a pot plant, a familiar object, a tree, a river or the clouds.

Listen to the sounds in your environment

Find a place to sit outside where you are unlikely to be disturbed. Close your eyes and focus your attention on everything you can hear. What sounds can you hear? Focus on one sound at a time. Listen for the sounds that are close to you. How many different sounds are there? Listen hard for the very soft and delicate sounds. Now do the same for the sounds that are further away. If a worry or feeling arrives, notice it and bring your attention back to the sound you were focusing on.

Be tactile

Sit on a park bench. Find several small objects. Close your eyes as you handle each one. Focus on the detail of the object. Its shape, temperature, contours, textures, indentations etc. How does it feel? How cool or warm is it? Is it rough or smooth? Absorb your attention in the object. If worries come, observe that they are there and guide your attention back to the object.

Use your senses

Find somewhere to sit where you are unlikely to be disturbed. In the same way that you practised focusing your attention on listening to sounds and observing an image, practise being mindful with your senses. Focus on one sense at a time. Don't do anything else when you are doing this. Focus on the details of what you can see, hear and smell.

What can you feel around your body? Can you feel the breeze on your face, or coolness on your nose or cheeks? Can you feel the sun on you? Can you feel the clothes on your body, the seat you are sitting on, your feet on the ground? What can you hear? Focus your attention on what you can hear close to you and then shift your attention to the sounds further and further away. If worries or images come, notice them and bring the focus of your attention back to the sound, smell or sights around you.

Listen to music

This more complicated exercise involves switching your attention.

Listen to a piece of music played by many different instruments, e.g. a big band, an orchestra, a full jazz band, a brass band, pop music or a big rock band and vocalist. Try to listen to the music in a different way from usual. Focus on the sound of the different instruments. Listen to their pitch, the tone of the instrument, how loudly or softly it is being played. Try to follow each instrument for a while, focusing on the sounds that each instrument is playing. Imagine each of the musical instruments being played; imagine the stings being struck, the key being pressed and the woodwind or horns being blown. Rather than focus on the meaning of the words sung by the vocalist, focus more on the tone of their voice, how the singing blends in or stands out from the rest of the instruments, etc. Notice the backing vocals; how do they sound? Listen to the voice or voices as a sound rather than words.

Internal sustained mindfulness exercises

Audio recordings relating to the following two exercises are available free online with this book.

Mindfulness of the breath

Find somewhere to sit comfortably and adopt a upright sitting position, keeping your spine straight as you can. Close your eyes and begin to focus on your breathing. Don't count your breathing or try to change it in anyway; just breathe as normal and observe your breath. Remember that your mind will drift away from your breath and this does not matter; gently bring it back and refocus on your breath. Allow your breath to flow at its natural depth and speed. Accept your breathing as it is. The pace or depth of your breathing may naturally change or it may not, just let it flow. Notice the breath going in through your nose; where can you feel the air? Feel the air go into your body and into your lungs. As you exhale, feel the air leave your body. Follow the breath in and out of your body with your attention.

When your attention wanders off to different thoughts, ideas, images, plans, dreams, fantasies or worries, gently bring it back to your breathing. After about 3–4 minutes, slowly open your eyes and continue with your day. Slowly build up this mindfulness practice to about 10 minutes a day.

Mindfulness to yourself

Mindfulness to yourself means being aware, as specifically as you can, of what is happening inside you. Your aim is not to change anything but just to notice the thoughts, worries, feelings or physical sensations as you experience them.

Sit comfortably in an upright sitting position and close your eyes. Start off with the mindfulness practice of your breathing outlined above. After a few minutes, allow yourself to notice how you are feeling physically. Scan your body and notice any signs of discomfort. Are you feeling tense or relaxed? Move your attention around your body. Notice any emotions you are feeling or experiencing. Just be aware of them and observe them; you don't need to label them or judge them. You may only be vaguely aware of them. Notice where those emotions are located in your body – your head, throat, chest, stomach? Observe if the physical sensations of your emotions stay in one place or move around your body.

Become aware of any thoughts or worries that come with the emotions. Be mindful of the thoughts, images, ideas, plans or worry in your mind. Observe them without judgment. Finally, bring your awareness back to your breath for a few minutes.

Tips for success and dealing with obstacles

There is more than one way to practise mindfulness but these tips may help you find a way that works for you.

- Set aside a regular time to practise your mindfulness. As with any new habit or behaviour it is easier to get started and to maintain progress by setting aside a day, time and place for mindfulness practice. Make sure that you will not be interrupted. If an external distraction occurs, such as the telephone or the doorbell ringing, pause what you are doing and go back to your mindfulness afterwards as soon as you can. Remember that you don't necessarily have to respond to distractions; just because the phone rings it does not mean you have to answer it.

- Be patient with yourself. Mindfulness is a skill that will develop as you practise. You will gradually find it easier to do, although, like all of us, you will find mindfulness practice easier some days than others. Practise mindfulness every day even if only for a few minutes.

- Start with short practices. When you first start practicing, start with a short session and gradually lengthen the time and frequency of your practice. A couple of minutes every day is better than 10 minutes once a week. As you become more experienced, you can gradually lengthen the amount of time you are mindful for. You can also gradually select other mindfulness practices to try.

- Focus on being mindful of one thing at a time. It is very difficult to focus on what is occurring outside you and inside you at the same time. The exercises in this book have been graduated so you can first practise being mindful of small, external things one at a time. It is easier to develop mindfulness skills by practicing on something that is not constantly changing. As you become more experienced with mindfulness, you can start to practise with more complex and changing events.

- Be non-judgmental. Focus on the immediate moment. Try not to judge or evaluate the moment, rather just passively observe it. Try not to decide if the internal or external events you are experiencing are good or bad, right or wrong, appropriate or inappropriate. Simply accept and remain open to your moment-by-moment experience.

- Don't avoid any feelings. When emotions are distressing it is tempting to avoid those feelings. While this is a natural tendency, suppressing or avoiding emotions can make them more intense when they emerge again later, and in the long term, avoidance contributes to maintaining anxiety. Emotional discomfort is a very normal human experience. Emotions can provide us with useful information; they motivate us and are important to our survival. Remember that even the most distressing feelings are not permanent and will pass. Emotions have been likened to a wave; at times becoming intense, then reaching a plateau and then subsiding. As you allow yourself to experience emotions, accept they are present rather than trying to push then away. Your ability to tolerate heightened emotional states will increase with practice.

- Keep going even when your mind is very active. Our minds tend to always be busy but sometimes it can feel like they are racing, out of control and jumping around from one thing to another, which can be distressing. Remember that the goal of mindfulness is not to be perfectly focused on the present all of the time, but to be able to notice when your mind is wandering or worrying and gently bring it back to the here and now. Expect and accept that your mind will wander off again and again; this does not matter because it is what our minds do. Each time you notice this happening, gently bring your mind, your attention, back to the moment you are in. The more you practise this, the easier it will become to refocus your attention.

Mindfulness even when you are busy

- Choose one activity that you can do mindfully during the day, for one or two minutes; for example, drinking a glass of water, walking, eating something you enjoy or something with different flavours, mindfully doing a relaxation exercise etc.
- Whichever activity you choose to do mindfully, be in the moment when you do it. Focus on all aspects of that activity: what you see, hear, smell, touch, feel or taste. Observe and describe rather than judge the moment.
- As other thoughts, images, worries and sensations come into your mind, notice them arrive and then refocus your attention on your mindful activity.

Worry postponement

One of the things you will have noticed is that when worry enters your mind, it is demanding. It wants as much of your attention as it can get and it wants it straight away, so it interferes with whatever you are doing. But worry can wait! Worry postponement is a strategy you can use to reduce the interference worry has in your day-to-day life. The steps are fairly easy but require some practice.

Step 1

Choose a regular time, not too close to your bedtime, and a place that is relatively quiet so you won't be disturbed during this exercise. Allow yourself up to 20 minutes for worrying while in this place. The place should be comfortable and free of distraction, but it needs to be somewhere you don't sit regularly (but not your bedroom) so that the only purpose of the chair is as somewhere to sit during the worry period. For example, this could be at 5 p.m. on the chair in the laundry.

Step 2

As soon as you become aware of a worry during the day, postpone thinking about it to the worry period. If you wish you can note down the worry theme you are postponing and put the note aside for the later worry period. Remind yourself that right now is not the time to worry and that you will have time to think about this later; there is no need to worry about it now. Remind yourself that later you will be able to give your attention to the worry without interruption but there are more important things for you to give your attention to at the moment. Use any of the strategies we have talked about in this chapter to help you refocus your attention on what you are currently doing. For example, bring your attention to the present moment and focus your attention on the activity you were doing, as mindfully as you can. Or use any of the detached mindfulness strategies to help move the worry to the back of your mind.

Step 3

When the time comes for your worry period, go to your worry place. If you wrote reminders about the worries you had during the day, take these with you. There are some important things to remember while you are in your worry place.

- Only worry about the topics you decided to postpone to the worry period.
- If you don't feel as if you need to worry about some of topics you postponed to this period, then do not make yourself worry about them.
- You do not have to spend the full time worrying if this is not needed, but it is important that you do not allow the worry period to exceed the 20 minutes set for worrying.
- Once the worry period is over, use the strategies described in Step 2 to help you refocus your attention on the here and now and move on to your next activity. Detach from the worry once the worry period is finished.

● If the worry period comes but you don't feel like you want to worry about any of the postponed worries, then you don't need to. Just carry on with your day, and if more worries come or come back, they can be postponed until the next worry period.

Like all the strategies in this book, worry postponement gets easier with practice. When you postpone worry, you are developing your attention flexibility further and will also experience a greater sense of control over worry. The activity of postponing your worry may also give you time to realize that you don't need to worry and also what else you need to do, or that what you need to do is some problem-solving rather than worrying.

When to choose thinking differently or mindfulness

As you may have realized, thinking differently and mindfulness are quite different approaches to managing worry. When you focus on thinking differently, you need to give attention to your thinking so that you can come up with more helpful ways of looking at things and of reducing the beliefs that maintain anxiety or trigger worry. In contrast, the aim of detached mindfulness and classical mindfulness is to achieve distance from your worry by reducing the attention you give to those thoughts or images. Thinking differently requires attending to the thoughts in order to change those thoughts, whereas detached mindfulness requires not focusing attention on worry.

When you are dealing with a belief about worry, unhelpful thinking styles or negative self-talk, the best strategy to choose is thinking differently. It can also be very helpful to use your attention flexibility skills to refocus your mind on your helpful self-talk.

When you are weighed down by worries, or when worry is interfering with your day-to-day life, choose mindfulness or detached mindfulness.

Unhelpful thinking: worries and wasps

Unhelpful thinking, such as unhelpful thinking styles, negative self-talk or even beliefs about worry, is much like being bothered by a wasp. You can use a number of methods to deal with the wasp, such as swatting it with a magazine, flicking it away with your hand or spraying it with insect repellent. This is similar to dealing with unhelpful thinking. You can swat or deal with the unhelpful thought by using some of the thinking differently tools.

But dealing with worry is different. Just as one wasp can be joined by other wasps and they begin to morph into a swarm, so anxiety thoughts can start to gather in numbers and become a swarm of worries – becoming worry.

The methods you would use to deal with one or two wasps, like swatting them, would not be effective with a swarm and might even irritate the wasps. The same is true for worry. The thinking differently tools are likely to be less helpful when there are too many worries or anxious thoughts to tackle and you may find yourself getting stuck.

Instead, when you notice your worrying occurring, use your mindfulness strategies; for example, observe the worry, let the worry come and go, and detach from the worry.

As with a swarm of wasps, don't run because they'll follow; don't try to push the wasps away as they'll hang around more; don't try to swat them as it may aggravate them.

Instead, just notice the swarm and let them go about their business, and eventually they'll move on – be mindful.

Luke's use of attention strategies

Luke was unsure about attention training and mindfulness when he first read about them. But as his previous ways of coping with anxiety and worry had not actually changed the anxiety or worry, he was open to trying new strategies. In addition, he had started to feel better about the exercise he was doing and the regular relaxation practice. Luke was busy, though, so he slotted his daily mindfulness practice into his lunchtime at work or university. Luke would sit outside and practise attention training or mindfulness, guiding himself to do this. He also used headphones at times to listen to audio versions of these techniques or put on music that had lots of instruments or was layered with various sounds. He also found he could do mindfulness during other breaks or if he was on the bus going to work. Over the weeks he kept practicing. If he missed a practice, he didn't beat himself up about it but just rescheduled it. Luke also began to notice that he was getting better at letting worries or images come and go, as well as noticing when his stories were running like a projector and he simply observed this process. Sometimes they just faded away.

Sarah's use of attention strategies

Sarah had been practising attention training regularly for several weeks. She found it hard to know if this was making her mind more flexible but she definitely noticed that she was more able to observe worries in her mind and then redirect her attention elsewhere. She didn't need to push them away; they came and went. Sarah practised mindfulness in the mornings once the house was quiet or she would go and sit in the local park and use all the different sounds – of birds, people, cars, wind, leaves rustling or water flowing in the stream – as elements in her mindfulness or attention training practice. If she had to drive to pick up the kids, she would get to the school early and practise while sitting in the car, using her stereo or winding the windows down for various sounds. Worries would come during her practices and she was able to treat them like something she was just observing. At times this was more difficult, but the frequency of the difficult times was lessening. She was also using the stories mindfulness metaphor frequently. Her worries or her metaphor for her worries were just adverts on her computer screen that she could observe but pay little attention to.

Sarah was gaining more evidence against her beliefs that worry was uncontrollable because of her ability to detach from it. Sarah also admitted to herself that she had been worrying less and nothing bad had happened. She was handling life's day-to-day tasks just fine, so she was really starting to doubt her beliefs that worry was helpful.

Chapter summary

In this chapter you have learned:

- about mindfulness, and begun to develop your own regular practice, increasing your ability to be in the moment
- how to use mindfulness strategies to help manage your worry
- a more flexible approach to your worries.

You will be starting to have a sense of being 'in the driving seat' rather than being driven by your own mental activity, worries, emotions and physical sensations. Remember to use thinking differently strategies for unhelpful thinking and beliefs about worry; in contrast, use mindfulness approaches for worry itself!

Activities for you to do

Before moving on to Chapter 10, make sure you:

- continue your attention training practice (Chapter 7)
- practise detached mindfulness with your worries every day
- find a time that you can practise mindfulness every day
- work your way through the mindfulness exercises in this chapter slowly and systematically, starting with the more simple external exercises and eventually moving on to the 'mindfulness to self' exercises. If you find mindfulness difficult, go back to a simpler exercise for a while or practise an attention training exercise.
- practise worry postponement.

Part 4 gives you the opportunity to practise all of the strategies you have been introduced to so far. The chapters in Part 4 help you to develop a strategy to reduce your worry and associated behaviours and introduce you to strategies you can use to manage anxiety triggers and increase your general wellbeing.

PART 4

Practice

Letting go of worry behaviours, using your strategies each day and building your resiliency

CHAPTER 10

Using your strategies each day

Overview

It's time to focus on tackling the safety behaviours and avoidance that you identified earlier in the book and on your Behaviour vicious petal. In this chapter you will learn about:

- behavioural experiments; these are a way of testing out your anxious predictions or thoughts about doing things differently
- letting go of unhelpful safety behaviours and any avoidance that keeps your worry and anxiety going
- how to design and construct behavioural experiments for yourself to test out what happens when you drop the use of avoidance and safety behaviours, in order to help you eliminate these worry behaviours in your life.

Stepping past safety behaviours and avoidance

In the Behaviours section in Chapter 4, you identified the safety behaviours and avoidance you might be using to cope with your anxiety and worry. We also looked there at how these behaviours might provide only short-term relief and actually maintain worry and anxiety, often making it worse in the long term. Now that you have been working on thinking differently and on your attention on thoughts and worry, it is time to focus more on changing behaviours that may be preventing you from making further progress. In fact, you have already been experimenting by responding to your thoughts and worry differently, and you may have noticed that this has resulted in less anxiety.

Behavioural experiments are information gathering activities designed to test the validity of your negative predictions or thoughts to see if they actually happen when you let go of old habits and safety behaviours. Behavioural experiments can also be about testing new ways of responding or doing things. These experiments are beneficial because they give you the opportunity to try something out rather than just reading or thinking about it. Behavioural experiments support letting go of avoidance and safety behaviours, but also change how you think by showing you that you can cope and that the worst doesn't happen. This in turn can reduce the physical sensations you experience with anxiety and the related distressing emotions. Behavioural experiments are a powerful way of tackling not only unhelpful behaviours, but worry and anxiety.

It is likely that unhelpful thinking, worry and anxiety will be trying to persuade you not to experiment with dropping the use of the behaviours (safety behaviours, avoidance, reassurance seeking, excessive checking) that you believe may be protective and reduce your anxiety. We certainly understand that doing some behavioural experiments might be hard for you, but try to see your anxiety and worry for what it is: catastrophizing, fortune-telling and emotional reasoning trying to convince you to remain as you are. These responses from your anxiety and worry are evidence that you are on the right track to tackling these problems. So if you're thinking of letting go of one of these worry behaviours and you start to get anxious predictions telling you that you won't cope, that something bad will happen, or that you shouldn't to do it and that you need to keep 'checking' or 'avoiding', it usually indicates that you are dropping the very unhelpful behaviours you need to. The fact that you're getting anxious thoughts or reactions about doing the behavioural experiment means you are certainly targeting the behaviours that keep your worry and anxiety going! Recognize that these anxious thoughts and reactions will happen and then mentally take a step back and be curious about what you may discover from doing a behavioural experiment. It's time to test out those anxious predictions.

Where do I start?

On Worksheet 10A, write down the safety behaviours, avoidance behaviour and any other worry behaviours, e.g. checking, reassurance seeking, that need to be tackled. Put the behaviours in the order you want to tackle them, on the worksheet. Start with the least challenging one first, with the most difficult last. Over the coming weeks you will work towards dropping the more difficult behaviours, e.g. number 1 will be the first behaviour you are going to tackle through a behavioural experiment, then number 2, and so forth until you reach the end of your list. If you are not sure how to order them, Worksheet 10A below gives some tips on how to do this. Also, it may be helpful to look at Sarah's Worksheet 10A, which lists six behaviours for her to work on.

Sarah's Worksheet 10A: Behaviours to tackle list

1. *Not ask Steve for reassurance for my worries (about 5/10 anxiety)*
2. *Don't text Steve when he is driving away with work or a bit late coming home to check he is okay. We've agreed that it's okay for me to text him at lunch once and okay to text if he is more than 90 minutes late home (6/10)*
3. *Not leave the room when news story on about cancer or if someone is talking about cancer. Don't try and mentally block it out either (6/10)*
4. *Not check my body daily for signs of cancer (7/10)*
5. *Don't go on the internet to look symptoms up on Google (7/10)*
6. *Don't keep texting or calling kids to see if they're okay when they are out. Stick to once to check they are where they're meant to be. Steve and I agreed it's okay to text if they are late getting home but not during the day continually or if they are out with other adults or families we know (8/10)*

Self-assessment ✓

Look at the Behaviour vicious petal that you completed in Chapter 4 and decide which behaviours from your petal you are going to try to drop. Making the least challenging behaviour to drop number 1, and list the other behaviours to work on in order of difficulty, working up to the most challenging.

If you are unsure about the order of difficulty, use the scale below to rate each behaviour according to how much anxiety you believe it will cause you not to use the behaviour or to behave differently.

1	2	3	4	5	6	7	8	9	10
No anxiety				Moderate anxiety					Maximum anxiety

Worksheet 10A: Behaviours to tackle list

1. _____

2. _____

3. _____

4. _____

5. _____

6. _____

7. _____

8. _____

9. _____

10. _____

Below are tables of common safety and avoidance behaviours, similar to the one in Chapter 4. Beside each type of worry behaviour there are suggestions of what you could do as a behavioural experiment. Keep these suggestions in mind as you develop your own behavioural experiments to tackle the behaviours you wrote down on Worksheet 10A. Also, if you notice in the table any other worry-related behaviours that you do, you can add these to your Behaviours to tackle list on Worksheet 10A.

Avoidance behaviours

Behaviour	Examples	Consequences of using it	Behavioural experiment to tackle this
Avoid new situations.	Don't go anywhere new or that you don't know well.	Fail to learn you might be fine and could cope.	Pick somewhere new to go. Use adaptive skills such as looking up directions, then go. Don't engage in worry about it.
Avoid making decisions.	You get others to solve problems for you or make your decisions.	Never learn that maybe you can problem-solve or make a good decision, so your confidence in yourself never gets a chance to grow.	Use problem-solving steps (Chapter 12) to work through to a decision. Develop an option to take. Put the decision in place. Remember, no one makes the 'right' decisions all of the time.

Avoid responsibility.	Avoid taking on a new position or task at work or taking a course, as you believe you'll get it all wrong.	Get stuck in a rut and don't learn to have confidence in yourself or see you do have the abilities to achieve things in life.	Don't avoid! Gradually take on responsibility (as long as you are not already overloaded). If you need support with a new skill, ask for mentoring or for someone to show you how. Then give it a try yourself.
Delay doing things, procrastinating to avoid anxiety or worry.	Things don't get done, or when it comes to the crunch it seems too hard or the original issue has become a bigger task or problem.	Annoys others and you get frustrated with yourself because you don't achieve as much as you would like.	Think about what needs to be done. Break it into steps and then make a start. One step at a time!
Sleeping too much to avoid anxiety and worry.	Going to bed early, sleeping later than normal, or napping in the day.	You end up over-tired and don't learn you might be able to cope better than you think.	Reduce your sleep time to an appropriate level. Increase your exercise during the day and use strategies from Chapters 6–9 to deal with worry or anxiety.

Behaviour	Examples	Consequences of using it	Behavioural experiment to tackle this
Don't watch TV or read newspapers; avoid anything you believe will trigger worry.	Avoid TV in case you hear something about an illness you worry about having, or hearing about a car accident because you think your family will be in one.	We can't avoid day-to-day information all the time and trying to do so keeps you preoccupied with avoiding the very thing you are trying not to see, hear or think about. Then if you do by chance see something, it leads to worry, anxiety and beliefs you won't cope, or to superstitious thinking that this is a sign the 'bad thing' will happen.	You do not need to expose yourself to numerous unpleasant news items. But try to spend some time not avoiding these things. If a news item etc. triggers unhelpful thoughts or worry, use strategies from Chapters 6–9 to manage this.

Safety behaviours

Behaviour	Examples	Consequences of using it	Behavioural experiment to tackle this
Be overly protective of loved ones, not letting them go out or do much.	Not taking kids to the beach or local pool in case they drown.	Family frustrated with you, and you don't see they may actually be okay. Can lead to those around you (children) becoming anxious about the world too.	Gradually be less protective. It's important that children are educated about being safe, but think what small steps you can take towards being less protective. Think about other parents who may not have worry and what they think is appropriate but sensible for their children.
Be overly cautious to stop mistakes from happening, or try to do things perfectly.	Being overly slow and careful when writing an email or doing your work.	Takes you forever to do things. Don't learn that you don't need to be so cautious all the time and that you might be more capable than you think. Trying too hard	Don't check excessively. Check something over once and move on to the next task.

Behaviour	Examples	Consequences of using it	Behavioural experiment to tackle this
		to be perfect is exhausting and you'll feel down when you don't meet your overly high standards.	
Use alcohol or food or misuse drugs to avoid feeling anxious or worried.	Drinking most evenings to shut down the worry.	Substances usually make worry and anxiety worse when they wear off and also are not good for your mood, weight or physical health.	Reduce your use of substances. Use the thinking differently and attention strategies from Chapters 6–9 for worry. Increase exercise and use more of the strategies from Chapter 5 to increase your overall ability to manage stress.
Over-use the internet, shopping or gambling as a means of escape or distraction.	Spending too much time on the internet or shopping.	This costs you time and money, and may lead to feelings of guilt and a reliance on these coping strategies. You then worry about what you've been doing too!	Reduce your internet use or use of other unhelpful behaviours. Test out your beliefs about coping by using thinking differently and attention strategies from Chapters 6–9 for worry.

Use lists excessively.	Having lots of 'to do' lists.	The lists never end and you don't learn that you can rely on yourself to get things done without writing everything down.	Try to act *as if* you don't need lots of lists. What would be appropriate? Keep *one* list and that's it!
Plan excessively to reduce uncertainty.	When going away or doing anything new, you spend hours on the internet finding out all the details and trying to be certain you've covered all the bases.	Loss of time, and you will probably get very anxious if you feel things aren't going to plan. You don't learn that a little planning is okay and that maybe you will cope with whatever comes your way!	Limit the time you spend planning. Ask a couple of people you know how much time and effort they might put into planning and use that as an indicator for yourself. If they only spend 30 minutes looking into something, then do that yourself. See what happens! Try doing something without planning! Like going somewhere new or doing something different.

Checking and reassurance-seeking behaviours

Behaviour	Examples	Consequences of using it	Behavioural experiment to tackle this
Repeatedly check on your loved ones because you think danger is just around the corner.	Keep texting or calling a loved one to check they are safe when they are out.	This breeds doubt because it keeps you preoccupied with the worry that if you don't check on them, something bad has happened or will happen. It's frustrating for them to have to respond to you each time. Repeatedly checking on someone won't make them any safer and if you can't get hold of them, your anxiety will sky-rocket!	Drop this repeated checking. Reduce it to a minimal amount. If you are unsure what would be appropriate, ask the person you are checking on what they think would be a reasonable frequency, or ask a person who does not worry what they think would be a realistic amount.
Repeatedly check a task or your work to ensure there are no mistakes.	At work you go over things repeatedly, or at home you monitor yourself and everything you do for errors.	Slows down your performance. Can irritate you and others. You don't get to learn that checking once is enough.	Don't check excessively. Check it over once and move on to the next task.

Search the internet for information on serious illnesses.	Find online information about symptoms to see if the sensations you are having are okay or not.	Being flooded with misleading information. You will always find something that feeds into your beliefs that you have a serious illness. This rapidly increases your worry and anxiety!	Don't look on the internet for information on illness. Drop this altogether and develop your ability to tolerate the uncertainty.
Check your body repeatedly for signs of a serious illness.	Prodding or feeling your body for lumps or signs of a serious illness, e.g. cancer.	Prodding will only irritate your skin, leaving soreness and redness, which you may interpret as symptoms of a serious illness, e.g. cancer.	Let this go. Stop physically checking (except for regular self-examination as recommended by a doctor). Notice if you are mentally scanning your body for signs of illness or even anxiety. Catch this scanning early and interrupt it. Redirect your attention to whatever else you are doing. Let the urge to check or scan fade into the background of your awareness and ride out the discomfort.

Behaviour	Examples	Consequences of using it	Behavioural experiment to tackle this
Ask others repeatedly for reassurance about your worries.	Keep asking someone if you will be okay or for their reassurance about your decisions.	Asking once for someone's opinion is okay but more than that and you will fail to gain confidence in yourself, your ability to make decisions and your ability to believe in yourself. Repeatedly asking keeps you preoccupied with your worries and anxious if you don't get the answers you want. Stops you learning to cope with uncertainty. Can frustrate others too.	Drop reassurance seeking. If it's a problem or decision that you need support with, problem-solve it using the steps in Chapter 12. If it's a worry or unhelpful thinking, don't seek reassurance. *Don't keep asking.*

When using a behavioural experiment to test out letting go of any of the behaviours above, remember to use the strategies you've been practising from previous chapters to deal with worry and anxiety that may arise during your experiment, e.g. thinking differently, worry postponement or mindfulness. It's important that you ride out the worry and anxiety during your behavioural experiments as if it's a wave. As you are letting go of behaviours that you believe may protect you or reduce your anxiety, it's not uncommon for anxiety to increase before or while you do your behavioural experiment. This is normal and it will pass – but the only way to discover this is by testing it out!

Let's get started on your first behavioural experiment! Use Worksheet 10B and follow the steps below.

Behaviour changing strategy ♘

Use this worksheet to work on the first behaviour listed in your Worksheet 10A. You will need to complete a new worksheet for each behaviour you work on.

Follow the detailed explanations after the worksheet about what to put in each part of the table. You could also look at the example of a completed Worksheet 10B after the explanations for ideas on how to fill one in.

Worksheet 10B: Behavioural experiment worksheet

Date	
1: Experiment *(What behaviour or avoidance am I tackling? What am I going to do differently? How will I manage any difficulties?)*	
2: Prediction *(What do I think will happen? How much do I believe it will (rate 0% = not at all, to 100% = completely believe it)? How would I know if it had happened?)*	

3: What happened? *(What I did. What actually happened?)*	
4: What did I learn? *(Was my prediction accurate? Re-rate the prediction. Is there a different way of thinking?)*	

Step 1: Experiment

Pick one of the behaviours from your Worksheet 10A. Start with number 1 as your first behavioural experiment. Try to make the experiment challenging and testing but achievable. Don't make it too tough, but not too easy or undemanding either. To be effective in testing your anxious predictions, there needs to be some anxiety! The experiment needs to raise your anxiety level to 4–7 out of 10 (where 10 = maximum anxiety while doing the experiment, and 0 = no anxiety).

Opposite '1: Experiment', write down the following.

- The specific safety, avoidance or worry behaviour that you want to tackle.
- What, specifically, you want to test out or do differently. If the target behaviour you want to work on is unclear, it will either be hard to do the experiment or difficult to know whether or not you have made progress. For example, if someone wrote down 'Worry less', it would be hard to measure what this actually means and what amount is considered worrying less; but writing 'I will drop reassurance-seeking today' is specific about what they are going to do and for how long.
- What you will do differently instead of using the worry behaviour you are targeting. For example, if you were going to drop

reassurance-seeking you might write, 'I will drop reassurance-seeking by not asking my family or friends to answer questions about my worries. Instead I will redirect my attention toward engaging in the activity I am doing and ride out the uncertainty'.

● How you might handle any barriers or problems that might occur; for example, 'If I get anxious I can refocus my attention, remember this is my anxiety using emotional reasoning on me, remember times when I have been able to ride the worry out and things have turned out okay'.

Step 2: Prediction

Opposite '2: Prediction', write down your thoughts or predictions about what you think might happen when you drop your avoidance, safety behaviour, reassurance-seeking or checking. When you were completing Step 1 or thinking about this experiment, what negative or anxious thoughts went through your mind? What prediction are you making about letting go of the targeted behaviour, not avoiding or doing things differently? Use the following steps to develop your prediction.

● Write down exactly what you think or predict will happen. Be as clear as possible; for example, 'I will not cope or get through the day' or 'The worry will not stop and will drive me crazy'. If you have more than one prediction, number them.

● Be careful not to be vague or put down predictions that are not clear about what you think the consequences or the worst will be. For example, the prediction, 'I'll get anxious or panicky' is difficult to test out because you may indeed get anxious; this would be normal because you are letting go of behaviours you believe have protected you. So think about what would happen if you get anxious or panicky. What is the worry or unhelpful thinking style (e.g. fortune-telling) saying to you about what will happen if you do not avoid or use a safety or other worry behaviour? Think about what the bottom line is. Ask yourself 'If I get anxious or worried what is the worst that could happen to me?' or 'If I drop this behaviour, what will happen?' The answer maybe something like, 'I'll be anxious all day and won't be able to achieve anything', 'I'll go mad from the anxiety' or 'If I don't check on my loved one, something bad will have happened to them'.

- After writing down your prediction, rate as a percentage how much you believe this prediction will happen, where 0 per cent = you don't believe it at all and 100 per cent = you completely believe the thought. This will show you how strongly you hold the anxious prediction. Your prediction or belief might not be proved completely wrong with the first experiment, as doing a behavioural experiment once may not give you enough credible evidence to counter your anxious prediction, let alone disprove it. Sometimes the evidence may be enough to reduce the strength in your belief a little and sometimes it may reduce the strength a lot. Remember that these worry behaviours have had months or even years to take hold, so you may need to repeat experiments a number of times to tackle them completely. So rating the strength of your beliefs or predictions about dropping these behaviours helps to you see if the predictions are weakening and losing their hold on you; if they aren't, it means you need to do this experiment a few more times to weaken the prediction. For example, if 'I'll be anxious and not able to achieve anything' has a rating strength of 90 per cent, it may need to be tested a few times, and over time we would expect the belief rating to reduce as you find your anxiety lessens and you learn you can achieve things.

- Lastly, how would you know if the prediction had occurred? Write down a couple of ways that the prediction could be measured if it were to occur. It is best to use concrete terms that can be measured. For example, for the prediction 'I'll be anxious and not able to achieve anything', you would write down a description of what would count as not achieving, such as: 'Not being able to make the kids' lunches', 'Not able to have a conversation with a friend' or 'Not able to exercise'. For the prediction 'I'll go mad with anxiety', you might write that this would mean, 'I won't be able to speak', 'I won't be able to know what day it is' or 'I'll be locked up somewhere'.

You have now completed Steps 1–2, so it's time for you to try the experiment. Good luck!

Step 3: What happened?

Complete the section opposite '3: What happened?' once you have begun or completed the experiment. It can be written up during the experiment if it runs over a period of time, like over a few hours or a day, or otherwise immediately after you've finished it. It is important to write things down soon after you have let go of the behaviour so you capture the events while the experiment is still fresh in your mind and before your memory clouds what actually happened.

In this section of the worksheet, observe and record the outcome of your behavioural experiment. Use the following steps to help you.

- Notice what happened. Note whether you dropped the behaviour you were working on. What did you actually do?
- Write down what went well for you? How did it turn out?
- Even if things did not go as well as you would have liked, it is still important to write down what happened so you can reflect on this, learn from the experience and plan what to do differently in the next behavioural experiment for tackling this behaviour. Make sure that unhelpful thinking isn't influencing how you interpreted what happened. For example, 'It went badly' would be black-and-white thinking, whereas 'I was only anxious for the morning rather than the whole day' would be more objective and a better reflection of what really happened.
- It might be useful at this stage to talk through what happened with your support person so that they can help you reflect objectively on what you did and what to put down on your worksheet. This is a good way to prevent unhelpful thinking or difficulties in remembering what happened from interfering with your recall and observations of what you actually achieved.

Step 4: What did I learn?

Now you have tried the experiment, the first thing to do is to recognize the hard work and effort you have put into this experiment. Regardless of how the experiment went, it is important to acknowledge to yourself that, despite apprehension, you have challenged your worry and anxiety by doing things differently, by changing your behaviours and taking on your anxious predictions about letting go of these behaviours. This is often a tough and tiring task, so well done!

When the experiment is over, it is important to reflect on what happened and how this fits with your initial predictions. Opposite '4: What did I learn?', write down what you have learned from your experiment and the meaning of this with regard to your worry and anxiety. Use the following steps to help you.

- Think about the outcome. How does this fit with your original prediction? For example, 'I learned that I can cope without worrying all day and that the anxiety won't be there all day'. Also, re-rate your prediction from the second column with a percentage to see if the strength of your prediction has changed.
- Based on what you have learned, are there any different or alternative ways of viewing worry or anxiety? For example, 'My worry passes, I can cope, and I did not go mad or crazy' or 'I had some anxiety initially when I dropped this worry behaviour but it was okay. It came and went and it did not take me over'. The questions below may help you to discover other outcomes from doing your behavioural experiment:
  - Did you learn anything new from your experiment?
  - How do the outcomes fit with your beliefs about worry. What does it mean for your 'Worry helps me' or 'Worry harms me' beliefs?
  - How does it fit with your unhelpful thinking styles and negative self-talk?
  - What happened to your anxiety and worry symptoms?
  - Does what you have learned about dropping your worry behaviour change your views about worry and anxiety in general? Does what

you have learned about your original prediction change how you think about your anxiety or worry? What does this mean about your worry and anxiety in the future?

- Can you relate or apply what you learned to letting go of other behaviours or how you perceive your anxiety generally?

● If things did not go as well as you would have liked, read through the trouble-shooting tips later in this chapter. Watch out for unrealistic or overly high expectations about your progress or the outcome you achieved. Don't minimize what you did. Think about what you learned from the experiment and how this could inform what to do differently next time.

Example of a completed Worksheet 10B

Date	Tuesday
1: Experiment	I will drop reassurance-seeking by not asking my family or friends to answer questions about my worries. Instead I will redirect my attention to engaging in the activity I am doing and ride out the uncertainty.
	If I get anxious I can refocus my attention, remember this is my anxiety using emotional reasoning on me, remember times when I have been able to ride out the worry and things have turned out okay.
2: Prediction	1) I will not cope or get through the day – 60%
	2) The worry will not stop and will drive me crazy – 80%
	3) I'll be anxious and not able to achieve anything (e.g. making meals, holding a conversation) – 90%

3: What happened?	I was only anxious for the morning rather than the whole day.
	I did not go mad. The worry stopped or faded to the background naturally or when I used my strategies.
	While I was anxious, at times I was able to function and able to do things at home.
4: What did I learn?	My predictions weren't true. My ratings decreased:
	1) 40%
	2) 55%
	3) 70%
	I learned that I can cope without worrying all day and that the anxiety won't be there all day.
	Some evidence against my beliefs that worry will harm me.
	My worry passes. I can cope, and did not go mad or crazy.

Once the behavioural experiment is completed, do it again to keep decreasing the strength of your anxious predictions and associated safety behaviour. Then move on to another experiment. Tackle another behaviour on your list!

Whenever and wherever an opportunity to do a behavioural experiment arises, whether you're at home or out and about, grab the opportunity and do it! If you can use a behavioural experiment worksheet, do so, but even if you haven't got one, still test out doing things differently. Remember to reflect on what you learned or discovered too. The more behavioural experiments you do the better.

An important point

Because your worry and anxiety have probably been around for a while or have set themselves up in your life, behavioural experiments need to be repeated. This gives these new ways of behaving a chance to take hold in your life and develop as helpful ways of going about your day-to-day life or responding to unhelpful thoughts and worry. This will also give you the chance to collect evidence against your anxious thoughts and predictions, as well as helping you to see that you can cope. It is important to repeat behavioural experiments until you start to see that you no longer need the safety or avoidance behaviours, reassurance-seeking or excessive checking. Keep going until the strength of belief in your anxious predictions starts to weaken, moving closer towards 0 per cent!

Troubleshooting

What happens if the behavioural experiment didn't work or you were too anxious?

- When you decided on the experiment did you have a specific enough prediction to test out? Was it clear to you what you were actually going to do?
- Did you rate your degree of belief in the negative prediction before and after the experiment to see if this changed to any degree?
- Was the level of the experiment too difficult or not difficult enough? If it's too hard, you might find you are too anxious, but if it's not challenging enough you won't be testing out your prediction so you'll be putting in a lot of effort for little gain. Try to make the experiment challenging and testing but achievable: not too hard and not too easy. If you're unsure how to work this out, remember that you want the experiment to raise your anxiety to 4–7 out of 10 (where 10 = maximum anxiety) while doing the experiment.
- Apart from the avoidance, safety or worry behaviour you're trying to drop in the behavioural experiment, has any other safety or

worry behaviours interfered with the experiment? If the experiment wasn't as effective as it could be, was it because another subtle safety behaviour or avoidance crept in or you unintentionally used one to reduce your worry or anxiety? This will affect the outcome of your experiment. It's okay – this sometimes happens – but try the experiment again without using any safety or avoidance behaviours at all.

- Have another go!

Below are examples of behavioural experiments that Luke and Sarah completed.

Luke's behavioural experiment

Date	Sunday
1: Experiment	Not to drink beer to cope with worry and anxiety about work tomorrow and the week ahead. Instead I'm going to use mindfulness with my thoughts. Will do some exercise in the day and use relaxation close to bedtime.
2: Prediction	1) My worry will be out of control 85% (it won't stop). 2) My worry will keep me up all night 90% (will know if this has happened because I will be awake all night).
3: What happened?	Didn't drink on Sunday. When I started to notice worry I used mindfulness. Also remembered that over the past week or two when using worry postponement my worry has not been there all the time. Had some worry over the day, about 60% of what I normally do. But it did pass at times. Took me a bit longer to get to sleep than usual but I did get to sleep without having to rely on alcohol.

4: What did I learn?	1) My worry was not out of control. It was there at times but was less than I expected it would be without using alcohol. It did go away at times. My original prediction dropped to 60%.
	2) I can get to sleep without using alcohol. The relaxation technique and exercise in the day seemed to help. Need to test this out more. But shows that the worry was unpleasant but did not harm me. Original prediction now is 65%.
	Need to repeat this again for more evidence that worry passes.

Luke found that by dropping his use of alcohol he was able to test out if his worry would be uncontrollable. He exercised during the day and at night directed his attention to talking with his girlfriend and watching television. When unhelpful thoughts or worries popped into his head he used detached mindfulness rather than trying to push the thoughts away or focusing on them. Luke let the worries come and go. He thought of them as noisy kids in the background, like the kids he would hear on the bus to work sometimes, who he could tune out and direct his attention away from. When Luke went to bed he was bombarded with thoughts about the week ahead at work and at university. This started to make him feel anxious but he noticed that these were good examples of the fortune-telling and catastrophizing unhelpful thinking styles, trying to convince him things were going to be terrible. Luke remembered what he had learned about his 'Worry helps me' beliefs, that worry would not make him more prepared for the week ahead. He observed these worries in his mind and then started his progressive muscle relaxation and chose to notice his worry coming and going as he did this. Soon after this he managed to fall asleep. The following morning he completed his behavioural experiment worksheet and reflected on what he had found – that his worry did indeed pass and it was not uncontrollable. He decided to repeat this experiment over the next few weeks to chip away at his beliefs that worry was uncontrollable and he also picked another behaviour to tackle using the behavioural experiment approach.

Sarah's behavioural experiment

Date	Monday to Friday
1: Experiment	Don't ask Steve for reassurance for my worry. I will first work out whether it's a worry I'm having or a problem. If it's a worry I won't ask Steve about it. Instead I will ride out the uncertainty! Use my strategies for thinking differently and detaching from worry.
2: Prediction	1) If I don't ask Steve then the worst will happen, my worry will come true. 95% 2) I will be overwhelmed by anxiety and I will be forced to ask Steve about my worries to make the anxiety go away. 100%
3: What happened?	Was really hard some days. Monday I had about five worries and caved in on one and asked Steve. Was mad with myself. Rest of the week was better. I was able to not ask on Tuesday. On Wednesday I slipped again and asked Steve. But on Thursday and Friday I did not ask at all. This made me anxious but it did pass, then returned with the next worry but then passed again. None of my worries about bad things happening came true so not asking for reassurance didn't make these worries happen. It was just catastrophizing!
4: What did I learn?	1) Worries did not come true. Belief dropped to 85%. Need to test this out some more. 2) I did feel very anxious and asked Steve for reassurance but the times I didn't the anxiety did pass. Felt pleased I achieved this. My belief I'll be overwhelmed has dropped to 75% which is surprising but good. I need to test this out more, but I now think that I don't have to ask Steve questions every time I have a worry and the anxiety does move on.

Sarah spent a week working on not asking her husband for reassurance. This was difficult for her and she was not able to do it all of the time. But she did manage to reduce her reassurance-seeking and on some days didn't use it at all. Sarah found that the work she had been doing on her attention, such as attention training and mindfulness, appeared to help make her worries less 'sticky', so they moved on without plaguing her. She also remembered that beliefs that 'Worry helps me' were a trap for her and they were false. Sarah found evidence for this because a couple of times during the week she was sure that something had happened to her kids but she did not ask Steve for reassurance and the worries came to nothing. Sarah found it really interesting that the times she did ask for reassurance her relief from the anxiety and worry was short-lived. She began to notice that not asking for reassurance became less difficult and the anxiety and worry faded and she felt more confident in herself. She was beginning to see that worry was not a good coping strategy for her. Sarah decided to continue with this experiment for another two to three weeks to help her really develop her skills of letting go of worries and not relying on reassurance from others.

Chapter summary

In this chapter you learned about

- behavioural experiments, a key way of letting go of behaviours that have been maintaining your worry and anxiety by testing out different ways of responding to unhelpful thinking, worry and anxiety
- how to develop a list of worry-related behaviours to tackle
- how to develop behavioural experiments to support you in dropping the safety behaviours and avoidance that maintain your worry
- how to use behavioural experiments to test your anxious predictions about dropping worry behaviours and evaluate whether you need these behaviours any more. You also learned to reflect on your ability to cope.

Activities for you to do

Before moving on to Chapter 11, make sure you:

- continue to use your Worksheet 10B to set up behavioural experiments for yourself
- keep repeating these until your anxious predictions weaken and you discover you don't need that avoidance, safety, reassurance-seeking or checking behaviour any longer
- keep tackling the other worry behaviours listed on your Worksheet 10A.

Chapter 11 will introduce you to different methods of managing anxiety triggers: Five ways to wellbeing and Five steps for effective coping. These strategies are valuable means of increasing your overall day-to-day physical and mental health, which can make you more resilient to stress, worry and anxiety.

Managing anxiety triggers

Overview

In addition to the anxiety management strategies we have talked about so far in this book, keeping well also requires that you actively pursue a balance between all of the competing demands on you – family, work, relationships – and purposely manage stressors and those things that can trigger your anxiety. This is challenging for all of us and for most of us it does not occur without directed attention and effort. In this chapter you will learn about some key ways to manage your anxiety triggers and stressors.

Five ways to wellbeing

'Five ways to wellbeing' refers to five actions that research evidence has shown it is essential to build into our day-to-day life for our wellbeing and the wellbeing of our families and community. These are to connect, take notice, keep learning, be active and give.

Connect

Feeling connected to others is a fundamental human need. Social contacts can provide support and contribute to self-worth. Make time to connect with those around you, your family, friends, colleagues or your community. Consider broadening or strengthening your social connections. Become involved in a group or local club. Smile at a stranger!

Take notice

Developing more awareness of the here and now also contributes to increased wellbeing and can reduce depression and anxiety. The importance of being mindful was covered in Chapters 7 and 9. Practise increasing your awareness of what is in your environment. Take notice of what you see, hear, smell and feel. Practise focusing your attention on the here and now. Even frequent, short mindfulness practice can have great benefits. For example, take the opportunity to sit quietly in a busy place, like a shopping mall or airport, and just observe or be mindful about what you can see or hear around you. Or find a spot outdoors somewhere, like in a park, near a river or on a beach, and be mindful.

Keep learning

Set yourself to learn something new. This can increase your confidence and your wellbeing. Learning something new does not just refer to formal education, but could be doing anything that stimulates your curiosity. Try something new or rediscover an old interest. Give yourself a new challenge or try a new activity. For example, memorize a new word every day, try out a new recipe or broaden your knowledge on any topic. Seek out new experiences; dare yourself to try something new. This is a good way to challenge uncertainty and see that you can manage it! Learning is also a good way to improve your brain's health, no matter what age you are.

Be active

As Chapter 5 emphasized, physical activity is very beneficial. As little as 10 minutes of physical activity can increase your wellbeing and lower anxiety and depression. The physical exercise does not have to be strenuous. Do whatever activity you can manage for as long as you can manage between three and five times a week. Walk, jog, cycle, swim, play an active game with your kids or friends, do some gardening or dance.

Give

Give someone your time. Taking time to smile, say thank you or provide a listening ear can be incredibly rewarding. It feels good to give, and everybody has something to offer. Do something kind or helpful for someone else: a family member, a friend or a stranger. Do some voluntary work or join a community group. Take an opportunity to support someone else. Give a compliment – take time to acknowledge when someone has done well.

Variety is important. The research suggests that repeating the same activity is not as beneficial as mixing things up a bit and keeping your five ways activities 'fresh'. So when you think about the five ways, think about a range of options, like a five ways menu of activities. It is not necessary to complete each of the five ways all at once, which could be too much. Think about what you can manage in your own daily life; it is better to take some small steps. Don't make the five steps overwhelming or stressful. Strive for a balance, so that any five ways activity you choose will be easily maintained over the following days, weeks and months. Maybe some of the strategies you are using to tackle your worry and anxiety can double up and count as five ways activities, e.g. mindfulness practice, exercise or socializing with friends. Start to note down your ideas on Worksheet 11A.

Behaviour changing strategy

Think about how you can begin making the five ways part of your everyday life and write down your ideas in each category. You don't need to come up with all your ideas at once; gradually add to and build on your ideas for wellbeing. Of course, the most important point is that you follow through on your ideas and make a plan to put them into action!

Worksheet 11A: Five ways to wellbeing

Connect	
Take notice	
Keep learning	
Be active	
Give	

(Adapted from 'Five Ways to Wellbeing', New Economics Foundation website)

Have a look at Luke's Worksheet 11A to give you an idea of how to use it.

Luke's Worksheet 11A: Five ways to wellbeing

Connect	Already seeing Mark when we play squash and go surfing.
	Catch up with family more at the weekend, maybe have them over for dinner.
	Join work's social touch-rugby team for activity but there's lots of socializing too.
Take notice	Started to do more of this through my mindfulness practice - just need to keep it up.
	Could do this more when I go surfing. Like noticing the scent of the sea, the warmth of the sun, the sound of the waves and feel of the water. This makes me feel alive but is calming too.
Keep learning	Don't have time for this now as doing studies at university, so I guess that covers it.
	But could try to learn more about something not too time-consuming.
	Amanda likes cooking so we might try making some different meals together. I really enjoy photography so I could learn more about that and combine it with going to the beach to surf maybe.
Be active	Feel I have this covered with exercise, squash, touch-rugby and surfing. I have a few things to choose from now so just need to make sure I keep doing it and make the time.
Give	Time is an issue for me to volunteer as already trying to make a lot of changes with tackling my anxiety. I could help my mum and dad out a bit more when they get stuck using their computers or need a hand with their gardens - plus that would be connecting too.
	I could try to give people I care about more compliments too, like Amanda.

Practical advice ⇨

Helpful habits I: Lifestyle

Lifestyle factors are very important for maintaining wellbeing and managing stress. In addition to the five ways to wellbeing, a healthy diet, sufficient exercise and sleep are essential.

A healthy diet

Eat regularly throughout the day from a wide variety of food groups.

- Choose fewer refined (processed), high-sugar foods and drinks.
- Eat more wholegrain foods, cereals, pulses (legumes such as beans, chickpeas and lentils), fruit and vegetables.
- Include some protein (e.g. meat, fish, eggs) at each meal.
- Include oily fish (for omega-3 fatty acids) in your diet.
- Maintain a healthy weight.
- Maintain an adequate fluid intake (water).
- Keep within the recommended limits if you drink alcohol; if you are unsure about these, look at the websites listed in Chapter 15.

Exercise

As you read in Chapter 5, there are many benefits to regular exercise. In addition to helping you manage anxiety, exercise can help you maintain to your general wellbeing. It's a great stress reduction tool!

Sleep

There is no agreement on exactly how much sleep we need. Not only are sleep needs very individual, they also vary with age. There are many reasons for having trouble getting to sleep or having disturbed sleep, including physical discomfort, distress, worry and anxiety. Some of the factors that can contribute to poor sleep are present long before you go to bed. If you are having trouble getting to sleep or having disturbed sleep, look at the Practical advice box 'Sleeping well' at the end of this chapter for help in improving your sleep. Make sleep a priority.

Stress reduction

In addition to the anxiety management strategies already covered, the five ways to maintain wellbeing and lifestyle factors, managing anxiety triggers also require us to actively manage stressors.

Stress occurs when the demands of life outweigh our ability to cope. What stresses people and how they respond varies according to the individual, and the kinds of demands that are stressful for one person may not be stressful for someone else. So it's not helpful to evaluate negatively how stress affects you in comparison to others you know. It is important instead for you to identify the things that may be stressful for you so you can better manage stressors. Similarly, the ability to cope varies from person to person and although the things people do to cope may have similarities, these are also very individual.

Reducing stress requires three steps:

1. becoming aware that stress is a problem
2. becoming aware of what is stressing you
3. following strategies to manage and reduce the effects of stress on you.

Sources of stress

Our environment continually bombards us with the need to adjust and adapt; for example, we must continually adapt to changing seasons, weather, noise and traffic, to name a few. While there are many different types of stressors, stress usually comes from three basic sources:

- our social world places considerable competing demands upon us, e.g. work deadlines, domestic tasks, demands for our time and attention, relationships, and caring for loved ones

- our physiological status can also be a source of stress; lack of sleep, illness, pain, injury, poor nutrition, hormones, aging etc can all contribute to raising our stress levels
- our own thoughts and unhelpful coping strategies not only contribute to anxiety, but also to stress or the worsening of stress and anxiety.

If you want help in identifying your particular sources and levels of stress, look at the social readjustment rating scale (www.emotionalcompetency.com/srrs.htm) developed by Thomas Holmes and Richard Rahe of the University of Washington School of Medicine. The scale is easy and takes only a few minutes to complete. It asks about a wide range of common stressors that might have occurred in the past year and then gives you an idea about the impact stress has had in your life during that period.

Common signs of stress

Many of the signs of stress are similar to the emotional and physical responses and unhelpful thinking experiences you notice when your anxiety increases. This is because stress and anxiety affect your body, mind, emotions and behaviours in much the same way. In Chapter 1 we talked about how each aspect of our day-to-day functioning is affected by anxiety. Like anxiety, stress that is unchecked can lead to problems, including triggering and increasing worry and anxiety, and mood problems.

Worksheet 11B lists 50 common signs of stress. Read through this and identify your signs of stress, ticking each one.

Self-assessment ✓

Go through these common signs of stress and put a tick next to any signs that you are experiencing because you are currently stressed or are becoming stressed.

Worksheet 11B: Fifty common signs of stress

1	Frequent headaches, jaw clenching or pain	
2	Gritting or grinding teeth	
3	Stuttering or stammering	
4	Tremors or trembling of lips or hands	
5	Neckache, back pain, muscle spasms	
6	Lightheadedness, faintness, dizziness	
7	Hearing ringing, buzzing or 'popping' sounds	
8	Frequent blushing or sweating	
9	Cold or sweaty hands or feet	
10	Dry mouth or problems swallowing	
11	Frequent colds, infections or herpes sores	
12	Rashes, itching, hives, goosebumps	
13	Unexplained or frequent 'allergy' attacks	
14	Heartburn, stomach pain, nausea	
15	Excess belching or flatulence	
16	Constipation or diarrhoea	
17	Difficulty breathing, frequent sighing	
18	Sudden attacks of panic	
19	Chest pain, palpitations or rapid pulse related to stress or anxiety	
20	Frequent urination	
21	Diminished sexual desire or performance	
22	Excessive anxiety, worry, guilt or nervousness	
23	Increased anger, frustration or hostility	

24	Depression, or frequent or wild mood swings	
25	Increased or decreased appetite	
26	Insomnia, nightmares or disturbing dreams	
27	Difficulty concentrating, racing thoughts	
28	Trouble learning new information	
29	Forgetfulness, disorganization or confusion	
30	Difficulty in making decisions	
31	Feeling overloaded or overwhelmed	
32	Frequent bouts of crying or suicidal thoughts	
33	Feelings of loneliness or worthlessness	
34	Little interest in appearance, poor punctuality	
35	Nervous habits, fidgeting, foot-tapping	
36	Increased frustration, irritability or edginess	
37	Over-reaction to petty annoyances	
38	Increased number of minor accidents	
39	Obsessive or compulsive behaviour	
40	Reduced work efficiency or productivity	
41	Lies or excuses to cover up poor work	
42	Rapid or mumbled speech	
43	Excessive defensiveness or suspiciousness	
44	Problems in communication or sharing	
45	Social withdrawal and isolation	
46	Constant tiredness, weakness, fatigue	
47	Frequent use of over-the-counter drugs	
48	Weight gain or loss without dieting	
49	Increased smoking, alcohol or drug use	
50	Excessive gambling or impulse buying	

(From the American Institute of Stress website)

Effective strategies to cope with stress

There are five important ways to cope with stress in an effective way: explore and clarify your feelings; identify and manage your thoughts; identify and prioritize the problem or stressors; identify your internal and external coping resources; and identify the barriers to effective coping and your strategies for overcoming these.

Explore and identify feelings and needs

Becoming more aware of your feelings and needs is the first step to resolving a problem or coping with a stressor. Understanding how you are feeling about a situation or what your needs might be in any given situation gives you the option to express your feelings directly and assertively rather than acting them out in aggressive or self-destructive behaviours. Although this can sometimes be challenging, honestly acknowledging your feelings and talking about those feelings can be helpful.

Identify and manage thoughts

Take time to become aware of your unhelpful thoughts. If you need to remind yourself about the basic cognitive principles (specifics about thoughts and our thinking), go over Chapter 4 again. Is your self-talk negative and unhelpful? Are you using unhelpful thinking styles about the stressor? Have you got into a pattern of worry? Are unhelpful beliefs about worry ('worry harms me', 'worry helps me') keeping your worry going and intensifying your stress? Use the strategies outlined in Chapters 6 and 8 to take control of your unhelpful thinking about the current stressful situation. Think differently or use mindfulness to detach from worry if it's kicked in. Remember, we cannot always change a situation but we can control how we respond to it by taking charge of our thinking or attention to worry.

Identify and prioritize the problems or stressors

Take time to identify the problems or stressors. Make a list of all the issues that have consumed a lot of mental, emotional and physical energy in the past week or so. Put the items on the list in order according to how much energy they consumed. Give priority to the problems that have consumed the most energy and are most urgent. Clarify your needs in each situation.

Get support by communicating your thoughts and feelings about the problem to someone you trust or to your support person. If you feel overwhelmed, try reaching out to get support before you explore your feelings or thoughts or before you act to alleviate the problem. Talking things over with someone else can help you to get a better perspective on the situation. This is not using reassurance-seeking for worries, but problem-solving. It is appropriate if you are getting support or talking an issue over with someone to find ways to resolve the problem. If you start to ask the same thing repeatedly, then make sure you aren't reassurance-seeking rather than constructively solving an issue or problem.

Identify internal and external coping strategies

Complete Worksheet 11C, which helps you identify your coping resources or strategies. You may already use some of the coping strategies listed in the worksheet but there will be others that you can try out. We all rely not only on our internal coping resources to some degree but also on external resources. Expand your options for coping; try something on the list you have not thought of before as a coping resource. It can also be helpful to talk to others you know and ask them what their coping strategies are. What do they do to cope with stress in healthy and productive ways? You will see there is room on the worksheet to add coping strategies as you become aware of them.

Self-assessment ✓

Put a tick beside the coping resources and strategies that you use, and add some of your own.

Worksheet 11C: Coping resources and strategies

Internal coping resources and strategies	
Intelligence	
Energy	
Sense of humour	
Organizational ability	
Resourcefulness	
Confidence	
Creativity	
Persistence	
Assertiveness	
What other internal coping resources do you have?	
External coping resources and strategies	
Connect with others	
Ask for assistance – family, friends etc.	
Contact a support or a service agency	
Take time to relax	
Take time off	

Go away for the weekend	
Meditation or prayer	
Relaxation practice	
Breathing practice	
Visualization	
Monitor unhelpful thinking and then think differently	
Time management	
Exercise	
Practise mindfulness, be focused on the present	
Open up and communicate with others	
What other external coping resources do you have?	

Luke read over the checklist of signs of stress in Worksheet 11B and recognized a number of the signs applied to him. What stood out the most was neckache, headaches, decreased sexual desire, sleep problems, feeling overwhelmed, over-reacting to things, increased alcohol use and, of course, worry and anxiety! He showed the sheet to Amanda and she said that she experienced some of those signs herself, which helped Luke realize that it wasn't just him who struggled with stress at times. Luke filled out Worksheet 11C, which helped him to consolidate and recognize the ways he had of coping with and reducing stress.

Luke's Worksheet 11C

Internal coping resources and strategies	
Intelligence	
Energy	
Sense of humour	√
Organizational ability	
Resourcefulness	√
Confidence	
Creativity	
Persistence	√
Assertiveness	√
What other internal coping resources do you have?	
At work I can be patient when doing tasks. *I work well with others.*	
External coping resources and strategies	
Connect with others	√
Ask for assistance – family, friends etc.	√
Contact a support or a service agency	
Take time to relax	
Take time off	
Go away for the weekend	
Meditation or prayer	√
Relaxation practice	√
Breathing practice	√
Visualization	
Monitor unhelpful thinking and then think differently	√
Time management	
Exercise	√

Practise mindfulness, be focused on present	√
Open up and communicate with others	
What other external coping resources do you have?	
Supportive girlfriend and friends. *Got some parks nearby. I can enjoy walks there, plus the beach.* *Good people at work who are happy to give me mentoring or guidance with my work if I ask.* *If I needed it, the university has a therapy service for students.*	

Identify barriers to effective coping and strategies for overcoming them

There can be many barriers that get in the way of effective coping. These can include:

- lack of information
- lack of time
- deadlines and other demands
- insufficient resources, e.g. limited money, lack of support at work or home.

It is important to identify and address the barriers to coping effectively. Remember, it is okay to ask for assistance and advice if you are working on solving a problem constructively rather than just looking for reassurance for worry.

Worksheet 11D will help you to work through the five steps for effective coping, including dealing with any barriers in your way. Some of the coping resources you listed on Worksheet 11C may help here, and you can also look at Luke's worksheet below.

Behaviour changing strategy

Write down:

1. your feelings about the situation and your needs
2. the unhelpful thoughts you need to manage
3. prioritize the problems or stressors, giving the highest priority to those which are the most pressing or those you need to address first
4. identify the coping resources you have available that might be particularly helpful for each of the problems or situations; Worksheet 11C might give you some ideas here

5a. the barriers to coping effectively with the situation

5b. how you can overcome each barrier.

Worksheet 11D: Five ways to effective coping

1 My feelings and needs	
2 My unhelpful thoughts	
3 Problems and stressors	
4 My coping strategies	

5a Barriers to effective coping	
5b Strategies for overcoming barriers	

Ineffective coping strategies

Isolation

Withdrawing from other people and isolating yourself is a common reaction to stress. Avoiding can seem like a good option, especially if you feel overwhelmed and believe you won't be able to cope with others or their questions about how you are. The problem is that withdrawing leaves you with no support and it is much harder to maintain perspective or an objective point of view when you are alone. Being around others who are supportive means you benefit from positive interactions and you are also exposed to non-critical views that are alternatives to your own, which may be negatively shaded if you're battling stress. These interactions help you to think differently and encourage positive emotions.

Focusing harder on the stressor

It is common when faced with a stressful problem to work harder on the problem or spend too much time thinking (or worrying) about the problem in an attempt to resolve things. However, this typically happens at the expense of sufficient rest and exercise, eating well and time with others. As you already know from reading this book, rather than alleviating stress, unhelpful thinking or over-thinking things and worry contributes to increasing stress.

Substance use

It is common for people to use substances, whether alcohol or other drugs, as a coping strategy, to try to escape from problems by temporarily alleviating stress. Unfortunately, any stress reduction is short term; the problems remain and can also be made worse by substance use. For example, alcohol slows down the brain and central nervous system processes; it can impair a person's motivation and ability to problem-solve. Several studies have also shown that alcohol isn't conducive to getting a good night's sleep; alcohol may help you to fall asleep more quickly but the restful and restorative part of sleep is disturbed, causing poor concentration and daytime drowsiness that makes dealing with stress even more difficult. This can contribute to more worry and anxiety too. Over time, heavy drinking or use of other substances has adverse effects on both physical and mental wellbeing.

Unhealthy diet

Overeating generally or eating too much of particular types of food, such as sweets or fast food, is a common way of managing stressors but is unhelpful in the long term. Stress seems to affect food preferences and has been associated with food cravings. Researchers have linked stress to weight gain. It is also common for some people to stop eating or eat very little when under stress or when anxious.

The importance of a balanced diet when managing stress has already been mentioned. Without a balanced diet our bodies become more stressed, with physical and emotional consequences. In short, overeating to fulfil emotional needs or as a distraction from problems can become an unhealthy cycle that makes the problems or sources of stress worse! If this is the case for you, start working on gradually balancing your diet.

Overspending

Sometimes when we are stressed, our spending habits can spiral out of control. This usually occurs because we take shortcuts when life becomes hectic; we might spend more on take-aways or by eating in restaurant rather than cooking at home, or buy ready meals rather than food to cook ourselves. We may spend more on treating ourselves to clothes, electronic devices or other material things in an attempt to relieve the stress we are feeling, as a way of escaping it. Although treats and new purchases might temporarily make you feel better, in the long run, overspending can cause more stress and worry than it reduces.

Internet use

While surfing on the internet can provide some distraction and relieve stress, excessive use or spending too much time online can cause problems. Research shows that too much internet use can result in increased procrastination, avoiding solving problems, neglecting other responsibilities at home and work, decreased productivity, reduced social involvement and increased loneliness. All of these increase rather than reduce stress.

Acting aggressively

Acting aggressively towards other people, either verbally or physically, is common when people are trying to manage the emotions they experience when they feel under stress. Hurting others only creates further problems, like regret, and increases social isolation.

Luke and the five ways to effective coping

After reading through the ineffective coping strategies Luke realized that he used some of these. He knew he worried more when stressed and that this usually led to him procrastinating about what needed to be done. This was particularly true at work and university when he felt stuck with some task or another. Luke knew that when he was procrastinating he would go onto the internet at work or at home and lose time surfing through irrelevant webpages rather than working on what he needed to.

Luke also knew he was drinking more alcohol than normal, having too much coffee and too many energy drinks, and eating junk food because he felt too busy to cook. Luke realized that he could still make a healthy sandwich or take fruit and yogurt to work rather than spending money on unhealthy foods.

Luke was stuck at the moment with a university essay that was due, so he tried using Worksheet 11D to help get him back on track.

1 My feelings and needs	*Feel anxious and stuck in regard to an essay due in at university next week.*
2 My unhelpful thoughts	*'I can't do this.' 'I'll fail.' Can't stop thinking about it and it being due - WORRYING!*
3 Problems and stressors	*Unsure of what I am meant to be writing about.* *Trouble getting to the library to get the books I need for the essay.* *Amanda wanting to go away this weekend when I need to be working on this essay.*
4 My coping strategies	*I am resourceful and persistent.* *Supportive friends and Amanda is supportive.* *Thinking differently skills.* *Mindfulness skills.*
5a Barriers to effective coping	*Need to understand more what I'm writing about.* *Lack of time!* *Unhelpful thinking and worrying.*

5b Strategies for overcoming barriers	*Make a time to speak with or email the lecturer about the essay requirements.*
	Talk with workmate Ryan who is doing the same course about using the books he has. Also, we helped each other with our assignments before when one of us is stuck about what to do. He might be able to give me some guidance on this essay.
	Talk over with Amanda about going away the following weekend instead of this weekend. She'll be disappointed but she's understanding and to make up for it I can let her choose where we go and I'll do the cooking while away.
	Remember worry is NOT helpful.
	Can use thinking differently skills for my unhelpful thinking and negative self-talk.
	Use mindfulness for worry.

Practical advice ⇒

Helpful habits II: Sleeping well

- **Avoid alcohol, cigarettes, and other drugs.** You will sleep better if you limit your intake of substances that contain caffeine and alcohol in the four to six hours before going to bed. Coffee, chocolate and some prescription and non-prescription drugs contain caffeine. Also, eating sugary food close to bedtime can result in a drop in blood sugar during the night which contributes to wakening. Alcohol can make you feel sleepy initially, as it slows down your brain activity, but it also changes important sleep brain patterns so you can end up having a worse sleep.
- **Establish a regular sleep and wake cycle.** Try to keep to a regular sleep/wake cycle. It is particularly important to get out of bed at roughly the same time each morning. Also, don't go to bed until you are tired or sleepy.

- **Avoid naps during the day.** Don't take a nap during the day, even if you have had less sleep during the previous night. If you can't manage without a nap during the day, sleep for less than one hour and before 3 p.m.
- **Create a healthy sleep environment.** Make your sleeping area as free from distraction and noise as possible, and as comfortable and conducive to sleep as you can. You will sleep better if you keep the bedroom at a cool temperature and free of strong light.
- **Develop a bedtime routine.** Try to develop a bedtime routine that you follow every night. Consider a light (and caffeine-free) snack before bed to prevent waking from hunger. Try taking a hot bath about 90 minutes before bedtime. A hot bath will raise your body temperature and the drop in temperature following the bath can leave you feeling sleepy. Empty your bladder just before you go to bed.
- **Exercise, but time it carefully.** Exercise in the morning or afternoon can improve the quality of sleep, but avoid exercising for at least two to three hours before going to bed.

Once you are in bed

- Only use your bed for sleeping and sexual activity. Avoid watching TV, doing work, making phone calls, using the internet, arguing etc in bed.
- Don't clock-watch, i.e. don't monitor how long it takes to go to sleep or how much sleeping time will be left before you have to get up. Turn your clock around or cover it.
- Avoid co-sleeping with children and pets, as most of the time both contribute to disturbing your sleep.
- Don't worry if you can't sleep. Practise a relaxation strategy such as progressive muscle relaxation or the slow-breathing technique (Chapter 5) to become relaxed, and mindfulness or detached mindfulness (Chapter 9) to disconnect from your worries.

If you can't get to sleep or you wake in the night

- If you have not fallen asleep after 20 minutes, get out of bed and do something relaxing until you feel tired enough to go to sleep.

- Don't expose yourself to bright light; light tells your brain it is time to wake up. So don't use the TV, computer or smartphone, which all produce too much bright light.
- If you wake in the night and don't get back to sleep naturally, do not try to force yourself to go back to sleep until you feel sleepy again. Get up and do something relaxing.
- Practise focusing mindfully on your breathing.
- Don't worry if you can't sleep – worrying about sleeping will keep you awake.
- Practise detaching from your worries using mindfulness exercises, metaphors or mindfulness of breath (Chapter 9).

Chapter summary

In this chapter you have learned:

- the role the five ways to wellbeing activities, plus diet, exercise and sleep have in maintaining your wellbeing
- how you can action the five ways to wellbeing in your day-to-day life
- what changes to make, if necessary, to your lifestyle: diet, exercise and sleep routines
- how to identify the common triggers for your stress and your personal signs of stress
- how to identify your internal and external coping resources
- how to use the five steps for effective coping to improve how you manage problems and stressors.

Activities for you to do

Before moving on to Chapter 12:

- start to try out the activities on your Five Ways to Wellbeing worksheet (Worksheet 11A)
- consider whether you need to make changes to your lifestyle (Chapter 15 lists online resources to help with this)

- complete the Social Readjustment Rating Scale and the 50 common signs of stress questionnaire (Worksheet 11B) to help you identify your sources and signs of stress
- use Worksheet 11D to implement the five steps to coping effectively with stress.

In Chapter 12, you will learn what resilience is and how to increase your resilience so that you become fully ready to face life's challenges and take life's opportunities. This will also boost your overall health and wellbeing. Research has shown that resilience is something we can learn and that certain activities enhance our levels of resilience. Chapter 12 looks at ways of doing this, including more on constructive problem-solving.

Building resilience

Overview

Resilience refers to our ability to tolerate or absorb disturbance in our lives and gain back our balance, or to maintain relatively stable and healthy levels of functioning despite disturbance. While disturbance to balance can be difficult, it can eventually result in people developing a greater capacity to adapt and cope.

What contributes to resilience?

Several key factors contribute to our levels of resilience, including stress management, our social connections and culture, our self-efficacy, problem-solving and our flexibility. Here are some ideas about how you can use them to increase your resilience.

Stress management

In Chapter 11, you learned about your sources of stress, common signs of stress, your particular signs of stress and ways to handle stress so you can better manage your anxiety. Dealing with your stress has more advantages than just managing anxiety. Being proactive and keeping your stress manageable will also help you to develop and increase your overall resilience. If it has been a while since you read Chapter 11, look back over the stress management section to check that you are still actively and effectively managing stress.

Social connections and culture

Our resilience arises not only from within us but also from those around us, e.g. our family, friends, the groups we belong to and our culture. Culture refers not only to the ethnic group we belong to, but also to culture in the broadest sense; particular ways of life, attitudes and behaviours, and also spirituality or religion, traditions, values, standards and laws are all elements of our culture.

Being involved with others and being connected with our culture promotes our resilience and it is essential to maintain these connections even when we are busy or stressed. Being cared for and caring for others is not only how we maintain our wellbeing but also how we develop resilience.

Self-efficacy

Increasing self-efficacy is also a good way to increase resilience. Self-efficacy means having confidence in one's ability to manage and complete tasks and reach goals, i.e. the belief you have in yourself and your capabilities. Strong self-efficacy increases your self-confidence, helps you succeed with challenging problems, increases your motivation and commitment to solving problems and helps you recover quickly from setbacks and disappointments. A sense of self-efficacy can be learned and also enhanced in a variety of ways. One of the most effective ways to maintain or increase your self-efficacy is through managing the negative self-talk that can undermine your confidence and increase your anxiety (see Chapters 4 and 6).

It is also important to remind yourself about the strengths and abilities that you have; research shows that it is our own accomplishments make the biggest contribution to our self-confidence. So having a go at new activities and being persistent even when that activity is challenging is really important for developing our self-efficacy. Observing how other people succeed at activities and challenges can also help you develop more knowledge and useful skills.

This will increase your self-belief that you can succeed with something. Having good people around you who encourage you and remind you of your particular abilities is important, because their support makes it more likely that you will succeed and their beliefs in you will increase your self-efficacy. Encouragement and feedback from others can help you start a tricky activity, persist at it and increase your belief in your own abilities. Don't wait for encouraging support, ask your support person(s) and those around you for specific feedback on your achievements and for encouragement.

In many ways the principle of self-efficacy is simple. The more we try out new things and succeed, the more our sense of achievement and our self-confidence increases. Worksheet 12A can help you identify your strengths; first do it by yourself and then with the help of someone who knows you well and cares about you.

Self-assessment ✓

Read through the words below that describe strengths people can have. Circle, underline or highlight the words that you think apply to you, i.e. the strengths that you have. Then ask someone who knows you well and cares about you to circle, underline or highlight the strengths that they see in you. Don't minimize your strengths.

Worksheet 12A: Strengths identification

Energetic	Focused	Observant	Planning
Empathetic	Instructor	Practical	Disciplined
Wise	Creative	Hospitable	Writing
Pragmatic	Protective	Originality	Tactful
Versatile	Precise	Different	Peacemaker

Resilient	Empowering	Enthusiastic	Loyal
Strong	Coach	Motivated	Trustworthy
Tolerant	Humble	Capable	Adviser
Skillful	Mentor	Ingenuity	Forgiving
Dedicated	Humility	Playful	Industrious
Evaluating	Teaching	Kindness	Social
Careful	Courageous	Intelligent	Vitality
Athletic	Inspiring	Artistic	Volunteering
Adventurous	Brave	Caring	Curiosity
Modesty	Strategizing	Listening	Gentle
Verbalizing	Appreciative	Spiritual	Independent
Coordinating	Communicating	Fairness	Logical
Hopeful	Straightforward	Honest	Integrity
Compassionate	Orderly	Directive	Organizing
Discovering	Innovating	Knowledgeable	Persistent
Hardworking	Persuasive	Presenting	Spontaneous
Fast	Authentic	Speaking	Clever
Outgoing	Assertive	Committed	Ambitious

Warmth	Determined	Loving	Accurate
Confident	Lively	Explaining	Attentive
Open	Mercy	Understanding	Preparing
Balancing	Responsible	Scheduling	Optimistic
Imagining	Thrifty	Counsellor	Patient
Purposeful	Steady	Willpower	Flexible
Friendly	Thoughtful	Idealistic	Entertaining
Resourceful	Managing	Learning	Encouraging
Perseverance	Visionary	Charming	Generous
Serious	Gratitude	Fixing	Relaxed
Leadership	Respectful	Educated	Considerate
Helpful	Teamwork	Humorous	Happy
Reliable	Prudence	Adapting	Researching

Sarah's strengths

Sarah easily recognized that her self-efficacy had always been low. She identified that much of her anxiety and worry was tied to her lack of belief in herself and in her ability to achieve things or make the 'right' decision. However, she had been working on dropping her reassurance-seeking behaviour and was gaining more belief in her ability to decide things or do things without needing constant reassurance from others. Sarah had also been working on reducing her fear of uncertainty by doing activities that weren't planned; this gave her the chance to see that things turned out okay and that she did cope with the challenges that arose. She read Worksheet 12A and was quietly surprised that she was able to find a number of strengths in herself. Sarah noted that among her strengths were having warmth and being empathetic, compassionate, hardworking, friendly and creative – and increasingly brave too! Sarah had not really evaluated herself in this way before and it was good to recognize that she actually did have a lot of positive characteristics. Sarah worked out too that she did not need to worry about others as a way of showing she cared because she showed her caring side in many other ways that was highlighted by the strength identification exercise.

Problem-solving

As we know from earlier chapters, our thinking can keep us stuck and stop us from problem-solving effectively. Sometimes, despite working on our unhelpful or negative thinking, we are still confronted with problems that need to be solved. Outlined below is a simple five-step plan to help you work through a problem to reach a decision or to resolve the problem.

Step 1: Define the problem

The first step in any problem-solving is identify what the problem is, defining the nature of the problem and outlining it clearly and in as much detail as possible. Specific problem details will include the situation, circumstances, timing, behaviours and actions of you and others. Defining the problem can sometimes be a lengthy task in itself, especially when problems are complicated and interwoven, so it may take time to gather all the information you need. Be patient. You may need to drill down a lot to help you split the problem into smaller parts, but if you take the time to understand the problem fully, you are much more likely to be able to find a way to resolve it.

Step 2: Brainstorm the options

Your next aim is to think as broadly as you can in order to come up with as many possible solutions as possible. You can do this on your own but sometimes brainstorming with others you trust can be very helpful. Different people will have different ideas and expertise and might approach the problem in different ways, and they can share their ideas with you. This is a time to be creative and innovative with your ideas. Be as open as possible in your thinking; it is better to put all your ideas down, no matter how impractical they might seem at first.

Step 3: Evaluate and decide on the best solution(s)

Once you have listed all the possible solutions, the next stage is to analyse and evaluate them to find the best solution(s) for your problem. When analysing the solutions, think about the solution that seems to have the best fit for solving the problem. Also think about the best timing, time constraints, budgets, resources, how practical each solution is and what the consequences of each solution might be. At this point it is also important to consider what will happen if nothing is done to solve the problem. Will solving this problem cause other people problems? Sometimes the best solution to one problem can create many other problems. If this is the case, the solution that has the least adverse or negative consequences might be the best solution.

Step 4: Carry out the solution(s)

Next, implement the solution you have decided. Be specific about how, when and where you intend to put your solution into action. Think about any resources you might need, including support from others.

Step 5: Evaluate the outcome

After you have implemented the solution(s), the final step is to review the outcomes of your problem-solving, usually over a period of time.

Sometimes this means getting feedback from others who were involved in the solution or keeping a record yourself of how things are going. Check to see if any unforeseen issues or new problems occurred when you carried out the solution.

Worksheet 12B will help you to work through the five steps of problem-solving.

Behaviour changing strategy

Think of a problem or issue you need to resolve, and work out your solution(s) using the five-step approach.

Worksheet 12B: Problem-solving

Step 1: Identify and define the problem

_____

_____

_____

_____

_____

_____

Step 2: Brainstorm possible solutions

1. _____

2. _____

3. _____

4. _____

5. _____

6. _____

7. _____

8. _____

9. _____

10. _____

Step 3: Evaluate and decide on the best solution(s)

1. _____

2. _____

3. _____

4. _____

5. _____

6. _____

7. _____

8. _____

9. _____

10. _____

Step 4: Carry out the solution(s). Decide on:
How:

_____

_____

When:

_____

_____

Where:

_____

_____

Resources:

_____

_____

Supports:

_____

_____

What else do I need to take account of to action my solution?

_____

_____

Step 5: Evaluate the outcome

_____

_____

_____

_____

_____

_____

_____

_____

_____

_____

_____

_____

Luke's problem-solving

Luke had a big presentation coming up at work that he was worried about and he was procrastinating over it. He completed Worksheet 12B as follows.

Step 1: Identify and define the problem

Presentation at work in six weeks to upper management. Anxious and worrying about it.

Step 2: Brainstorm the options

1. *Don't do it.*
2. *Leave it until closer to the time.*
3. *Try and get someone else to do it.*
4. *Just get on with it.*

Step 3: Evaluate and decide on the best solution(s)

1. *This would not be good as it will make me look like I'm not doing my job and I don't really have a choice.*
2. *Yes, done this before many times. While I do work well under pressure sometimes, this creates lots of anxiety for me and sleepless nights as the due date approaches. So it's an option but not a good one as it will result in stress and worry.*
3. *Yes, I could do this but it will annoy others in my team and it will look like I'm not pulling my weight.*
4. *Yes, I need to do it. Just need to plan it out in a way that means I'll be productively working on it rather than worrying.*

Step 4: Carry out the solution(s). Decide on:

How:
Get my diary out and set aside a two-hour block each week to start working on it so that the week before I give the presentation it should almost be done and I won't be stressing over it.

When:
I will organize my diary later today and have the two-hour blocks booked in for Tuesday mornings.

Where:
I will work on this in my office but will shut the office door so that I don't get interrupted. Will turn my phone and email off too as they are good at side-tracking me!

Resources:
Got all the resources I need to write it. I will ask Ryan to review my presentation slides before I give the presentation.

Supports:
Just getting Ryan to review my presentation beforehand and use his feedback.

What else do I need to take account of to action my solution?
There are some other things I need to watch out for. First, that unhelpful thinking doesn't try to lead me into thinking it's a good idea to put-off working on this presentation when my two-hour block rolls around. Watch my negative-self talk telling me 'I won't do a good enough job' and also not to buy into beliefs that worry helps me if I find myself worrying about it. If I start to worry about the presentation, I need to remind myself this isn't a helpful strategy and that I have time set aside to get on top of this presentation. Then detach from the worries using mindfulness.

Step 5: Evaluate the outcome
I'm two weeks into the preparation of the presentation. Have stuck to my two-hour preparation blocks per week. Unhelpful thinking styles have tried to interfere with my focus when I working on this, such as saying 'The presentation won't go well'. But I've seen these thoughts for what they are - rubbish.

I have been able to step back from worrying when it's kicked in during the week about not having the presentation done as I know I've got it problem-solved by setting aside the blocks of time. I have been able to detach from this worry okay!

Sarah's problem-solving

Sarah had been feeling stuck socially. She spent some time with her friend Maria but wanted more time with others. She worked through the problem-solving steps on Worksheet 12B and found them quite helpful.

Step 1: Identify and define the problem
Feeling socially isolated.

Step 2: Brainstorm the options
1. *Spend all my time with family and my friend Maria.*
2. *Spend more time with the mums at the school.*
3. *Join the local walking group.*
4. *Leave things as they are.*

Step 3: Evaluate and decide on the best solution(s)
1. *Could do this but it would be relying too much on my family. Would be too dependent on Maria also and she does enough with me already. This option doesn't allow me the chance to meet others and it is not fair on Maria.*
2. *I've tried this over the years. I get on okay with a couple of them but I have different interests to most of them and they're a bit focused on school issues and I want to talk about different things. So while I could try and spend more time with the mums I get on with, this isn't a good option really.*
3. *Yes, been thinking about this and I see them all out walking, then they go for a coffee afterwards so that would be good. Would help with physical fitness too. So far this would be the best way forward.*
4. *I'm feeling a bit in a rut and needing some time with people other than my family. This is not the best option.*

Step 4: Carry out the solution(s). Decide on:
How:
I can email the walking group organizer tonight and find out the steps to joining. They go walking a number of times a week so I could pick a time that works for me.

When:
I will email tonight and start walking with them later this week.

Where:
I know they usually start at the local park and it's close by.

Resources:
Got my shoes and walking gear so that's all good. Just need to ensure I have enough in my purse each week for a coffee, as that appears to be where they socialize a lot.

Supports:
Don't need too much support for this. I could tell Steve what I'm doing, that way I've told someone I'm doing it, which makes me more likely to do it. Might need to get a decent umbrella.

What else do I need to take account of to action my solution?
Just need to make sure I know the start day and time. Remember to try and make conversation with the others there when I first go as getting to know new people can take a bit of work. Remember I may not hit it off with every person but it's likely I will connect with some of the other walkers. They always look relaxed and like they are enjoying their walks and chats.

Step 5: Evaluate the outcome
Went on Thursday afternoon for the first time. It was a little awkward at first when I got there as I didn't know anyone. But once we started walking a couple of people talked with me for most of the 45-minute walk. Then when we got to the local café, Jen introduced herself and started talking to me, we had a bit in common. A few people said they'd see me next week and they're organizing a club get-together, picnic I think, in a month for everyone's families so I think this will be good for me as a way to meet other people.

Flexibility

Flexibility is an essential part of resilience. Flexibility enables you to adapt to situations with awareness, openness and focus, to problem-solve effectively and take appropriate actions. By learning how to be more flexible you will be better equipped to respond when faced with problems and challenges. With practice, you can increase your psychological flexibility (thinking and problem-solving). Practise becoming more comfortable in different situations at a pace that is challenging but not overwhelming. Give yourself small but clear and specific goals that will broaden your experiences in novel situations. Mindfulness practice can also help you increase your psychological flexibility (see Chapter 9), by helping you to become less judgmental and to take a more objective stance toward your own thoughts, feelings and situations. This can free you up to be not only more accepting of situations, yourself and others, but also more flexible in your approach to responding to or resolving those situations.

Uncertainty and mindfulness

As you read in Chapters 4 and 6, uncertainty is one factor that can maintain anxiety, and it can also undermine our resilience. As well as the methods of managing uncertainty already described in this book, you can also use some of the mindfulness strategies from Chapter 9. Below are some steps for applying mindfulness to uncertainty.

Be aware

First, be aware of and acknowledge the presence of worries. You can't let go of something if you don't know you have it in the first place. So notice and acknowledge that you are worrying, perhaps by saying to yourself: 'Here comes a worry' or 'A worry has arrived' or 'I'm noticing I am worrying'.

Don't respond

When you notice you are worrying, it is important not to respond to your worries. The most common response is to engage with your worries, chase them around or try to control them in some way. Instead, observe your worries with interest. Don't respond to them. Don't judge them or react to them. Describe to yourself the thoughts, feelings and sensations you are experiencing at that moment. Allow your worries to just be, without responding to them or trying to change them in any way.

Let go

After fully acknowledging, observing and describing the worries you have in your mind, you can make the decision to let them go. Think of letting the worries pass by like clouds moving slowly across the sky or leaves floating on a stream. Perhaps view them as a worry story. Release the worries and let them wash over you. You might do this by saying to yourself: 'My worries are not facts, realities or truths ... they are just thoughts ... they aren't helpful to me ... I'll just let them go'.

Be present-focused

Once you have told yourself to let the worries go or pass by, it is important to focus your attention on the present moment. When you worry, you are focused on the future and on the bad things that could happen. If you focus instead on what is happening in the present moment, it is impossible to worry or get caught up in a whirlpool of uncertainties.

Give it a try. Why don't you start by noticing your breathing and what it is like at this moment? Draw your attention to all the different physical sensations you feel as you inhale and exhale. Notice the physical sensations you have in your body as you are standing or sitting. Become aware of how your body makes contact with the environment around you (e.g. the chair, the ground, the air) and what these sensations of touch and pressure feel like. For example, notice how your feet feel in your shoes or sandals. Do they feel warm or cold? Do they feel dry or a little clammy? Wiggle your toes a little – how does that feel? Worries may try to grab your attention, but don't worry if this occurs. Remember, your task is not to chase the worries away but to refocus your attention on your current breathing.

Now, what did you observe about yourself during this exercise? Did you notice that there was less room in your mind for worries when you were focused on the present moment? Being present in the moment may seem a strange concept at first, but it is about increasing your awareness of your breathing, body and surroundings in the moment as they are happening – something we rarely stop to do. This is something that requires practice, but by focusing on the present moment, you will allow your worries to pass you by.

Deal with a wandering mind

When trying to focus on the present, it is important not to get frustrated when you find your mind wandering away from your breathing or bodily sensations to worrisome thoughts. This is natural and normal, and will occur. Just congratulate yourself for recognizing that your mind has wandered and return your attention to the present again and to what it was you were focused on. Do this as often as you need to.

Sarah's experience of uncertainty and mindfulness

Sarah found the section on uncertainty and mindfulness valuable because it brought together and consolidated much of what she had read earlier in the book. She had identified through the development of her worry vicious flower that her family's safety was a worry theme for her. This worry theme was worsened by the unhelpful thinking associated with it about some catastrophe happening to them. These unhelpful thoughts or images would activate her beliefs that 'worry helps me' so that she then believed she needed to worry about something happening to her family to prevent it from happening. Then the worry would start: stories of bad things happening over and over. Sarah's attention would get caught up in this and she would try to look for certainty.

Sarah began to recognize that the unhelpful thinking was catastrophizing and trying to make her anxious. She also chose to think differently about her 'worry helps me' beliefs. Sarah knew worry didn't help and it did not prevent bad things from occurring. It did not give any certainty, that's for sure. She then used mindfulness to detach from the worry and focus on the present moment. Sarah was aware that over time she was getting better at doing this. She also noticed she was hunting for certainty less often and could let this urge go.

Assertiveness skills

Assertiveness is a term used to describe a style of communicating. We are being assertive when we communicate our thoughts and feelings in an open, honest way without violating the rights of others. Being verbally or emotionally abusive, actively aggressive or passive-aggressive (e.g. trying to get your way through manipulation, being difficult or using the 'silent treatment') violates the rights of others.

Being assertive means asking for what we need or want, saying no to others' requests or demands, experiencing and expressing of a wide range of emotions, and expressing a broad range of opinions.

Non-assertive communication can take different forms, as the table below shows.

Non-assertive communication	Definition	Verbal and non-verbal examples
Aggressive	Standing up for your rights at the expense of someone else's rights. Acting superior. Being threatening or abusive.	Staring the other person out. Being sarcastic or condescending. Put-downs, threats, sexist or racist remarks. Stand-over tactics.
Passive	Failing to express honest feelings, thoughts and beliefs.	Not saying what you mean. Apologizing inappropriately. Agreeing when you do not agree.

For most of us being assertive takes practice. Sometimes our upbringing and previous experiences mean that we have not learned to be assertive. Being unassertive has harmful effects on our self-efficacy. The more we act in an unassertive manner the more our self-esteem erodes and the more likely it is that our stress levels will increase. An inability to express our feelings and thoughts can lead to internal tension and conflict that affect our mental and physical wellbeing. Being unassertive also makes it very difficult to have your needs met, achieve your goals and have control over your life.

Being assertive is a very important contributor to increasing your resilience. Being assertive can increase your self-efficacy, self-esteem and self-confidence. The more we practise assertiveness, the more confident we feel and the easier it becomes to be assertive. By being more assertive you increase the likelihood that you get what you need or want and become free to live a confident, happy life.

Managing unassertive thinking

Unhelpful thoughts and negative self-talk can make it difficult to be assertive. Here are some common examples:

- They should know what I want.
- If I assert myself they will think badly of me.
- If I ask for what I want they will be angry with me.
- It is rude and selfish to say what I need or want.
- It is embarrassing to say how I feel or what I think.
- If I let people know how I feel, they can take advantage of me.
- They will say no if I ask for what I need.
- People should keep their feelings and thoughts to themselves.
- I shouldn't burden others with how I am.
- If I am assertive I will upset the other person and ruin the relationship.
- Others' needs are more important than mine.
- I should always try to please others and be helpful.

Now look at the list 'My assertive rights' below. These assertive rights are the rights and expectations that every human being has. Many of the assertive rights were first proposed by Manuel. J. Smith in his 1975 book *When I Say No I Feel Guilty*.

My assertive rights

- I have the right to say no, without feeling guilty.
- I have the right to express my own opinion.
- I have the right to be listened to and to be taken seriously.
- I have the right to be respected and treated with dignity.
- I have the right to make mistakes and be responsible for them.
- I have the right to change my mind.
- I have the right express my feelings.
- I have the right to ask for what I want.
- I have the right to make reasonable requests of others.
- I have the right to like or not like something.
- I have the right to disagree with someone else's opinion.
- I have the right to say 'I don't know'.
- I have the right to say 'I don't understand'.
- I have the right to decide what I am responsible for.
- I have the right to be successful and to acknowledge it.
- I have the right to privacy.
- I have the right to be alone and to be independent.
- I have the right to change myself and be assertive.

Our rights and responsibilities

Our rights come with responsibilities. For example, while we have the right to express our opinions, we also have a responsibility to respect that others have that right too, and their opinion may differ from ours. Behaving in an assertive way still means we are responsible for the consequences of our behaviour. Remember too that communication is not just about what we say, it is also how we say it – our non-verbal communication. Non-verbal communication includes all the other ways you communicate, e.g. the tone of your voice, your facial mannerisms and body gestures. Non-verbal communication can quickly turn what you thought was an attempt at assertive communication into aggressive or passive communication. To make sure you are using assertive non-verbal communication, keep a natural facial expression, good eye contact, a calm voice and speak at a normal volume and pace. Try a relaxed but active or alert body posture.

Worksheet 12C helps you to look at the thinking that prevents you being assertive and how you can think differently and more assertively.

Behaviour changing strategy

Write in the first column some of the thoughts that get in the way of you being assertive. Using the techniques described in Chapters 6 and 8, manage these unhelpful thoughts by thinking differently, and next to each unassertive thought write a more helpful assertive thought. Use the assertive rights list above to help you. The table also has an example.

Worksheet 12C: Managing unassertive thinking

Unassertive thinking	Helpful thinking
e.g. If I assert myself they will think badly of me.	e.g. I am entitled to ask for what I want and make reasonable requests of others.

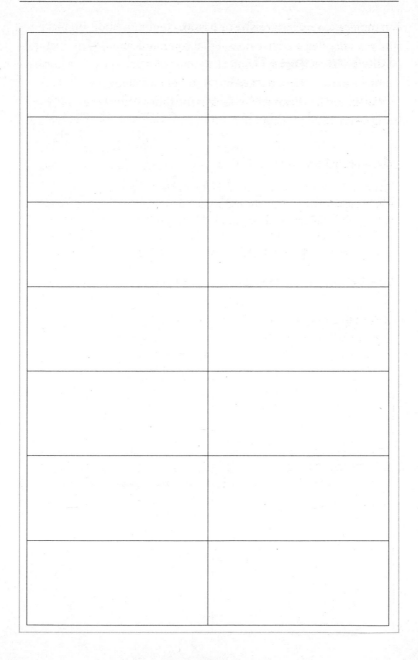

Have a look at Luke's Worksheet 12C too.

Luke's Worksheet 12C

Luke had a go at using Worksheet 12C to help with being more assertive at work, an issue he had been struggling with for some time. He had recently been asked by a senior work colleague, Dave, to take on a new project. Luke felt it was going to be too much for him and that it was an unreasonable request given his current workload. At the next staff team meeting, Luke knew Dave was going to push for Luke to take on the project and Luke wanted to disagree with this request in the meeting, but he was anxious about this. Luke used the worksheet to think differently about his unhelpful and unassertive thinking as a way of preparing himself more for the meeting.

Unassertive thinking	Helpful thinking
The rest of my work colleagues are busy so I should just get over it and do what I'm asked to do. Their needs are more important than mine.	I have the right to say no, without guilty feelings. I have the right to be listened to and to be taken seriously. It is reasonable for me to say no to more work being piled on me. While at times I fall into the trap of thinking others' needs are more important than mine, this is not true and I have the right to be treated as equal to others.
If I assert myself, they'll think I'm being full of myself or a whiner. They'll be annoyed with me.	I have the right to express my opinion. I have the right to ask for what I want. I have the right to express my feelings. If they get annoyed with me, that's okay. I can't make everyone happy all the time and trying to will lead to burn out!

They will say no.	I have the right to make reasonable requests of others.
	They might say no, but at least I will have voiced my concern about what they're asking me to do.
I'll get nervous and embarrassed and not be able to say what I need to.	I might get nervous. But if I think through what I'm going to say in the meeting that will help.
	I can talk to a work colleague beforehand about my strategy of raising this issue and addressing it in the meeting.
	I've seen Ryan get nervous in a team meeting before and it was fine. I don't think any less of him; it's understandable given our bosses are in the room.

Assertiveness techniques

Below are six assertive techniques for you to practise, but before you are assertive with someone, there are some important things to think about.

- Identify how you are feeling and what you are thinking.
- Identify what it is you need or would like. Is a compromise possible or is there an alternative outcome?
- If the situation allows, do some preparation. Think about what you would like to say. Rehearse what you are going to say and do. Sometimes it can be helpful to write this down.
- If the situation allows, choose the right time and place. Setting aside a time to talk with someone will work better than trying to assert your needs when the other person is busy, when there is insufficient time or when there are others around. Of course, this is not always possible as sometimes you need to be assertive in the moment.

Techniques

Be specific

Be as clear and specific as you can about what you want, your beliefs, opinions or feelings. It is often easier to be assertive if you focus on being simple, brief and direct. Address the facts; don't mind-read or speculate. Be clear and specific about the changes you would like made. Be polite and calm. Remember to monitor your non-verbal communication. Be straightforward and honest.

Use 'I' statements

Talk about your feelings and thoughts rather than starting or prefacing what you say with 'you'. 'I' statements say how it is for you without blaming the other person. 'You' statements tend to trigger predictably negative responses from others and escalate conflict. Compare, for example, 'You are holding up the project' with 'I feel frustrated when the project is not moving forward'. Or 'You take me for granted' with 'I feel taken for granted'. Or 'You made me angry' with 'I feel angry because …'. Examples of other types of 'I' statements' include:

- I feel too afraid.
- I feel sad.
- I don't want to …
- I would like …
- I don't like it when … because …

Listen carefully

Let the information flow both ways. Good assertiveness skills also require you to listen carefully and respectfully to the other person's point of view. Good listening includes:

- looking at the person when they are talking to you
- asking questions to clarify so that you understand the other person's point of view

- not interrupting when the other person is talking
- showing the other person you understand by reflecting back what they have said.

Acknowledge others

Try to understand and acknowledge the other person's feelings and point of view. Keeping a perspective about the other person's view and feelings while still asserting your needs or view will also help you not to over-react. If there is some truth in the other person's position, acknowledge this. Don't be defensive as this only heats up the situation. Acknowledge the truth and continue to assert your needs. For example, 'I understand you're not happy about the end result. However I believe it is unfair that I am being held solely responsible'. Don't over-apologise.

Be persistent ('broken record')

If you feel that you are not being heard, just keep repeating what you want in a calm manner. Speaking like a 'broken record' helps you to stay focused, ignoring all the side issues, and makes it more likely you will stay calm.

Say no

Many people find it difficult to say no. Not saying no can result in you spending a lot of time on things you don't want to do. Resentment, frustration and anger can develop as a consequence and impact negatively on the relationship. Some tips to saying no are:

- keep it brief – you don't need to provide lots of reasons
- be polite and warm in how you say no
- repeat ' no' if the other person persists or applies pressure.

Be brave and say no when you need to. Remember your rights; you have the right to say no without feeling guilty. Know that you can't do everything.

Now fill in Worksheet 12D; Luke's is below as an example.

Behaviour changing strategy

Use this worksheet to work through and prepare for a situation in which you would like to be more assertive, and to review afterwards how it went.

Worksheet 12D: Assertiveness

What situation do I want to be more assertive with?

_____

_____

_____

_____

_____

What unhelpful thoughts are barriers to me being assertive in this situation?

_____

_____

_____

_____

_____

What are my more assertive beliefs?

_____

_____

_____

_____

_____

_____

What are my specific needs, thoughts and feelings in this situation?

_____

_____

_____

_____

_____

Write down what you would like to say. Be as specific, clear and concise as possible. Then try your assertiveness out.

_____

_____

_____

_____

_____

Review how it went here.

_____

_____

_____

_____

_____

_____

Luke's Worksheet 12D

Luke had been asked at work to take on a new work project by a senior work colleague. He was unhappy about this because he believed it was too much for him given what he was already doing at work. After completing Worksheet 12C to help him say no to the extra work being asked of him, Luke found that he was able to think differently and had developed some helpful assertiveness thinking. He went on to do Worksheet 12D.

Worksheet 12D: Assertiveness

What situation do I want to be more assertive with?
More assertive at work by turning down the request by my senior work colleague, Dave, to take on a new work project. I am already overloaded at work and this seems an unreasonable demand.

What unhelpful thoughts are barriers to me being assertive in this situation?
On Worksheet 12C I wrote down some unhelpful or unassertive thinking including:

Their needs are more important than mine.

If I assert myself they'll think I'm being full of myself or a whiner. They'll be annoyed with me.

They will say no.

I'll get nervous and embarrassed and not be able to say what I need to.

What are my more assertive beliefs?
While at times I fall into the trap of thinking others' needs are more important than mine, this is not true and I have the right to be treated as equal to others.

I have the right to express my feelings. If they get annoyed with me, that's okay. I can't make everyone happy all the time and trying to will lead to burn out!

I have the right to make reasonable requests of others. They might say no but at least I will have voiced my concern about what they're asking me to do.

I might get nervous. But if I think through what I'm going to say in the meeting that will help. Also, I've seen others get nervous when the bosses are there; it's understandable and it's not something I judge them negatively for so it's unlikely they'll think poorly of me.

What are my specific needs, thoughts and feelings in this situation?

I need to state that what Dave is requesting is unreasonable given my current heavy workload. I need management to know that giving me this new project will lead to increased levels of stress. Dave is not my manager so although he is senior to me he does not have authority over me and is not fully aware of what work projects I am already involved in. I need them to have the project managed by someone else who has time to do this.

Write down what you would like to say. Be as specific, clear and concise as possible. Then try your assertiveness out.

'I believe that taking on this project would be an unreasonable demand on me given my current workload and responsibilities. I do not have the time to put into this project. It would be best managed by someone else in the team.'

If that isn't taken seriously I could add, 'I feel it is unrealistic to ask me to do this. If I have to take this on I will not be able to complete it by the proposed deadline and managing this project will lead to increased stress.' Then point out that, 'I also took on the last new project'.

Review how it went here.

I was quite nervous before the meeting but I reviewed my helpful assertiveness thinking from Worksheet 12C. I spoke to a work colleague before the meeting about how I should address this in the meeting and they gave me some additional points to raise, including that the last project that had been assigned also went to me.

In the meeting I pretty much stated the comments as above. Dave said he was not happy that I was trying to 'get out of it'. But most of the team agreed with the points I raised and validated my concerns so that was good. My boss did not completely agree with either Dave or me. However, he took on board what I said and recognized this project was too much for me and indeed for one person, so the project has been given to Jenna to manage with some support from Ryan

> *and me. So while I may end up doing some work on it, my role is limited – this is okay. Dave's a bit grumpy with me but he's like that with others and he gets over it.*
>
> *I learned that I can be assertive and express my opinion. It was difficult for me but I did it and it went okay. The main thing for me was actually being able to voice my concerns and see that some others agreed with me.*

Self-compassion

We can be incredibly hard on ourselves, beating ourselves up when we know we have made a mistake. We often compare ourselves to others, notice our shortcomings and feel inadequate, guilty or ashamed. Yet although there are areas in which we do well or in which we have particular strengths, there will always be someone who is smarter, better looking or more successful. Research suggests that we can increase our general wellbeing and resilience by developing a more self-compassionate attitude toward ourselves *and* we can still achieve, be successful and happy.

How do we develop self-compassion? The answer is to stop judging and evaluating ourselves. There is considerable evidence to show that self-criticism, despite being common, is not at all helpful. It does not help us achieve our potential; in fact, it only makes things worse. Self-compassion, on the other hand, fosters positive states of mind, such as happiness and optimism, and enables us to flourish and to increase our resilience. As Kristin Neff says, 'when we soothe our agitated minds with self-compassion we're better able to notice what is right as well as what's wrong so that we can orient ourselves toward that which gives us joy'.

Steps for developing more self-compassion

Compassion for others is the same as compassion for yourself. The first step is to recognize that self-criticism (negative self-talk) and judgment are costly. Stop trying to label yourself as 'good' or 'bad' and simply accept yourself. This involves softening your heart towards yourself.

Give yourself unconditional support and kindness, just as you might to a loved one.

Recognize and remind yourself that it is hard to suffer from anxiety, and it takes a lot of strength to make changes to reduce your worry and anxiety. Know that you are not alone; everybody makes mistakes and everybody experiences suffering at some time in their life. As Neff so eloquently writes, 'we are human and our ability to think and feel, combined with our desire to be happy rather than to suffer, warrants compassion for its own sake'.

It is important to understand that self-compassion is not self-pity or self-indulgence; rather, self-compassion involves wanting good health and wellbeing. Self-compassion makes it more likely that we will be proactive and change our situation in order to achieve. Self-criticism and judgment, on the other hand, leads to us feeling unhappy, anxious, dissatisfied, demotivated or too paralysed to change.

Self-compassion exercises

Here are two exercises to help you develop a more self-compassionate attitude towards yourself: Letter to yourself (Worksheet 12E) and Self-compassion diary.

Behaviour changing strategy ♘

Follow the instructions below and write a letter to yourself.

Worksheet 12E: Self-compassion – Letter to yourself

Imagine your ideal best friend: a friend who is unconditionally loving; someone you trust, who is kind, caring and compassionate towards you. This friend has known you all your life and has been with you through most of your life experiences. They know all of your strengths and your weaknesses, but they accept and love you just as you are. They know you are not perfect and they don't expect you to be. They know that you struggle with anxiety and that although you try to manage, sometimes it gets the better of you. They understand that your anxiety can be severe at times and that means you can't be the kind of person you would like to be, but they still love and accept you anyway.

Write a letter to yourself from the perspective of this best friend. Focus on what they would say to you about your worry and anxiety, the difficulties you have experienced and how you are managing and coping. What would your friend write that captures their love and acceptance of you? What would they write that shows their deep compassion and understanding about how difficult things have been or are currently? What would your friend write to remind you that you are only human, with strengths and with weaknesses like everyone else? What would they write to remind you to stop being so self critical, to think differently, and to be kind to yourself?

Once you have completed your letter, put it aside for a while and then go back and read it over. Does it capture the true essence of your best friend, their kindness, acceptance, compassion, love and total commitment to your wellbeing?

Read this letter regularly. Practise reading the words without judgement, accepting them as an honest and true response from someone who knows you very well and who loves and completely accepts you.

Self-compassion diary

Start a self-compassion diary. At the end of each day, take a few minutes to review the day's events and write down anything that you judged or criticized yourself for, or felt bad about. Write down a compassionate response to yourself. In that response, remind yourself that you are human. Let yourself know that you care about yourself, sooth yourself. Write yourself some kind, understanding words of comfort. Remember it is okay if you messed up and it is unlikely to be the end of the world, even though it might feel like it. You can always try again and do things differently next time.

Other exercises can be found at www.selfcompassion.org to help increase your self-compassion.

Luke's self-compassion diary

Luke found it very difficult to get his head around being compassionate to himself. He had always been quite hard on himself and he thought that was probably why he had had so much critical, negative self-talk bombarding him in the past. Luke had been working on thinking differently about himself and not buying into his negative self-talk. He had been detaching from worrying related to themes of failing too.

Luke wanted to work towards not being so harsh on himself while still pushing himself at times to do well in some things. He knew that lots of business people used 'coaching' statements to themselves to keep them on track and motivated. Luke recognized too that such statements need to be affirming rather than critical. So he worked on developing and using self-compassionate and encouraging responses to his day-to-day negative judgments of himself. He had an electronic diary that was private and he could type notes in each day. On most days, after work or university, he would reflect on his day and note down any negative self-talk or judgments that had occurred. Luke would then become his 'compassionate coach' and respond to this negative self-talk.

On Monday, for example, he made an error at work that his boss picked up on and Luke experienced an attack from his negative self-talk. He saw the negative self-talk for what it was at the time, which weakened it somewhat. But later that day, using his self-compassion diary, he wrote 'You're okay, mate, you're only human, and we all make mistakes. You learned from where you went wrong today and have worked on resolving the issue.' Also, on Wednesday, Amanda had been really short with him and Luke later reflected on this in his diary noting, 'It's fine, this was not about her not wanting me but about her having a really rough day at work. We all have difficult days and this was one for her and it's not about her being upset with me. She did apologise later too.'

Over time Luke found that because he had been using the self-compassion diary, these supportive thoughts and responses started being more accessible to his mind during the day; they started to occur more naturally. He was more able to consider these ways of thinking about himself rather than negative self-talk. He was thinking differently!

Chapter summary

In this chapter you have learned:

- what resilience is, and how you can increase your resilience
- what your strengths are, which you can rely on to increase your self-confidence and self-efficacy
- five steps to problem-solving that you can use in day-to-day life
- how to use mindfulness to manage uncertainty
- to practise being present-focused
- what assertiveness is, how to manage unassertive thinking, and how to use some assertiveness techniques
- how to develop a more compassionate attitude toward yourself.

Activities for you to do

Before moving on to Chapter 13, make sure you have a go at the following if you haven't already.

- Identify your strengths (Worksheet 12A)
- Use the five steps to problem-solving (Worksheet 12B)
- Read 'My assertive rights' and work on how to manage unassertive thinking (Worksheet 12C)
- Work on becoming more assertive (Worksheet 12D)
- Keep up the self-compassion! Write a letter to yourself (Worksheet 12E) or a self-compassion diary.

Part 5 will focus on maintaining your progress, how your support person(s) can help you and extra resources that you might find helpful. In Chapter 13 you have the opportunity to reflect on what you have learned so far and the progress you have made, review your early goals and develop new goals to keep you moving forward.

Progress

Maintaining your progress towards change and supporting yourself for the future

CHAPTER 13

Maintaining progress

Overview

This chapter is your opportunity to look back, review what you have learned and congratulate yourself on the progress you have made. It also provides an opportunity to make plans for the future so that you keep moving forward and continue to make progress.

What have I learned?

To help you review what you have learned, complete the quiz below on tackling worry and anxiety. This is not an exam! It's just a simple way for you to see whether you picked-up some of the key points and to help you to remember them. You will find the answers at the end of the book. It doesn't matter if you don't get them all right; most people won't. The quiz will give you an opportunity to update what you know.

Self-assessment ✓

Read each of the statements below. If you think the statement is true, circle 'True'; if you think the statement is false, circle 'False'.

Quiz : Tackling worry and anxiety

1	Anxiety disorders are one of the most common illnesses.	True / False
2	All anxiety is bad.	True / False
3	The physical sensations of the flight, fight or freeze response are normal physical sensations. It's our anxious thoughts that are the problem.	True / False

4	Worry is a core feature of anxiety.	True / False
5	If someone is worrying about a number of things and finding it difficult to control these worries and their anxiety, they may have generalized anxiety disorder.	True / False
6	Using alcohol or drugs to escape worrying is okay and won't make anxiety worse or keep it going.	True / False
7	Anxiety is directly linked to thinking, which impacts on how we feel emotionally and physically.	True / False
8	A goal of the cognitive behavioural self-help approach to anxiety is to learn how to recognize unhelpful thinking and respond differently to that thinking.	True / False
9	If all you do is just believe in yourself you will get over anxiety.	True / False
10	Emotion, physical responses, beliefs about worry, attention and behaviour can act as triggers for worry.	True / False
11	'Worry helps me' beliefs occur when we believe that worry may be helpful in some way.	True / False
12	Avoidance and safety behaviours are effective and long-term ways to stop worrying and anxiety.	True / False
13	The progressive muscle relaxation technique is a good way to reduce stress and general levels of anxiety.	True / False
14	The slow-breathing technique is about taking big, deep breaths.	True / False

15	Regular participation in exercise, slow breathing and relaxation techniques combined with other techniques in this book are the best approach to dealing with my worry.	True / False
16	Unhelpful thinking styles are experienced by most people, but occur more frequently when worry and anxiety are occurring.	True / False
17	Believing that I am weak or a failure because I have worry and anxiety is evidence of the unhelpful thinking style called labelling.	True / False
18	Holding beliefs that 'worry helps me' and 'worry harms me' keeps me stuck in worry.	True / False
19	Unhelpful thinking is uncontrollable.	True / False
20	Attention feeds worry.	True / False
21	Thoughts are just thoughts.	True / False
22	Spending time worrying about what might happen in the future is a type of helpful thinking.	True / False
23	Telling myself what I *should* do is always the best approach.	True / False
24	Taking time to rethink in a realistic and helpful way will reduce my worry and anxiety.	True / False
25	Mindfulness means being in the present moment.	True / False
26	Mindfulness practice can help reduce worry and anxiety.	True / False
27	Setting aside a regular time for mindfulness practice is not necessary to reduce worry and anxiety.	True / False
28	Behavioural experiments only target behaviours.	True / False

29	It's important to make sure the negative predictions in my behavioural experiments are general and not specific.	True / False
30	Repeating the same behavioural experiment is a good way to weaken the strength of my beliefs in my negative predictions.	True / False
31	Stress management is important for increasing my resilience.	True / False
32	The best way to increase resilience is to try only the things I know I can succeed at.	True / False
33	Being assertive means demanding what I want.	True / False
34	Being active is one of the five ways to wellbeing.	True / False
35	One of the first steps to managing my stress is to distract myself, e.g. by spending more time on the computer.	True / False
36	Working harder on the things that stress me will solve the stress.	True / False
37	Planning how I might overcome potential barriers to progress is not necessary.	True / False
38	My own self-talk can contribute to getting stuck.	True / False
39	Setbacks will occur; how I respond to a setback is what is most important.	True / False

What progress have I made?

Take some time now to reflect on the progress you have made so far. Look at Worksheet 3A listing your SMART goals (Chapter 3). These are the goals you have been working towards by using the cognitive behavioural approach in this book. Use Worksheet 13A to reflect on and evaluate your progress so far.

Monitoring progress

Write down:

- in the first column, each of your goals from Worksheet 3A.
- in the second column, the progress you have made towards each of your goals. Be as specific as you can about your progress. Transfer any notes you have made in the 'Progress' column of Worksheet 3A onto this worksheet. You might find it helpful to reflect on your progress with your support person(s), who can help you identify how you have progressed.
- in the third column, what you have learned in regard to each goal.

Worksheet 13A: My progress

Goal	Progress towards goal	What useful things have I learned?

Both Luke and Sarah completed Worksheet 13A to reflect on their progress and what they learned.

Luke's Worksheet 13A

Goal	Progress towards goal	What useful things have I learned?
Get to sleep easier at night.	I am still having trouble on the odd night getting to sleep because of worry. But I have found that the relaxation techniques and regular physical activity has helped greatly. I am getting to sleep quicker using detached mindfulness too, letting the worries come and go. The nights I can't get to sleep, I use the sleeping tips and get up until I'm tired. I occasionally also use worry postponement by noting to myself I can focus on this worry tomorrow.	I have learned that worry is not uncontrollable and I can get to sleep using regular routines, exercise and relaxation. I have learned I can detach from the worry by using mindfulness so that my attention is not on the worry.
Be less irritable with Amanda.	Definitely less irritable, I think because I am looking after myself better and exercising and cutting down my alcohol use. Better sleep too. Amanda has noticed I am more relaxed.	I have learned these strategies help me to be more well-balanced in myself and my moods. I have learned that being less anxious and worried means I have more attention and energy for others. I also have found through my behavioural experiments that I don't need to rely on alcohol to manage my worry and anxiety.

Goal	Progress towards goal	What useful things have I learned?
Be more confident in myself.	Feeling more confident and have better self-worth. Less hard on myself and less preoccupied with failure worries.	I have been using thinking differently to tackle negative self-talk and unhelpful thinking styles. Also, being more assertive with others has improved my confidence. Sometimes people don't respond positively to my assertiveness but that's okay. I have learned that I can do these things. The compassionate diary stuff has also shown me I can place attention on these helpful thoughts and that helps me feel good and undermines my negative self-talk.
Feel less controlled by worry.	Feeling much less bothered and controlled by worry now that I have some strategies. Sometimes it visits me and I have to work at detaching from it but overall I am 80% better.	I have learned that beliefs about worry are false! I had never before questioned my beliefs that worry helps me or harms me, but I now know these are unhelpful and bogus beliefs. I have learned through detaching from worry using mindfulness and worry postponement that I can manage my attention to my worry. I also feel more able to direct my attention away from worry so the attention training and

| | | mindfulness have been great. I may not be able to control all that goes on in my head but I sure can manage where my attention is directed to. |
| | | |

Sarah's Worksheet 13A

Goal	Progress towards goal	What useful things have I learned?
Have more energy and not be so tired.	My energy levels have got to 6-7/10 most days, which is better than the 2/10 it was. Noticing more able to do stuff with the kids and enjoy. I do still get tired but that's normal given having a family to juggle. But feel less drained by anxiety.	From doing more exercise, which I used to not like at all, I have found my energy has increased. I also have learned letting go of 'worry helps me' beliefs means less worrying and feeling less drained.
Feel less anxious and panicky, have less worry.	I still have periods of worry and anxiety. I need to keep working on this. But my worry is much less frequent and less intense when it arrives. I am also able to step back from it most of the time. Probably spend some days not worrying but then have some days when I worry 20%-30% of the day. So not down to the 10% I wanted but getting there.	I have learned that worry doesn't make me more prepared or prevent bad things from happening. I can't see into the future! I have been practising mindfulness regularly and I have discovered if I pay less attention to my worry it fades. It also seems to be coming to mind much less.

Goal	Progress towards goal	What useful things have I learned?
	My fear of my physical sensations has decreased a lot, I'm not afraid of them and now don't panic!	I have learned that through doing exercise and sitting with physical sensations that they are just physical sensations and not harmful. If I have a twinge or pain out of the blue I can feel the worry story of cancer start but I am able to see this for what it is. I have found that working on not seeking reassurance from Steve and not repeatedly checking my body helps stop the worry and the anxiety about my health getting out of control.
Not be so worried about getting a serious illness.	As above, I occasionally feel anxious when I have a sensation or pain that I think is 'odd'. But I am getting better at noticing this is catastrophizing and cancer worry stories.	I have learned that if I stop monitoring my body for illness I experience less doubt. The anxiety decreases too if I don't keep checking, or asking others for reassurance. I realize now that worry does not help me.
Be able to relax and not be beside myself with worry when the kids aren't home.	This has been a challenging goal. When the kids are out or with other family I am getting much better at only checking in once to see they are where they are meant to be. I am also better at not panicking if they aren't home right on time.	I have discovered if I don't text them repeatedly and don't give my worries the time of day, my anxiety before the kids go and while they're out is much less. I have learned they can go out and be safe with some guidance from me and Steve, some ground rules and common-sense information about being

		safe, but I don't need to go on and on at them about dangers or keep them home as this only makes them worried or annoyed.

Where do I go from here?

Take some time now to think about the next steps you need to take so that you keep moving forward. Look at the questions below. Think about your answers; talking about these with your support person(s) can also be helpful.

Questions about my progress

- Are there still times when I react to situations by worrying?
- Are there still times when I catastrophize?
- Are there still times when I worry too much?
- Are there times when it is difficult for me to control my worry?
- Are there some situations I am still avoiding?
- Are there any remaining avoidance, safety or other worry behaviours I can work on letting go?
- What circumstances am I still being too cautious about?
- Is there more I can do to improve management of my anxiety?
- Are there other things I can do to improve my management of stressors?
- How can I further increase my resilience?
- Are there different scenarios or situations in which I can practise my skills?

Future plans are a bit like New Year resolutions; we have every intention of carrying them out, but as the year goes on we get busy and distracted by other things. Committing to our goals becomes harder than we anticipated. Accept that this is the situation for most of us, so it is unlikely to be any different for you. Once you accept that making change is and will be challenging, you will be more able to work with that challenge and achieve your goals. Think very carefully about how you can arrange things in your life to reduce the size of the challenge, to manage the obstacles around the challenge, and to support yourself to stay committed to your goals. If it's a while since you read Chapter 3, have another look at the 'How to make progress' section.

Now start to develop new goals, using Worksheet 13B. It might be helpful to reread Chapter 3 first to refresh your memory about SMART goals and about strategies for overcoming barriers ('roadblocks').

Monitoring progress

Write down:

- the new SMART goals you want to work on in the future; be as clear and detailed as you can
- how you will measure your progress towards these new goals
- how you will overcome barriers to achieving your new goals
- the time-frame for achieving your new goals.

As you work on these new goals, make notes about your progress in the final column.

Worksheet 13B: My future SMART goals and progress

My SMART goal	Measure of progress	Strategy for overcoming barriers	Time frame	Progress toward goal

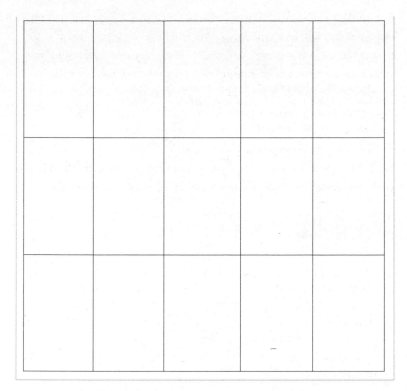

Here is what Sarah wants to work on in the future.

Sarah's Worksheet 13B

After reviewing her progress on Worksheet 13A, Sarah decided to keep two old goals that she believed she needed to keep working on. She also developed a new goal about going on holiday, as previously she had avoided taking the children anywhere in case something happened. Steve's brother lived overseas and had been asking them repeatedly to visit. Sarah thought that would be a good idea as they wouldn't have to find money for accommodation, just flights. Sarah wanted to work on tackling her worry about this so they could have a holiday, which they had never really had before.

My SMART goal	Measure of progress	Strategy for overcoming barriers	Time frame	Progress toward goal
Not be so worried about getting a serious illness.	*Not worry every time I feel a twinge or pain. Less than an hour a week worrying about cancer or other serious illness.*	*Use behavioural experiment worksheet for dropping monitoring and checking of body.* *Keep behavioural experiment going of not asking for reassurance from Steve.* *Practise attention strategies like mindfulness.* *When I get stuck I can reread the chapters on mindfulness and the section on beliefs about worry being helpful, when it's not.*	*3–4 months (it's marked on the calendar!)*	
Be able to relax and not be beside myself with worry when the kids aren't home.	*Not have worry bothering me when the kids are out and not repeatedly checking.*	*Set up more behavioural experiments around not texting and calling.* *Use detached mindfulness.* *When I get stuck I can remember that worry does not help me or prevent bad things from happening.*	*4 months*	

Organize a family holiday that includes flying and going somewhere I haven't been before, like visiting Steve's family who live overseas.	Progress will be made when we actually go somewhere!	I can break this into smaller steps with behavioural experiments that include us all going on weekend trips to places a few hours away by road that we haven't been to before. This will give me a chance to learn I can cope with uncertainty and to work on detaching from my worry before we go and once there. Money! I will need to pick up a few hours' extra work to save for a trip as money is tight. I could get some more clients with my hair styling. I can also use problem-solving steps to help me find ways of making the holiday more achievable.	In 10 months time	

Keeping motivated

Support

Talk to a friend or family member whom you can trust. Discuss your goals with that person, your plans for achieving your goals and your strategies for overcoming any barriers that might surface. Ask this person (or people) if they would be able to support you in staying committed to working on your goals. Let them know the specific steps you plan to take in the future. Discuss with them some of the specific ways they could support you, and in some detail about when or how that could happen. If you have more than one person to support you, it could be that you get different kinds of support from each person.

Monitoring progress

Write down what your support person(s) can say and do to support you. Also write down when and how they could do this.

_____

_____

_____

_____

_____

_____

_____

_____

_____

Prompt card

Write down the benefits of tackling your worry and anxiety on a small card. Look back at your Worksheet 1B in Chapter 1 to see whether these benefits are still valid, and add any more benefits you can think of. Keep the card in your wallet or purse, or pinned up in your office, car or somewhere else you will see it regularly. Set a reminder on your phone or computer to look at the card every other day, or just look at it when you need some support. You could also put an electronic copy on your phone.

Activities to support progress

Here are some activities to help you keep yourself on track and make progress.

Letter to yourself – 10 years in the future

Imagine you are 10 years in the future. Write a letter to yourself. In the letter, thank yourself for being brave, persistent and committed to achieving your goals. Tell yourself that you know it has been very hard and challenging at times, and that sometimes there have been setbacks, even quite major setbacks; but thank yourself for keeping going. Thank yourself for helping you get to where you are now (10 years in the future), and for all the progress you have made.

Self-talk

Practise being your own best friend or support. Earlier chapters have discussed how thinking can affect your feelings, your motivation being one of those feelings, and what you do. Chapter 7 looked at how you can have more control over your attention and the worries you focus on or give your attention to. These attention strategies not only help you manage worry but also give you the opportunity to focus your attention on helpful self-talk: the self-talk that will help you keep motivated and working on your goals even when it's tough.

Instead of focusing on the negative mental chatter in your mind, shift your attention to focus on helpful self-talk; for example, talk to yourself about what is going well and the progress you have made. Tell yourself what you *can* do rather than what you cannot do or what is difficult. Imagine you are your own best friend and give yourself some helpful advice that is realistic but compassionate and caring, just as you would do for someone else you care about and who you want to support. Or simply observe and acknowledge the supportive thoughts you have or even any positive thoughts you have about yourself!

Developing your own self-talk plan so that you are prepared and can practise helpful self-talk is a worthwhile thing to do. Use Worksheet 13C, which has examples of helpful self-talk statements to get you started on helpful self-talk statements as well as blank spaces for you to add your own helpful self-talk statements. Have another look at the section on self-compassion in Chapter 12 to assist you with this exercise. Don't be constrained by the number of blank spaces on the worksheet; if you have more ideas, write them down on another piece of paper. If you have trouble thinking of helpful self-talk, think instead about what you might say to someone else you care about (an adult or child) who is trying to make changes, learn something new or tackle something novel or difficult. Look back to Worksheet 12A in Chapter 12, where you identified your strengths. What are your strengths? Focus your self-talk on your strengths and how these strengths will help you keep making and maintaining your progress.

Behaviour changing strategy

Worksheet 13C: My helpful self-talk plan

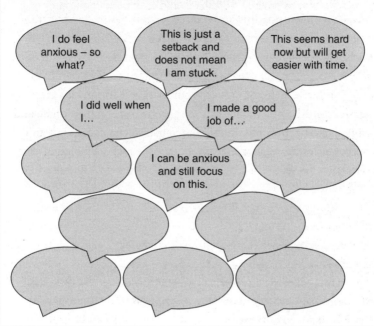

Sticky notes

Put some of the self-talk statements you have written down on Worksheet 13C on to sticky notes and pepper them around your home, office or anywhere else where you will be able to read them often.

Luke's and Sarah's self-talk sticky notes

Both Luke and Sarah had a go at developing self-talk sticky notes. They both used statements that they had developed when doing some of the thinking differently worksheets and also the strengths they had identified on Worksheet 12A.

Luke had two key helpful self-talk mantras: 'I am only human' and 'Worry is not helpful or harmful and I can get on in life without giving it my attention'. Sarah liked a few of the examples given on Worksheet 13C, but she developed some other helpful self-talk statements for herself that she kept on a card in her purse, on the inside of her bathroom cabinet door so she saw them every morning and on her phone. Sarah paid attention to these helpful self-talk statements often: 'I can show others I care through my kindness and saying it – I don't need to use worry at all to express that I care', 'I can't see into the future and I need to be focused on the here and now, not on worry stories' and 'I am brave and can tackle uncertainty and worry when it occurs'.

Dealing with high risk times

The risk of your anxiety increasing is higher at some times than at others. This usually occurs because a stressor considerably outweighs your resources, there are too many stressors or the stress has been going on for too long. At times like this it is often helpful to go back to the basic principles of anxiety management; for example, eat well, get sufficient sleep and exercise, reduce your alcohol use and practise slow breathing and progressive muscle relaxation. Focus on reducing unhelpful thinking by changing your self-talk or by using mindfulness strategies. High-risk times are also a good time to look at your blueprint for maintaining progress (see below) to make sure you are still regularly and actively keeping up with the important points on it. High-risk times are also times to ask for extra support from your family or friends and GP.

Dealing with setbacks

You will get stuck from time to time – everybody does. The important point here is to confront the roadblock as soon as you can. At times it may seem as if you have gone backwards, or like your anxiety has escalated to the level it used to be before you started working on it. Setbacks are not pleasant, but they happen to most of us when we initiate change. Setbacks are a good chance to review your skills and practise what you have learned. What is important is not that you had a setback but that you 'pick yourself up' and get going again. Remember, a setback means you have made progress; otherwise how could you have a setback?

Accept that setbacks will occur. When they do occur, take time to reflect on the setback. Ask yourself:

- How can I make sense of this?
- What can I learn from this?
- What could I do differently next time?
- What do I need to do now to move on?

By reflecting on your setbacks you can learn something new that you could use in the future to become more resilient than you were before.

The perils of all-or-nothing thinking

One of the particularly unhelpful thinking patterns that can turn setbacks into bigger roadblocks is thinking in 'all-or-nothing' terms, also known as black-and-white thinking (see Chapters 6 and 8). When we engage in black-and-white thinking we are thinking in extremes; there is no grey, no middle ground. Black-and-white thinking contributes to us feeling unmotivated, hopeless, shameful and guilty, and to being stuck, giving up and other unhelpful behaviours.

Examples of black-and-white thinking about your progress could be:

- 'This setback means I have failed.'
- 'This setback means I will never get better.'
- 'My anxiety has got worse and I will never be able to stay on top of it.'
- 'This is too hard for me!'
- 'My progress is too slow. I will never get there.'
- 'This means I am back to square one, where I started from.'

Rather than thinking in an all-or-nothing way, stop making black-and-white judgments. For example, alternative thoughts could be:

- 'Ten per cent of the time I get it wrong, not 100 per cent of the time.'
- 'I have had a setback, but it doesn't mean I have not made progress. Everyone has setbacks.'
- 'My anxiety has increased but this does not mean I have failed'.

Remember, the only way you can fail is if you give up!

Use Worksheet 13D to help you counter all-or-nothing thinking about your progress. If it has been a while since you read Chapters 6 and 8, revisit the section on unhelpful thinking styles. Look too at how Luke and Sarah used this worksheet.

Monitoring progress

Write down:

- in the first column, some of the all-or-nothing thinking you have had about your progress, or know that you might have when you have a setback
- in the second column, some alternative 'middle ground' thoughts.

Worksheet 13D: All-or-nothing thinking about my progress

All-or-nothing (or black-and-white) thinking	Alternative helpful 'middle ground' thinking

Luke's Worksheet 13D

All-or-nothing (or black-and-white) thinking	Alternative helpful 'middle ground' thinking
If worry or anxiety causes me problems for a few days I'm back to being controlled by worry and anxiety again.	*If I have a lapse and some worry or anxiety comes back for a few days, this is only a setback. It does not mean I am back where I started. It's a bit like an ex-smoker having a cigarette; it doesn't mean they're back to a pack a day! Same for me, a lapse of worry and anxiety does not mean all is lost. I just need to get back to tackling worry with my strategies and review my stressors.*
A setback means I am a failure.	*Lots of people experience worry and anxiety, they're not all failures. A setback is not a failure, just a normal lapse. Worrying about it or being self-critical will lead to more worry and anxiety. I need to focus on getting back on track!*

Sarah's Worksheet 13D

All-or-nothing (or black-and-white) thinking	Alternative helpful 'middle ground' thinking
If my worry or anxiety comes back I will lose control of it and it will never go away again.	*I've already had some times when the worry and anxiety have increased again. This is a common experience for people dealing with anxiety. But I've used my strategies and got back into exercise and it's started to decrease again. I need to*

remember not to catastrophize if I have a day or two with more anxiety than I'd like. Also remember that some anxiety is a normal human experience and not to panic about it, just use my thinking differently strategies for unhelpful thinking and mindfulness for worry.

Blueprint for maintaining progress

To maintain your progress you need to be very clear about the key things to remember and the key activities to keep doing to help you keep on moving forward. Creating a 'blueprint' for maintaining progress that is specific to you is really worthwhile. Some of the important things for you will be based on the exercises you have done as you worked through this book, but there will be other things that are important for your wellbeing that you are aware of and that also need to be on your blueprint.

This blueprint is one of the most important exercises in this book. Once you've completed it, keep it somewhere where you will see it regularly to remind you what you need to keep doing. Also, worry and worry behaviours like avoidance, safety behaviours and reassurance-seeking have a habit of creeping back, so your blueprint reminds you to keep on top of these things!

As you complete Worksheet 13E, it may be helpful to look back over the various worksheets you've completed throughout this book to remind yourself of what you've done. Also, look at the blueprints that Luke and Sarah completed to help you out.

Monitoring progress

Worksheet 13E: My blueprint for maintaining progress

What early experiences and other factors contributed to worry and anxiety being a problem in my life? (*Look at the bottom part of your worry vicious flower.*)

_____

_____

_____

_____

_____

What keeps my worry and anxiety going? (*Look at the vicious petals; think about the maintaining factors of emotion, physical responses, beliefs about worry, attention, behaviours.*)

_____

_____

_____

_____

What thinking differently points do I need to remember? (*Note down your new ways of thinking differently to tackle unhelpful thinking styles, negative self-talk, and beliefs about worry.*)

_____

_____

_____

_____

_____

What have I learned in this book or from other sources that have helped me to tackle my worry and anxiety? (*Note down what key strategy skills you've developed and what you have learned. Your Worksheet 13A will help here too.*)

_____

_____

_____

_____

_____

What do I need to keep doing? (*What are the key strategies you need to keep in place?*)

Examples:
Make self-care a priority and manage stress
Exercise regularly
Keep doing progressive muscle relaxation and slow breathing
Do a pleasurable activity each day
Practise mindfulness and detached mindfulness every day
Practise keeping my self-talk helpful and realistic – think differently!
Keep up good sleeping habits, eat well, watch the use of substances
Let others know how they can support me

Add others below:

_____

_____

_____

_____

_____

_____

How will I know when a setback occurs? What can I do? (*What would be your early warning signs of a setback? How would you know if worry or anxiety was becoming a problem again – what could you do? Your Worksheet 13D will help here.*)

_____

_____

_____

_____

_____

Luke's blueprint for maintaining progress

What early experiences and other factors contributed to worry and anxiety being a problem in my life?
It runs in the family, Dad is a worrier too.
Mum had high expectations of me – she meant well but I took these on myself.

What keeps my worry and anxiety going?
Feeling emotionally and physically overwhelmed, and then using emotional reasoning to believe that these emotions mean there is something to worry about.
Believing that worry helps me keep on top of things and will prevent me from failing.
Believing that worry is uncontrollable.
Focusing my attention on my worries or trying to distract myself, which never works.
Using alcohol to try to stop my worry.
Procrastinating on work and university assignments, avoiding emails.
Using mind-reading, magnifying and minimizing, and black-and-white unhelpful thinking styles.
Buying into negative self-talk that 'I'm a failure'.

What thinking differently points do I need to remember?

Worry doesn't help, it just keeps me stuck and I don't seem to get things sorted when I worry.

There have been times when my worry has stopped. It's not uncontrollable and it can't harm me.

Remember the disadvantages of believing worry is helpful. It only makes me go around in circles and not sort things and makes me anxious. Believing it's harmful just makes me worry about worry!

What have I learned in this book or from other sources that have helped me to tackle my worry and anxiety?

By thinking differently I can tackle my beliefs that I'll fail and feel more confident in myself and my self-worth.

Worry comes and goes. I can be mindful and it doesn't stay in my awareness so much.

Exercise and relaxation all make me less tense and resilient to worry and anxiety. Plus, I sleep better too.

I can be assertive - I may not get exactly what I want but at least I am heard, feel better in myself for speaking up, and sometimes my needs are met.

I don't need alcohol to manage my worry and anxiety.

What do I need to keep doing?

Keep surfing up with Mark.

Watch out for mind-reading with Amanda.

Keep compassionate and supportive statements to myself going and in my mind.

Watch out for black-and-white thinking. I am only human!

Make time for mindfulness in my diary.

Drop drinking in the week.

Be assertive at work when I need to.

How will I know when a setback occurs? What can I do?

My early warning signs would be that I am being self-critical, worrying about work and my studies noticeably, irritable with others and an increase in my drinking. Probably unhelpful thinking getting hold of me. Sleep becoming a problem again.

If this happens, I need to recognize it's a setback and I'm not back to where I started. Go over the strategies that have helped me and ensure they are back in place. Drop any safety behaviours or worry behaviours that I have started using again. Talk to Amanda too about how she can help me work on this.

If things get too much and I feel I can't sort it myself, I can talk to my doctor.

Sarah's blueprint for maintaining progress

What early experiences and other factors contributed to worry and anxiety being a problem in my life?

Nan got sick with cancer.
I was an anxious child too and worried a lot and probably learned this as a coping strategy.

What keeps my worry and anxiety going?

Interpreting feelings of dread to mean danger was heading towards me or my family.
Thinking physical sensations were a sign of cancer or something else serious.
Believing worry stopped me from getting unwell or would prevent danger.
Thinking that worry hurt my brain and would take me over.
Trying to push the worry away and also scanning my body mentally for signs of cancer.
Asking Steve for reassurance. Checking my body for signs of cancer, going on the internet to look up possible symptoms, and excessively checking up on the kids' safety when I don't need to.
Listening to worry telling me that my family and I are in danger.
Using the unhelpful thinking styles of blame and personalization, and lots of fortune-telling and catastrophizing too.

What thinking differently points do I need to remember?

I can't see into the future and worrying about it won't change a thing except to make me anxious.
Worry does not help me.
I can cope and I have in the past.
Worry is just anxiety talking and it isn't fact.

What have I learned in this book or from other sources that have helped me to tackle my worry and anxiety?

That I can train my attention to be less focused on worry.
That if I drop reassurance-seeking and checking, my worry and anxiety actually drop.
That I can use mindfulness to detach from my worry. Using a worry metaphor in my mindfulness such as seeing the worry as a computer screen pop-up or a worry story helps.
Worry does fade if I give it less attention!! I have learned through worry postponement that it is not uncontrollable.
Exercise is actually okay.

*Physical sensations are just sensations. I don't need to keep checking
my body for signs of illness.*

What do I need to keep doing?

Keep doing my walking!
*Use problem-solving steps when I can. If it's a worry then don't give it
my attention, detach from it.*
Remember my strengths.
Keep working on my goals and making progress towards our holiday.
*Drop reassurance-seeking and checking - this is crucial for me to
keep letting go.*
*Bring to mind that 'I am brave and can tackle uncertainty and
worry when it occurs' - I have the tools.*

How will I know when a setback occurs? What can I do?

*My signs of worry returning would be if I start getting worried about
cancer too much or if I find that when the kids go to school I am
getting caught in worry stories about their safety. Other signs would
be asking Steve for reassurance, checking up on the kids too much
and going on the internet about cancer.*
*I need to look over this blueprint and go over my useful strategies
again. Put things back into place if they've slipped. Reread the section
in this book about the factors that maintain my worry that I'm
struggling with and how to tackle them.*
*Talk to my support people, like Steve. Talk to my GP if I need to
or make an appointment to see a therapist trained in cognitive
behavioural therapy if I find the worry and anxiety is getting the
better of me.*

Chapter summary

In this chapter you have:

- reflected on the progress you have made so far and reviewed the
  things you have learned that have been useful to you
- identified some areas that you still need to work on to keep
  managing your anxiety
- started to think more about the future and identified some new
  SMART goals you would like to achieve

- developed plans to overcome the barriers that might get in the way of achieving your goals and found supports that you can rely on
- developed and strengthened your own helpful self-talk and have a plan for how to use this in your day-to-day life
- learned that setbacks are common, especially at high-risk times, and that what is most important about setbacks is how you respond to them
- completed your blueprint for maintaining progress and identified the important practices you need to keep doing regularly.

Activities for you to do

Before moving on, make sure you:

- review your progress and what you have learned so far
- develop new SMART goals for the future and find solutions for potential barriers
- complete the following activities:
  - write a letter to yourself
  - identify ongoing support
  - create a self-talk plan
  - put up self-talk sticky notes
  - create a wallet/purse card
- complete the All-or-nothing thoughts worksheet (Worksheet 13D)
- develop a blueprint for progress.

Chapter 14 has been especially written for your support people. In addition to providing tips and guidance for your supporters, it discusses ways of responding to someone with worry that are not helpful. If you believe that there is a family member or close friend who might like to help you work on tackling your anxiety and worry, ask them to read Chapter 14 – it's written for them. You might find Chapter 15 useful as it lists a number of additional resources for you.

CHAPTER 14

Advice for supporters of those tackling worry and anxiety

Overview

For the most part, this book has focused on teaching strategies and ways to manage worry and anxiety. In this chapter, we offer some guidance to those supporting someone who is trying to overcome their worry and anxiety. For you, the **supporter**, we outline how you can best help the person you are supporting, the **supportee**, to tackle their worry and anxiety.

First, thank you for taking the time to read this chapter about how you can provide support and enable your supportee to work on tackling their difficulties with anxiety and worry. You can make a big difference to them and their progress. It is helpful to acknowledge that the person does have a difficulty they are struggling with or that a change has occurred in their wellbeing due to their anxiety. Keep in mind that mental health problems are the same as any other physical condition, i.e. they are disabling conditions of the brain and its functioning. Mental health problems come with a range of physical and mental symptoms that are not the sufferer's fault. This is similar to someone with a broken leg; they don't cause the ongoing pain, it's part of the condition.

However, there are things that can either improve or worsen mental health issues. For example, expecting a person with worry and anxiety to overcome their anxiety quickly is unrealistic and can lead to them feeling pressured, causing more worry and anxiety. This is like asking the person with a broken leg to do too much walking before their leg is healed sufficiently. This would be unhelpful, would probably cause further injury, would keep the problem going and the person would remain unwell. To help the person with a broken leg recover and experience less pain, it is beneficial to give them time to rest and provide support as they gradually get back on their feet, build up their activity slowly and then walk again. The same is true for those with worry and anxiety problems; they need time to tackle their anxiety, to gradually gain confidence in themselves and to improve their wellbeing. This means reasonable time to put into practice the strategies in this book and time for the strategies to become effective.

Talking to the person suffering with worry about how they are coping can be useful. It may also be helpful for you to read Chapter 2, which explains what worry and generalized anxiety disorder (GAD) are. Indeed, ask the person you are supporting what you can do to help. They have been working through this book and developing a number of strategies to reduce their worry. They may even ask you to read parts of the book to give you further understanding and information about how to help them strengthen their resilience to worry.

Making changes and reducing anxiety take time so it is important to keep in mind that your persistence, much like the persistence of your supportee in using these strategies, will lead to gains over time. It may be that you are already doing positive things to help them reduce their worry, so keep that up! Below we provide specific guidance that may be useful for you in helping your supportee. These steps are intended to help you be a 'coach' for your supportee in tackling their anxiety and excessive worrying.

Before outlining the steps to being a good support person, it may be helpful to talk about some common, and unhelpful, ways of responding to a person's worry. We understand that you are trying to do the best that you can to support them but the list in the box may include some of the things that you might be doing. These actions may be well-intentioned attempts to reduce their anxiety and distress, but unfortunately some ways of responding to a person's worry can keep it going in the longer term.

Common but unhelpful ways of responding to someone's worry

- Trying to provide reassurance about their worries or anxious thoughts, e.g. saying it will be fine, or repeatedly giving answers that are intended to make them believe nothing bad will happen.
- Repeatedly responding to their checking of your or others' safety, e.g. if they are texting or calling more often than is necessary or reasonable to see if you are okay while away from home and you reply frequently. Or if they ask you to text or phone them often and you do so because you don't want them to worry.
- Helping them to avoid situations that trigger their worry, e.g. if they are worried they will be in a car accident so you drive them on back roads and avoid main roads. This means they don't learn that they'll be okay.
- Avoiding situations yourself so that they feel less worried about you, e.g. staying at home rather than going on journeys or outings in case you come to harm. The same would be true if they are being overly protective of other family members.

What can I do to reduce their worry?

So how can you help? A good starting place is to ensure that both you and the person you are supporting are ready to commit to change. If they are reading this book and you are reading this chapter, then you are probably both onboard with addressing their anxiety and worry. However, at times they may struggle to use the strategies recommended for managing worry and anxiety. It is also common for people to initially experience an increase in their anxiety when trying to change some of their worry and anxiety, which makes overcoming their difficulties more challenging. If they are struggling to work on their worry and anxiety, it can be valuable to do the following:

- Ask them, 'What might be the benefits of working on your anxiety?'
- Go over their Worksheet 1B on the benefits of tackling their worry and anxiety that they identified have for themselves in Chapter 1.

- If they are struggling to think of the advantages of the efforts they are making, perhaps point out what they achieved so far in working on their worry that has been useful and reduced their periods of worry or the severity of their worry and anxiety.
- Ask them, 'What can I do to help you put the tools from this book in place today?' or 'What are you working on from the book at the moment. How can I support you with that?'
- Ask them to share their goals with you from time to time. They set some specific, SMART goals in Worksheet 3A in Chapter 3. Review with them how they are moving towards each goal. If they are getting stuck with something, perhaps go back over the relevant section of this book with them to help them overcome that particular sticking point or barrier.

Managing avoidance

Avoidance is a core feature of anxiety problems. It is understandable that people will try to avoid what they believe will harm them or what they associate with their anxiety. But reducing avoidance is an effective step in tackling anxiety. If the person you are supporting is avoiding situations or anything else that triggers their worry or anxiety, there are steps you can take to help them overcome such avoidance.

- Help them to identify what they are avoiding.
- Don't force them to face what they are avoiding or throw them in the deep end. Help them to work out gradual steps towards managing avoidance behaviours. (Get them to explain safety behaviours to you!)
- Help them to set-up a behavioural experiment to tackle the avoidance (see Chapter 10).
- If the avoidance becomes problematic or its reduction is causing your supportee distress, consider guiding them to seek professional help from a cognitive behavioural therapy practitioner (see Chapter 15) or their GP.

Managing reassurance-seeking and checking

One of the more challenging issues for family members and supporters of those with worry and anxiety is the dilemma of providing reassurance. It seems to makes sense to offer reassurance or give them the answer they want to hear to reduce their anxiety, because you don't want them to be upset, stressed or worried. However, if the worry is leading to your supportee repeatedly asking for reassurance that things are or will be okay, remember that saying it will all be 'all right' or 'okay' will only provide short-lived relief. You may be aware that when you answer one worry it's usually replaced with another worry. The answer you give to their worry question or the reassurance they get from you is often fleeting and they are soon seeking more reassurance or asking more questions around their worries and anxiety. It becomes a vicious cycle! Also, watch out for worry leading to subtle reassurance-seeking or checking. These are less obvious ways in which worry leads the person to seek guarantees of safety or certainty. For example, the person with worry may ask how the traffic is rather than asking you straight out how safe the roads are today.

So what do you do? It is best not to respond to the worry itself; don't say 'It will be fine' or repeatedly text back to let them know you are okay. Instead, name the worry for what it is, e.g. 'This sounds like a worry' or 'This checking seems to be a worry behaviour'. Perhaps have a talk with the supportee about the role of reassurance-seeking and checking type behaviours and try to both agree that they will work on not asking you or others for reassurance. In this way you will help them think about and use other ways to manage potential worries, such as doing a behavioural experiment or using problem-solving, worry postponement or detached mindfulness.

Here are some questions and remarks that may help the person you are supporting to use adaptive responses to their worry and reassurance-seeking:

- 'This sounds like a worry. How can you respond to this instead of worrying more or asking others for reassurance?'
- 'Is this a problem or a worry? If it is a problem, how could you problem-solve it? If it's a worry what could you do?'
- 'This is just worry, it's not fact. This worry will pass just like the others have.' (Tip: perhaps point out a specific example from the past days or week when the worry or anxiety has passed or not come true and relate this to not needing to pay attention to worries.)
- 'We agreed together that it is unhelpful for me to give you reassurance. Let's instead focus on what you can do to detach from this worry.'
- 'If I give you reassurance now it may make you feel better in the short term but it is only keeping your worry going.'
- 'Because I care about you and I don't want to keep this worry problem going, I am not going to respond to this worry question. What can we do instead to help you manage this worry differently so that we don't feed it?'

It is fine to soothe them and give them a hug if they are really upset, but then encourage them to use strategies such as worry postponement or detached mindfulness that they have been working on using in this book.

Important point

Some checking or reassurance in our lives is appropriate, so we are not suggesting that the person you are supporting can never check on someone or ask for your opinion on something.

So where do you draw the line? Think about what is a reasonable number of times to check on something or someone. Also, what is a suitable amount of time between checking? Perhaps think about what people you know who don't have worry or anxiety would usually do.

When it comes to giving an opinion about a decision, perhaps give them your opinion *once only* (they don't need to keep double-checking) or help them to work through the decision or problem using the problem-solving steps from Chapter 12.

What else can I do?

Reflect and reward

Sometimes progress can be slow. This is often the nature of recovering from anxiety problems. It is helpful to measure your supportee's progress on an individual basis rather than against a set standard. When they make progress, it is important to reward and reinforce these gains. Ways to do this include:

- Get them to reflect on the past day or few days when they have been less anxious or worried. Ask them what they have done differently and bring to their attention to how this has helped to reduce their worry and their reassurance-seeking. Encourage them to keep on doing it!
- Congratulate them! What else could you say or do to give them positive feedback on their progress?
- If they have made good progress towards a goal or reducing their worry, perhaps ask them what they might like to do to reward themselves for their hard work. It doesn't have to be a big reward, just a token or treat to acknowledge their hard work and progress.
- Help them complete or review Worksheet 3A in Chapter 3 (SMART goals) and Worksheet 13B in Chapter 13 (My future SMART Goals and progress) to monitor their progress.

Increase overall wellbeing

It is important to work on reducing anxiety and worry by encouraging a good lifestyle balance. This can include a number of strategies and activities that you participate in with your supportee to increase their resilience to anxiety. The following are some key ways to do this.

- Help them to reduce their workload at home or at work. Sometimes people with worry are actually overloaded and are struggling under the load. Perhaps you can guide them to problem-solve difficulties in their life or help them to lessen what they have on their plate regarding their home, work or other demands.

- If there are any stressors or problems in the home that might be contributing to their anxiety, it might be worth trying to reduce these, e.g. getting budgetary advice, seeing if friends or family can offer support or solutions, family therapy.

- Help them to exercise or engage in physical activity. Exercise can reduce stress, anxiety and low mood. It increases a person's sense of achievement too.

- Support them in scheduling time and creating a quiet space to practise relaxation, slow breathing exercises, attention training and mindfulness.

- Help them to develop or maintain a healthy eating pattern and reduce consumption of alcohol, fast foods and overly processed food (see Chapter 11). There are many websites providing information about what makes for a healthy diet.

- Do some fun stuff that will contribute to them not focusing on their anxiety but on enjoying themselves. This can include recreational activities such as going to a movie, going for a walk or socializing.

- Get them to socialize. They may not feel up to this at times but one way to help us feel good about ourselves is to be around people who care about us. This can help to redirect the supportee's attention away from worry and on to what they are doing in the here and now. Socializing can give them the opportunity to have positive experiences with you and others that help to increase their self-worth and to develop affirmative beliefs about themselves. Such social interactions can chip away at the negative and unhelpful beliefs they may hold about their sense of self or their abilities to cope.

In Chapter 3, the supportee made a list of pleasurable activities they could do (Worksheet 3B). Ask them what sort of things they have been doing or would like to do. Use the space below to develop some joint and planned activities for fun, relaxation or exercise:

_____

_____

_____

_____

_____

_____

Important point

Sometimes the person with worry and anxiety will want time with you that isn't focused on working with them to reduce their anxiety and worry problems. It is valuable at times for the supportee to have time to enjoy others' company and not be focused on their worry and anxiety. So have some downtime and some fun. Of course, this all helps to increase wellbeing and resilience to worry!

Medication

If the supportee is taking medication for their anxiety or for other difficulties such as depression, encourage them and remind them to take their medication as prescribed. If they are not taking medication and their anxiety and worry does not seem to be improving or is worsening, ask them to talk to their doctor about medication as an option.

Sometimes the side-effects of medication can be problematic, frustrating or even demoralizing for the person taking them, which can upset them. Sometimes the side-effects can in turn affect relationships. For example, the medication might lead to side-effects such as sedation, increased appetite or reduced sex drive. The person taking the medication may view themselves as a 'failure' or 'weak' for taking medication. It is important to remember and remind them that medication can be beneficial and we would not want someone with diabetes not to have their insulin or someone with asthma not to have an inhaler. Medication for mental health problems is no different; these medications correct the imbalances in brain chemicals that are contributing to the anxiety. If your supportee is struggling with taking their medication, please support them in seeing their doctor.

Dealing with setbacks

Setbacks or relapse are common and it is rare for worry and anxiety to go away forever, even after treatment. At times, worry and anxiety might creep back in to someone's life. Don't be alarmed by this. Help your supportee to put back in place what they had done in the past to tackle their worry and anxiety. Also, go over their Worksheet 13E, the blueprint for maintaining progress, with them, and both of you could read the section on dealing with setbacks in Chapter 13.

Seeking help

If your supportee's worry and anxiety do not appear to be getting better, or you are concerned about the level of their anxiety, or a relapse of anxiety becomes problematic, go over their Worksheet 13E. This will help you to know what they can try for themselves. However, it is important to discuss with them the option of seeing a health professional for further help. Encourage them to seek more direct support if you or they think it is needed; this might be from a GP, accredited cognitive behavioural therapist or registered psychologist. Chapter 15 lists websites that provide more information about anxiety and where to find therapists who work with anxiety.

If your supportee gives up on working on their anxiety or does not want to seek further help, you can't make them but you could gently ask why they feel this way. This might enable you to identify what the barrier is and help them to work through it. Perhaps encourage them to know that more support may be helpful from a qualified therapist or their doctor if they are feeling anxious or stuck.

What is unhelpful to sufferers of worry?

At times, people around those with worry problems or anxiety may not understand the problem or may be worn out from trying to help. This is not uncommon and it is important not to be hard on yourself or others if this has happened. For some, frustration with managing someone's worry may lead to sarcasm or telling the person to 'snap out it'. Such a reaction can make a person's anxiety or worry worse as it can increase their stress and trigger worries about their relationships. If you or others are struggling to support the person or manage your interactions with them, try to hold back from commenting as it is the worry and anxiety that is the problem, not the person themselves.

There may be several reasons why the supportee struggles with anxiety, including past experiences and an inherited vulnerability to anxiety (anxiety can run in families just like asthma, arthritis or diabetes). If their worry is causing ongoing problems in your relationship with them or within family relationships, support them in finding a suitable therapist (see Chapter 15) or seeing their doctor.

Perhaps consider accompanying them to see their therapist at some point too; this may help in developing ways for your supportee to manage the worry more adaptively and give you guidance on how best to respond when the worry is interfering in your lives.

What about you?

Remember, being a supportive person to someone with anxiety, or any mental health difficulty, means you need to take care of yourself too! Don't let worry consume you! Supporting someone with anxiety and worry takes compassion and, at times, persistence, so it is okay to take time out and to do things for yourself. We all need to have time to recharge our batteries.

If you are struggling to cope with your own difficulties, or your supportee's anxiety is impacting on your relationship to the point where you feel unable to manage it or support them further, support them in seeking therapy from a registered mental health professional. Consider also whether therapy for you may be beneficial.

The tip sheet below sums up many of the main points in this chapter and can act as a quick reminder when you need it. Don't forget that your support is very valuable and you are an important resource for your supportee. Thank you.

Tips for supporters

- Help the supportee develop goals that are small enough to achieve, and support them in choosing the goal they want to work on first (see Chapter 3).
- Don't expect change to be major or fast; change takes time, particularly if people have been worrying for a long time. Be encouraging but let them set the pace!
- Help the supportee find more than one person to be a supporter if possible. More supporters mean more people to rely on but also more people to provide different perspectives and different kinds of support.

- Ask the supportee for some details about what you can do to be helpful. Don't make assumptions.
- Don't wait for the supportee to ask you for ongoing support; make a plan about when and how frequently you will meet to talk over how you can support them.
- Go through each chapter with your supportee and discuss the content together in order to gain an understanding of what they are working on, but also discuss with them how you might help them put the strategies outlined into place. Ask them also if they want you to check on how they are progressing with their exercises from each chapter.
- When helping the supportee to use the strategies in this book, try to do so in the way that it has been described here. Let them take their time and perhaps explain to you the steps that are needed so that the strategy is more likely to be helpful.
- Remind them to keep completing the worksheets in this book. Can you give them any support with these? For example, have they got any behavioural experiments that you can help them with?
- Provide support but don't tell them what to do. It is important that the person works things out for themselves.
- Remember that enduring change occurs when people do things for themselves.
- Provide encouragement but not reassurance. It is important that the person develops skills to manage uncertainty on their own.
- Always maintain a helpful and compassionate attitude when you are offering support.
- Don't get too caught up in talking about where their worry came from in the past. It is okay to briefly discuss this, but often there may not be a clear-cut answer. Instead, direct the conversation to what is keeping their worry and anxiety going now. Ask them about the maintaining factors of their worry and anxiety that they learned about when they did their worry vicious flower model. Get them to explain the processes in their worry vicious flower to you.
- People often don't realize when they are using unhelpful thinking. Ask the supportee if you can help them work through the worksheets recognizing unhelpful thinking (Chapters 6 and 8).

- If you notice the supportee using any of the safety behaviours mentioned in Chapters 4 or 10, help them to see that this is occurring and to develop ways to lessen and let go of them (e.g. design a behavioural experiment: Chapter 10)

- Get them to describe to you the difference between a worry and unhelpful thinking versus helpful thinking or problem-solving (see Chapter 8).

- When they are getting stuck with a problem (not a worry!), then guide them to problem-solve. Suggest they work through the problem-solving steps in Chapter 12.

- Gently coach them to remember to practise the strategies presented in this book, such as attention training and mindfulness. Try to help them find a quiet time and place, free of interruptions, to do these exercises.

- Lapses or setbacks are a normal part of making changes. When the person has a setback, remind them that it is normal and encourage them to get back on track again.

- It can be very beneficial to help them engage in practical activities that help their overall wellbeing and develop resilience against anxiety. Book a regular exercise time and go with them! Other activities might include getting them to socialize every so often.

- Help the supportee to see the progress they are making and engage them in talking about their progress. It is all too easy, for all of us, to focus on what is not going right.

- Reinforce their progress with praise, encouragement and a reward every now and then.

- *Look after yourself too!*

Chapter summary

This chapter's focus was on providing guidance for supporters of people who are working on reducing their worry and anxiety. In this chapter supporters have learned:

- how to support a person with worry and anxiety
- how to respond to their supportee's worries, reassurance-seeking or checking behaviours
- specific ways they can help their supportee, including participating in joint activities with them for leisure, relaxation or exercise – all good tools in reducing anxiety, worry and stress!

Chapter 15 lists sources of further support for or more information on worry and anxiety. These can be useful for both the person tackling their worry and anxiety and those supporting them.

Useful resources and further help

This chapter outlines further resources to help you tackle your worry and anxiety. There are many reliable online sources of information on anxiety and related problems, and also some very good online self-help treatment courses. Many of the websites outline cognitive behavioural activities or exercises that you can do. Using evidence-based strategies, which have the same underlying principle to reduce worry and anxiety and improve wellbeing, will be the most effective for you. The resources listed are beneficial and informative as well as being complementary to the work you are doing in this book.

Sometimes worry and anxiety do not improve sufficiently or get worse, or if it feels too difficult to tackle on your own and some assistance is needed. If this is the case, then contacting a support group, seeing a cognitive behavioural therapist and/or talking to your GP about options for further help can be both valuable and sensible. GPs can also discuss with you whether an anxiety medication may be beneficial.

Online mental health and CBT resources

MIND (UK)
www.mind.org.uk
Provides trustworthy and reliable information, advice and support to empower anyone experiencing a mental health problem.

SANE (UK)

www.sane.org.uk

Offers emotional support and information to anyone affected by mental health problems through a helpline, email services and an online support forum where people share their feelings and experiences.

Fear fighter (UK)

www.fearfighter.com

An online cognitive behavioural approach for helping people with anxiety and phobias.

Ecouch (Australia)

https://ecouch.anu.edu.au

A interactive online self-help programme with units for generalized anxiety and worry, social anxiety, depression, relationship breakdown and loss and grief. Provides information about evidence-based strategies, including cognitive behavioural therapy, as well as information on physical activity and relaxation techniques.

Mycompass (Australia)

www.mycompass.org.au

An online self-help service that aims to increase resilience and wellbeing for people aged 18 years and older. Includes facilities for monitoring and tracking moods and modules to help manage stress, anxiety or depression.

MoodGYM (Australia)

https://moodgym.anu.edu.au

A free self-help programme to teach cognitive behavioural therapy skills to people with anxiety and depression. Provides interactive and downloadable resources.

This way up (Australia)

https://thiswayup.org.au

Provides online education and interventions for depression and anxiety.

Beyondblue (Australia)

www.beyondblue.org.au

Focuses on improving mental health across the whole lifespan. Provides online resources on anxiety, depression and other mental health issues, and information about finding therapeutic help in Australia.

AnxietyBC (Canada)

www.anxietybc.com

Provides free, downloadable self-help resources managing anxiety for youth, young adults, adults, new mothers and children.

Getselfhelp (UK)

www.getselfhelp.co.uk

Provides online cognitive behavioural therapy information, resources and self-help worksheets for various mental health problems including anxiety.

Blackdog Institute (Australia)

www.blackdoginstitute.org.au

Provides online materials for people with mood disorders (depression and bipolar disorder).

Centre for Clinical Interventions (Australia)

www.cci.health.wa.gov.au

Provides online self-help resources and information for mental health problems including anxiety, depression, social anxiety, panic attacks, worry, health anxiety, body image issues, improving assertiveness and overcoming perfectionism and procrastination.

Other support

Support groups

There may be an anxiety support group in your area. Contact details may be available from your local community health centre or GP. There are also online support groups and forums for people with anxiety. Mutual support groups, often conducted by people who have experienced similar problems, not only provide an opportunity to connect with others but are a good source of useful information.

Many of the websites listed in the previous section list support groups, and an excellent online resource for finding local support groups worldwide is **Mapigator** (www.mapigator.com), which also provides information useful for improving your wellbeing, such as information on local free events, parks and leisure spots, and community facilities and resources.

Cognitive behavioural therapy

If you have tried the self-help material in this book and find that you have not improved sufficiently or you are getting worse, it is time to contact a cognitive behavioural therapist who will be able to help you in person.

Your GP will be able to refer you to a cognitive behavioural therapist. Let your GP know that you have been using this self-help book and that the best-practice therapy for anxiety problems is cognitive behavioural therapy (CBT).

It is expected, and therefore common practice, for professional CBT therapists to belong to a professional body. Not all accredited therapists are CBT therapists so it is important to ask about this. The websites below are those of the professional bodies in Australasia, Europe and the USA, which provide guidance on finding an accredited CBT therapist.

Australia

The Australian Clinical Psychology Association (ACPA)
www.acpa.org.au/find-a-clinical-psychologist/

Australian Psychological Society (APS)
www.psychology.org.au/FindaPsychologist/?utm_source=Homepage&
utm_medium=Sidebar%2BTile&utm_campaign=FaP

Europe
European Association for Behavioural and Cognitive Therapies (EABCT)
http://eabct.eu/find-a-therapist/

New Zealand
New Zealand College of Clinical Psychologists (NZCCP)
www.nzccp.co.nz/for-the-public/find-a-clinical-psychologist/

New Zealand Psychological Society (NZPsS)
www.psychology.org.nz/community-resources/find-a-psychologist/#
cid=884&did=1

United Kingdom
British Association for Behavioural and Cognitive Psychotherapies
(BABCP)
www.cbtregisteruk.com/Default.aspx

Metacognitive Therapy Institute (MCT-I)
www.mct-institute.com/advice-treatment

USA
The Anxiety and Depression Association of America (ADAA)
www.adaa.org

Association for Behavioral and Cognitive Therapists (ABCT)
www.abctcentral.org/xFAT/

Other countries
Ask your GP to recommend a CBT therapist or look online for
your country's professional or accrediting body for CBT therapists
or clinical psychologists. The Anxiety and Depression Association
of America website has a search tool for therapists in a number of
countries outside the USA.
http://treatment.adaa.org/finding-help/advanced-search/?Show
Advanced=Y

Medication

Research shows that cognitive behavioural therapy is the most effective approach for managing anxiety, but if symptoms are severe some medical treatment can be helpful. Some types of antidepressants can help people manage anxiety even if they are not experiencing depression. Medication works by changing the brain's chemicals, such as serotonin, noradrenaline and dopamine which have been shown in research to be implicated in anxiety. There are many different types of anxiety medication. You will find some information about medication on the websites below. Your GP or a psychiatrist will be able to advise you and answer your questions about medication for anxiety.

National Institute of Health
www.nhs.uk/Conditions/Anxiety/Pages/Treatment.aspx

Beyondblue
www.beyondblue.org.au/the-facts/anxiety/treatments-for-anxiety/medical-treatments-for-anxiety

American Depression and Anxiety Association
www.adaa.org/finding-help/treatment/medication

Websites

Attention training and information on metacognitive therapy
www.mct-institute.com/attention-training-recording-and-guidance-notes

List of pleasurable activities
www.lmgroeszpsychotherapy.com/uploads/9/7/5/2/9752967/big_list_of_activities.pdf

Physical activity, exercise and healthy eating
As well as information about exercise, physical activity and nutrition, some websites provide helpful tools such as a calorie counter or a work-out tracker.

New Zealand

www.heartfoundation.org.nz/healthy-living/exercise-and-fitness

www.health.govt.nz/your-health/healthy-living/food-and-physical-activity/physical-activity/how-much-activity-recommended

UK

www.gov.uk/government/publications/uk-physical-activity-guidelines

www.mentalhealth.org.uk/help-information/mental-health-a-z/E/exercise-mental-health/

www.nhs.uk/livewell/fitness/Pages/Fitnesshome.aspx

www.nutrition.org.uk

USA

www.cdc.gov/physicalactivity/everyone/guidelines/index.html

www.fitness.gov/be-active

www.webmd.com/fitness-exercise/default.htm

Guidelines for recommended alcohol limits

Australian National Health and Medical Research Council (Australia)

www.nhmrc.gov.au/health-topics/alcohol-guidelines

Health Promotion Agency (New Zealand)

www.alcohol.org.nz

National Health Service (UK)

www.nhs.uk/change4life/Pages/alcohol-lower-risk-guidelines-units.aspx

National Institute on Alcohol Abuse and Alcoholism (USA)

www.niaaa.nih.gov/alcohol-health/overview-alcohol-consumption

Assertiveness

www.cci.health.wa.gov.au/resources/infopax.cfm?Info_ID=51

Self-compassion

www.self-compassion.org

www.centerformsc.org

Emotional competency

www.emotionalcompetency.com/srrs.htm

Mindfulness

NHS (UK)

www.nhs.uk/conditions/stress-anxiety-depression/pages/mindfulness.aspx

Get self-help resources (UK)

www.getselfhelp.co.uk/mindfulness.htm

The free mindfulness project

www.freemindfulness.org/download

Be mindful – Online mindfulness course

www.bemindfulonline.com

Metacognitive Therapy Institute

www.mct-institute.com/metacognitive-therapy

Worksheets, audio recordings etc. from this book

www.teachyourself.com/howtodealwith

Further reading

Wilding, C., *How to Deal with Low Self-esteem* (London: John Murray, 2015)

Epilogue

Experiencing worry and anxiety difficulties is not uncommon, so remember you are not alone and you're only human! One of the outcomes of many people having anxiety conditions is that considerable research has gone into developing evidence-based interventions for treating worry and anxiety. In this book we have covered many proven cognitive behavioural strategies to help you tackle your worry and anxiety.

Remember, reducing anxiety and worry is hard work, but persistence and repetition does pay off. Systematically and regularly working your way through the information, techniques and strategies in this book will be beneficial. It's likely that your worry and anxiety has been around for some time and has been maintained by the factors outlined in your worry vicious flower. So you need to give the strategies you have learned in this book an opportunity to take hold and work. This sometimes means trying things repeatedly. It's like learning any new skill, such as riding a bike, skateboarding or riding a horse; over time you'll get better at it. There will be a fall here and there, even when you're a pro! While the fall can hurt, you can either let it knock your confidence and not have another go, or you can reflect on the fall and what you can learn from it and do things differently next time; then get back on the horse again!

Remember, daily practice is optimal. Even very small steps will result in helping you progressively make substantial change so you can live the life you deserve.

'The journey of a thousand miles begins with one step.' Lao Tzu

References

American Institute of Stress, '50 common signs and symptoms of stress' at www.stress.org/stress-effects (retrieved June 2015)

American Psychiatric Association, *Diagnostic and statistical manual of mental disorders,* 5th edn (DSM–5) (Arlington, VA: American Psychiatric Publishing, 2013)

Asmundson, G. J., Fetzner, M. G., DeBoer, L. B., Powers, M. B., Otto, M. W. and Smits, J. A., 'Let's get physical: A contemporary review of the anxiolytic effects of exercise for anxiety and its disorders', *Depression and Anxiety, 30* (2013), 362–73

Baxter, A., Scott, K., Vos, T. and Whiteford, H., 'Global prevalence of anxiety disorders: a systematic review and meta-regression', *Psychological Medicine, 43* (2013), 897–910

Beck, A. T. and Dozois, D. J., 'Cognitive therapy: Current status and future directions', *Annual Review of Medicine, 62* (2011), 397–409

Beck, A. T., Rush, A. J., Shaw, B. F. and Emery, G., *Cognitive therapy of depression* (New York: Guilford Press, 1979)

Beesdo-Baum, K., Jenjahn, E., Höfler, M., Lueken, U., Becker, E. S. and Hoyer, J., 'Avoidance, safety behavior, and reassurance seeking in generalized anxiety disorder', *Depression and Anxiety, 29* (2012), 948–57

Bennett-Levy, J., Butler, G., Fennell, M., Hackmann, A., Mueller, M., Westbrook, D. and Rouf, K., *Oxford guide to behavioural experiments in cognitive therapy* (Oxford: Oxford University Press, 2004)

Borkovec, T. D., Alcaine, O. and Behar, E., 'Avoidance theory of worry and generalized anxiety disorder', in R. G. Heimberg, C. L. Turk and D. S. Mennin (eds.), *Generalized anxiety disorder: Advances in research and practice* (New York: Guilford Press, 2004), 77–108

Borkovec, T. D. and Ruscio, A. M., 'Psychotherapy for generalized anxiety disorder', *Journal of Clinical Psychiatry, 62 (Suppl. 11)* (2001), 37–45

Bromet, E., Andrade, L. H., Hwang, I., Sampson, N. A., Alonso, J., De Girolamo, G. and Iwata, N., 'Cross-national epidemiology of DSM–IV major depressive episode', *BMC Medicine, 9* (2011), 90

Castaneda, R., Sussman, N., Westreich, L., Levy, R. and O'Malley, M., 'A review of the effects of moderate alcohol intake on the treatment of anxiety and mood disorders', *Journal of Clinical Psychiatry, 57* (1996), 207–12

Cavanagh, K., Strauss, C., Forder, L. and Jones, F., 'Can mindfulness and acceptance be learnt by self-help? A systematic review and meta-analyses of mindfulness and acceptance-based self-help interventions, *Clinical Psychology Review, 34,* (2014), 118–129

Clark, D. A. and Beck, A. T., *Cognitive therapy of anxiety disorders: Science and practice* (New York: Guilford Press, 2011)

Dudley, R., Kuyken, W. and Padesky, C. A., 'Disorder specific and trans-diagnostic case conceptualisation', *Clinical Psychology Review, 31* (2011), 213–24

Dugas, M. J., Gagnon, F., Ladouceur, R. and Freeston, M. H., 'Generalized anxiety disorder: A preliminary test of a conceptual model', *Behaviour Research and Therapy, 36* (1998), 215–26

Hayes-Skelton, S. A., Roemer, L., Orsillo, S. M. and Borkovec, T. D., 'A contemporary view of applied relaxation for generalized anxiety disorder', *Cognitive Behaviour Therapy, 42* (2013), 292–302

Herring, M. P., Lindheimer, J. B. and O'Connor, P. J., 'The effects of exercise training on anxiety', *American Journal of Lifestyle Medicine, 8* (2014), 388–403

Hirsch, C. R. and Mathews, A., 'A cognitive model of pathological worry', *Behaviour Research and Therapy, 50* (2012), 636–46

Holmes, M. and Rahe, R., *The social readjustment rating scale* (Seattle, WA: University of Washington School of Medicine, 1981)

James, W., *The principles of psychology* (New York: Dover, 1950), vol. 1, 403–4

Jayakody, K., Gunadasa, S. and Hosker, C., 'Exercise for anxiety disorders: Systematic review', *British Journal of Sports Medicine, 48* (2013), 187–96

Kabat-Zinn, J., 'Mindfulness based interventions in context: Past, present and future', *Clinical Psychology: Science and Practice, 10* (2003), 144–156

Kessler, R. C., Petukhova, M., Sampson, N. A., Zaslavsky, A. M. and Wittchen, H. U., 'Twelve-month and lifetime prevalence and lifetime morbid risk of anxiety and mood disorders in the United States', *International Journal of Methods in Psychiatric Research, 21* (2012), 169–84

Moorey, S., 'The six cycles maintenance model: Growing a "Vicious Flower" for depression', *Behavioural and Cognitive Psychotherapy, 38* (2010), 173–84

Neff, K., *Self-compassion: Stop beating yourself up and leave insecurity behind* (New York: Harper Collins, 2011); quotations from pp. 12 and 13

New Economics Foundation, UK, 'Five Ways to Wellbeing' at www.neweconomics.org/projects/entry/five-ways-to-well-being (retrieved June 2015)

Newman, M. G., Llera, S. J., Erickson, T. M., Przeworski, A. and Castonguay, L. G., 'Worry and generalized anxiety disorder: A review and theoretical synthesis of evidence on nature, etiology, mechanisms, and treatment', *Annual Review of Clinical Psychology, 9* (2013), 275–97

Nitschke, J. B., Heller, W., Palamieri, P. and Miller, G., 'Contrasting patterns of brain activity in anxious apprehension and anxious arousal', *Psychophysiology, 36* (1997), 628–637

Pittaway, S., Palmer, D., Milne, R., Arowobusoye, N., Patrick, H., Cupitt, C. and Holttum, S., 'Looking at things from all angles', *A report on the randomised comparative clinical trial of three forms of cognitive behavioural therapy for mild-moderate depression and anxiety provided on a self-help basis* (London: Bexley Care Trust, 2008)

Salkovskis, P. M., 'The importance of behaviour in the maintenance of anxiety and panic: A cognitive account', *Behavioural Psychotherapy*, *19* (1) (1991), 6–19

Salkovskis, P. M., 'The cognitive approach to anxiety: Threat beliefs, safety-seeking behaviour, and the special case of health anxiety and obsessions', in P. M. Salkovskis (ed.), *Frontiers of cognitive therapy*, (New York: Guilford Press, 1996), pp. 48–74

Salkovskis, P. M., Warwick, H. and Deale, A. C., 'Cognitive-behavioral treatment for severe and persistent health anxiety (hypochondriasis)', *Brief Treatment and Crisis Intervention, 3* (2003), 353–368

Sarris, J., Moylan, S., Camfield, D., Pase, M., Mischoulon, D., Berk, M. and Schweitzer, I., 'Complementary medicine, exercise, meditation, diet, and lifestyle modification for anxiety disorders: A review of current evidence', *Evidence-Based Complementary and Alternative Medicine, 2012 (809653)*, 1–20

Schmidt, N. B., Richey, J. A., Zvolensky, M. J. and Maner, J. K., 'Exploring human freeze responses to a threat stressor', *Journal of Behavior Therapy and Experimental Psychiatry, 39* (2008), 292–304

Smith, Manuel J., *When I say no I feel guilty: How to cope, using the skills of systematic assertive therapy* (Toronto and London: Bantam, 1975)

Smits, J. A. and Otto, M. W., *Exercise for mood and anxiety disorders: Therapist guide* (New York: Oxford University Press, 2009)

Sylvers, P., Lilienfeld, S. O. and LaPrairie, J. L., 'Differences between trait fear and trait anxiety: Implications for psychopathology', *Clinical Psychology Review, 31* (2011), 122–137

Wells, A., 'A metacognitive model and therapy for generalized anxiety disorder', *Clinical Psychology and Psychotherapy, 6* (1999), 86–95

Wells, A., *Metacognitive therapy for anxiety and depression* (New York and London: Guilford Press, 2009)

Wells, A. and King, P., 'Metacognitive therapy for generalized anxiety disorder', *Journal of Behavior Therapy and Experimental Psychiatry*, *37* (2006), 206–212

Wilkinson, A., Meares, K. and Freeston, M., *CBT for worry and generalised anxiety disorder* (London: Sage, 2011)

Quiz answers

Chapter 4 quiz

1 Emotion

2 Emotion

3 Thought

4 Thought

5 Thought

6 Emotion

7 Emotion

8 Thought

9 Thought

10 Emotion

11 Thought

12 Emotion

Chapter 13 quiz

1 True (Ch. 1)

2 False (Ch. 1)

3 True (Ch. 1)

4 True (Ch. 2)

5 True (Ch. 2)

6 False (Ch. 2)

7 True (Ch. 3)

8 True (Ch. 3)

9 False (Ch. 3)

10 True (Ch. 4)

11 True (Ch. 4)

12 False (Ch. 4)

13 True (Ch. 5)

14 False (Ch. 5)

15 True (Ch. 5)

16 True (Ch. 6)

17 True (Ch. 6)

18 True (Ch. 6)

19 False (Ch. 7)

20 True (Ch. 7)

21 True (Ch. 7)

22 True (Ch. 8)

23 False (Ch. 8)

24 True (Ch. 8)

25 True (Ch. 9)

26 True (Ch. 9)

27 False (Ch. 9)

28 False (Ch. 10)

29 False (Ch. 10)

30 True (Ch. 10)

31 True (Ch. 11)

32 False (Ch. 11)

33 False (Ch. 11)

34 True (Ch. 12)

35 False (Ch. 12)

36 False (Ch. 12)

37 False (Ch. 13)

38 True (Ch. 13)

39 True (Ch. 13)

Index